D0359808

SOCIAL JUSTICE
AND PREFERENTIAL TREATMENT

SOCIAL JUSTICE

&

PREFERENTIAL TREATMENT

*Women and
Racial Minorities in
Education and
Business*

edited by

WILLIAM T. BLACKSTONE

&

ROBERT D. HESLEP

THE UNIVERSITY OF GEORGIA PRESS
ATHENS

Set in 11 on 12 point Linotype Garamond No. 3
Printed in the United States of America

Library of Congress Cataloging in Publication Data
Main entry under title:
  Social justice and preferential treatment.

  Papers presented at a conference held at the University of
Georgia, February 13–15, 1975, and sponsored by that
university's Dept. of Philosophy and Religion and Dept. of
History and Philosophy of Education, together with the Georgia
State Committee for the Humanities.
  Bibliography: p.
  1. Civil rights—United States—Congresses. 2. Affirmative
action programs—United States—Congresses. 3. Equality—
Congresses. 4. Social justice—Congresses. I. Blackstone,
William T. II. Heslep, Robert D. III. Georgia. University.
Dept. of Philosophy and Religion. IV. Georgia. University.
Dept. of History and Philosophy of Education. V. Georgia.
State Committee for the Humanities.
JC599.U5S594   323.4'0973   76-28921
ISBN 0-8203-0421-2

Contents

79778

Preface

ALL BUT ONE of the papers in this volume were presented at a conference titled "The Policy of Compensatory Justice for Women and Racial Minorities in Education and Business." The exception is the article written shortly after the conference by Professor Tom Beauchamp, who participated in the meeting as a session chairperson. The conference was held at the University of Georgia, February 13–15, 1975, and was co-sponsored by the University (department of philosophy and religion and department of history and philosophy of education) and the Georgia State Committee for the Humanities. The meeting was designed to focus on a moral and legal issue of major contemporary import—discrimination against racial minorities and women, past and present, and the appropriate response—moral and legal—to that discrimination.

Some have argued that policies of mere non-discrimination or benign neutrality with regard to race and sex will not overcome the injustices of the past. In fact, mere non-discrimination "would perpetuate indefinitely the grossest inequalities of past discrimination," argued J. Stanley Pottinger of the U. S. Office of Civil Rights. Much more must be done to overcome current inequalities and the effects of past injustice, it is argued, than simply the elimination of arbitrary discrimination; and the Federal Government has initiated the policy of "affirmative action," which requires the active recruitment for employment opportunities of those classes of persons—women, blacks, and other minority groups—who have been discriminated against in the past and who still suffer from current discrimination.

There has been much controversy over affirmative action programs. Some contend that affirmative action amounts to an official policy of reverse discrimination or preferential treatment on the basis of sex or race and, hence, discrimination against majority members of society. It is claimed that colleges, universities, and businesses are being forced to quota hiring or to racial or sexual discrimination in admissions and employment. This in itself violates the Civil Rights Act, it is argued. It results also in a lowering of academic standards and, in general, a system in which individual merit is relegated to secondary importance to equality of result. Furthermore, some contend affirmative action principles vest rights in groups rather than in individuals, a policy contrary to the Fourteenth Amendment and our political traditions.

Others deny that these results are entailed by affirmative action principles. Those principles require the active recruitment of women and racial minorities but not racism or sexism in employment, nor a lowering of standards, nor a vesting of rights in groups as opposed to individuals. The Office of Civil Rights recently has recognized that a number of colleges and universities have engaged mistakenly in reverse discrimination, perhaps due to a misunderstanding of affirmative action guidelines, and Peter Holmes, of the Office of Civil Rights of HEW, issued a memorandum to 2800 college presidents saying that reverse discrimination is illegal and that the person with the best qualifications should be employed regardless of sex or race. Yet there continues to be controversy over whether affirmative action programs require quota hiring on the basis of sex and race.

Quite apart from the issue of the proper interpretation of affirmative action principles and guidelines, moral philosophers and legal scholars have debated whether reverse discrimination or preferential treatment (either as a mode of compensating for past injustice or attaining current social justice) is consistent with, justified by, or required by (or all three) our moral commitment to equality and social justice. They also have debated whether discrimination in favor of certain groups as classes of persons is consistent with, justified by, or required by our constitutional principles. The moral issues at stake are complex enough, given conflicting interpretations of the principle of equality and conflicting frameworks for moral assessment. The waters get even muddier when we turn to the interpretation of the constitutional principles at stake. This is evidenced by the fact that the DeFunis-Odegaard case (involving the academic admissions policy at the University of Washington Law School) elicited three volumes of *amicus curiae* on both sides of the issue.

Despite the fact that the conference was originally conceived to dwell upon compensatory justice as an orientation to remedies of discrimination against women and racial minorities, it is obvious from the content of the papers that the overriding issue of distributive justice in our society received equal attention. And properly so, for distributive justice in our society is the generic issue at stake.

Our purpose, then, in putting together a conference on the question of compensatory justice and sexual and racial discrimination was to focus on the complex moral, philosophical, and constitutional issues at stake (especially in the areas of education and business) and to shed a little light on these issues where there is already more than enough heat. Therefore we assembled through the generous support of the Georgia State Committee for the Humanities and the University of Georgia a group of scholars in law and philosophy, businessmen, and academic administrators to examine and engage in dialogue on the multiple facets of this complex question. These papers constitute the conference's formal presentations. They represent divergent and conflicting views of the problem. But they contribute, we believe, to the clarification of the issues of principle at stake and, to that extent, they contribute to the resolution of this moral and legal controversy.

ACKNOWLEDGMENTS

The editors and the publisher gratefully acknowledge permission to reprint essays or portions of essays from the following sources: William T. Blackstone, "Reverse Discrimination and Compensatory Justice," *Social Theory and Practice: An International and Interdisciplinary Journal of Social Philosophy*, 3 (1975); Ruth Bader Ginsburg, "Realizing The Equality Principle," *University of Cincinnati Law Review*, 44 (1975); Robert D. Heslep, "Preferential Treatment in Admitting Racial Minority Students," *Educational Theory*, 26 (1976); and Richard Wasserstrom, "The University and the Case for Preferential Treatment," *American Philosophical Quarterly*, 13 (1976).

SOCIAL JUSTICE
AND PREFERENTIAL TREATMENT

Introduction

A COMMON THEME of the papers in this volume is the justifiability of preferential treatment of women and racial minorities. The authors approach this issue from several perspectives—that of the history of racial and sexual discrimination in this country and its debilitating impact on millions of persons; that of moral theory, theory of justice, and constitutional theory; that of the educational and business establishments; and that of official government policy as embodied in Equal Opportunity and Affirmative Action Programs. Different and conflicting views emerge, but it would be misleading to set forth a hard classification of the stances taken, pro and con, because each author approaches the issue from different perspectives and the conclusions drawn are subtly and carefully qualified. But, roughly speaking, Professors Wasserstrom, Edel, Beauchamp, and Wilson argue in favor of policies of preferential treatment for women and racial minorities, though on quite different grounds. On the other hand, Professors Blackstone, Rusk, Ginsberg, Heslep, Greene, and Banner argue against such policies—again from different perspectives and with qualifications.

In the initial essay "The University and The Case for Preferential Treatment," Professor Richard Wasserstrom recognizes that there is a "bewildering array" of arguments offered by different persons or groups for the preferential treatment of minorities and women in admission or employment at universities. The response of many academicians and universities, he suggests, has been a "strategy of accommodation" which permits internal peace and business as usual. But these changes in admission and employment are desirable not just on strategic grounds but for very good reasons. Those reasons may not always be sufficient reason for admission or appointment. Nor are they equivalent to the claim that a quota system should be used. Still, they are relevant and significant considerations which justify preferential treatment for minorities and women under certain circumstances.

One basic argument offered by Wasserstrom challenges the traditional view that identifiable skills, competencies, or abilities alone are relevant to membership (admission or employment) in the academic community. Several key premises operate in this argument. (1) The unreflective use of the performances of white, middle-class males as our standards of excellence is problematic. There may be other standards for excellence which are free of cultural biases. (2) Traditional criteria for being a successful student or faculty member may not be entirely adequate. The role-model function of miniority students or faculty might be seen as part of the relevant criteria. (3) A minority admissions (and appointments) program might rest on the value of such admissions to students of higher education and on the grounds that minority groups are appropriate recipients of this good considering the wrongs suffered by such groups in the past. (4) More fundamentally, Wasserstrom argues, even after the conventional conception of qualifications is challenged, we must also challenge the assumption that merit as based on qualification is the sole or proper test for desert. We cannot simply assume that the best qualified person to perform a certain task is automatically the one who deserves to be appointed or admitted; for there are other criteria for desert, namely, the needs of and advantages to minority members. Furthermore the possession of certain abilities or disabilities is often beyond the control of the individual. They are due to socio-economic class, environment, and inherited traits which cannot themselves be said to be deserved or undeserved. These are all relevant considerations, Professor Wasserstrom suggests, which must be weighed along with other considerations in the decision to preferentially admit or appoint a minority candidate.

A second argument which Wasserstrom offers for the preferential treatment of minorities and women in higher education is quite uncommon. The thrust of the argument is that the university itself will benefit from the presence of minority students and faculty. The argument is not that their presence will help solve the problem of racism in our society (though this may be true); nor is it that minority members will provide important role-models (though this is true); nor is it that minority members (or women) are more effective teachers in certain courses—courses in which teacher sensitivity to current and past discrimination is essential (though this may be true). Rather it is that a minority presence (faculty and students) on a university campus is instrumentally related to the fulfillment of an essential function of the university —the quest for truth. Wasserstrom suggests that race and sex are such central features of our experience that they determine in basic ways the manner in which persons perceive and respond to the world. If sex and race have a significant effect upon the evolution of entire academic disciplines—the way in which problems are formulated and defined in those disciplines—and consequently on what comes to be believed and labeled as knowledge, then the addition of minority persons to the student body and faculty will increase the probability that important truths will be discovered, for minority persons and women would conceive of problems and issues in new and different perspectives, furthering the quest for truth and knowledge.

Wasserstrom admits that there are no hard data supporting this thesis. It is an untested theory involving the sociology of knowledge. Many may be quite skeptical about it. Yet, if it is true, it constitutes forceful grounds for preferential treatment of minorities and women, given the current dominance of the educational establishment by middle-class white males. Surely the thesis deserves careful study particularly in academic disciplines like law, philosophy, sociology, psychology, and political science—where normative components often play key roles.

Professor Robert D. Heslep, the author of "Preferential Treatment in Admitting Racial Minority Students," undertakes a primarily critical task: he seeks to assess two received arguments which have been employed to justify the policy of preferential treatment in admitting racial minority students to colleges and universities. He calls one "the argument from compensatory justice" and the other "the argument from educational enrichment." To some extent Heslep's article may be viewed in relationship to other pieces in this volume. For example, his discussion of the argument from compensatory justice takes a position which seems generally compatible with many points made by Professor Blackstone in his essay; and his examination of the argument from educational enrichment seems to be in disagreement with that portion of Wasserstrom's paper which contends that racially variegated colleges and universities, even when created by preferential treatment, will help such institutions fulfill their traditional role of seeking the truth.

According to Heslep, the argument from compensatory justice has two variations. One of them holds that racial minority students should be extended preferential treatment in higher education admissions because such treatment will compensate these students for injuries, or violations of rights, which they have suffered. This variation plainly involves rectificatory justice. The other variation maintains that racial minority students should be given preferential treatment in higher education admissions because such treatment will compensate these students for losses suffered. This variation obviously appeals to distributive justice. With special attention to factual and normative claims embedded in these two variations on the argument from compensatory justice, Heslep locates and formulates what he takes to be weaknesses in the two variations. He questions, for example, that admissions by preferential treatment will be something deserved and, therefore, something that will be a compensation. The argument from educational enrichment, Heslep explains, holds that racial minority students should be granted preferential treatment in admissions to colleges and universities because such institutions need, for sound educational reasons, racially and culturally varied student bodies and because preferential treatment is required to provide higher education with racial minority students in significant numbers. Of the various difficulties which Heslep attributes to this argument, the one which he finds the most severe is that admissions by preferential treatment might defeat the educational enrichment which such treatment was supposed to serve.

After his discussion of these arguments Heslep recommends that the attempt to justify the policy of preferential treatment be abandoned and that another policy be entertained, viz., a policy of admitting racial minority students on the basis of standards which are different from but equivalent to the standards by which whites are to be admittted. He points out that, if this policy can be justified, it will accomplish what the policy of preferential treatment was meant to attain: the enlarged enrollment of racial minority students in colleges and universities. He allows that a defense of this policy would take a lengthy and complex argument and, thus, declines to undertake such a defense here.

Professor William Blackstone in his article "Compensatory Justice and Reverse Discrimination" uses the famous *DeFunis* case as a point of reference for discussing the appropriateness of policies of reverse discrimination. He finds that there are moral and constitutional arguments on both sides of this issue but the overall weight of the arguments leads him to the conclusion that policies of reverse discrimination are inappropriate. Compensation and remedy to those who have suffered from past institutionalized injustice, he agrees, are required by our moral and constitutional value commitments, just as the elimination of racial and sexual discrimination is required. But that compensation must be racially and sexually neutral (even if sex and race are utilized, quite legitimately, as criteria for identifying those who suffer from past injustice), and the process of eliminating racial and sexual discrimination to effect distributive justice cannot itself justifiably violate the principle of non-discrimination which it seeks to establish.

The scope of Blackstone's concern for compensatory justice is broader than the classical sense of this concept in which compensation is seen as remedy for wrongful injury. He suggests that a kind of compensation for natural inequalities—those due to the unfortunate or fortunate (economic or otherwise) circumstances of one's birth—is called for if we are to bring to fruition genuine equality of opportunity. Current reward procedures on the basis of merit are unjust because the competition is stacked against the disadvantaged. Our moral and constitutional commitment to distributive justice requires this sort of compensatory move as well. But the basic thrust of Blackstone's essay is an assessment of the moral arguments for and against compensatory measures in which sex or race are dispositive criteria for according compensation. He does not challenge the need for the justification for compensatory measures such as special education, training and tutorial programs, apprenticeships, day-care centers, and the use of non-standard criteria for the assessment of ability or potential in which race and sex are not the dispositive criteria.

The moral arguments for and against reverse discrimination he breaks down into two categories, those based on an appeal to justice and those based on an appeal to social utility. In both categories he considers the arguments for and against policies of reverse discrimination. There are justice-regarding arguments in favor of reverse discrimination based on the demand for economic justice; there are justice-regarding arguments against such policies based on procedural justice. But the overall weight of the arguments from justice against reverse discrimination are stronger than those in favor, he argues.

The same procedure of balancing is followed by Blackstone in assessing arguments involving the appeal to social utility. There are utilitarian arguments in favor of reverse discrimination. The most notable is that such policies, though containing elements of injustice, will in rectifying major social injustices overcome those factors which create social discord and disorder and maximize human welfare. And there are utilitarian arguments against such policies: namely, that official invidious discrimination against majority members of society would result in wholesale non-cooperation and an undermining of the basic institutions of society. The latter, for Blackstone, are the more forceful reasons of social utility. The overall balance of both reasons of justice and those of utility, he argues, is against policies of reverse discrimination.

The inappropriateness of reverse discrimination does not mean that compensatory measures designed to overcome the effects of past institutionalized injustice are inappropriate. Such measures, Blackstone argues, can be formulated in a racially and sexually neutral way. In fact, he argues, the Federal Government's equal opportunity and affirmative action programs not only do not permit but absolutely forbid reverse discrimination (even though some implementors of those programs have engaged in reverse discrimination). Substantial progress in overcoming the effects of past injustice and in assuring equality of treatment has been made by those programs, though much remains to be done. Blackstone is optimistic that national attention and a reallocation of national resources to emphasize compensatory measures designed to overcome the effects of past institutionalized injustice and the vigorous enforcement of non-discriminatory policies and affirmative action in recruitment will result in reasonable progress toward the goal of distributive justice.

Professor Tom Beauchamp's contribution, "The Justification of Reverse Discrimination," is best seen in juxtaposition with that of Professor Blackstone. He agrees with Blackstone that policies of reverse discrimination violate basic principles of justice and equal protection and that this is a *prima facie* reason against such policies. But he disagrees with the conclusion that such policies are inappropriate and unjustifiable. In spite of the fact that such policies violate equal protection guarantees and significantly injure some persons, they are justified (permitted and even required morally) not simply to compensate for past wrongs (though past wrongs do create special obligations to so act) but to eliminate present discriminatory practices against women and racial minorities. Policies of reverse discrimination are required to effect *current* distributive justice.

The crucial premise which leads Beauchamp to this conclusion is a factual one. It is apparently a disagreement on this factual premise which leads Blackstone and Beauchamp to disparate conclusions on the justifiability of reverse discrimination because they agree on the normative principles at stake—equality, distributive justice and compensatory justice. Beauchamp even agrees that there is a heavy presumption against policies of reverse discrimination on the justice-regarding and utilitarian grounds cited by Blackstone and others: namely, the fact that such policies could produce a series of injustices, provide advantages to some who do not deserve them, increase racial hostility, lower standards in important institutions, and reduce social and economic efficiency. These, it is agreed, are powerful reasons against policies of reverse discrimination. But Beauchamp argues that there are other more powerful reasons which override these and those reasons are tied to his assessment of current facts involving sexual and racial discrimination. What are the facts as he sees them? Current racism and sexism are so all pervasive in our social and institutional life that they continue to "warp selection and ranking procedures" and preclude genuine equality of treatment. Progress has been minimal and more policies of non-discrimination will not do the job. Beauchamp cites impressive evidence from historical, linguistic, sociological, and legal sources to document his assessment of the fact of inaction and non-compliance with non-discriminatory guidelines and of the social depth of sexism and racism in our society. To overcome such in-depth attitudes of sexual and racial discrimination and to assure equality of treatment for all within reasonable time limits (not a hundred years hence) we must have policies of explicit reverse discrimination and quota requirements, at least until the threshold of visceral racism and sexism is overcome. Such policies, Beauchamp argues, are necessary for an acceptable rate of progress and that progress in ultimately ridding our society of racism and sexism is the morally overriding consideration which justifies the temporary evils of reverse discrimination. In contrast to Blackstone he interprets equal opportunity and affirmative action guidelines as permitting, even requiring, reverse discrimination. If Beauchamp's assessment of the facts is correct, a strong moral burden is placed on anyone like Blackstone who would argue for mere non-discrimination and (racially and sexually) neutral compensatory measures.

In his essay "Preferential Consideration and Justice" Professor Abraham Edel takes the problem to be investigated as being "how to increase participation of women and racial minorities in education and business in ways compatible with our conception of justice." He holds that the problem can be more profitably discussed in terms of preferential consideration than in those of compensatory justice or of reverse discrimination. The concept of compensatory justice sets an overly narrow framework within which to examine the problem; on the other hand that of reverse discrimination is so value-laden as to preclude discussion of many issues related to the problem. While, for Edel, the concept of preferential consideration simply refers to a phenomenon, viz., that of deciding whether or not to give preference to this or that, it certainly does not exclude normative questions since it is characteristic of preferential considerations that they may be said to be just or unjust. Thus, he holds the problem to be investigated is how to apportion, by preferential consideration, to women and racial minority members the goods as well as the burdens of education and business in a just way. Plainly, Edel sees the problem as one of distributive justice.

The extant theories of justice, Edel submits, may be classified as utilitarian and non-utilitarian. Utilitarian formulae refer to "the kind of life that action according to the formulae will make possible." Non-utilitarian theories look for "an independent or autonomous structure of justice inherent in human life and personal relations, antecedent to any pursuit of the good and setting limits on the direction the latter may take." Edel, however, suggests that a theory of either type alone is not adequate for "the massive pressure of our contemporary world problems and the basic demands of the peoples of the globe" and he recommends that utilitarian and non-utilitarian theories not be regarded as opposing theories but as different models of justice. Accordingly, he proposes two models of justice to use in determining the justness of preferential considerations in distributing goods and burdens among women and racial minority members: the collective welfare model (utilitarian) and the individual rights model (non-utilitarian). Occasionally there might be clear-cut cases where one model applies and the other does not, but often there will be cases where both apply. In the latter cases preferential considerations must deal with the questions raised by each model.

To find and formulate the grounds of preferential consideration in a given area of activity, Edel points out, one must specify the standards relevant to the area, explore these criteria in the light of "underlying aims," understand the complex conditions under which the involved selection is being made, and predict the consequences of action along the lines of the given standards *vis-à-vis* the given underlying aims and the given conditions. To assure that the grounds of a preferential consideration are just one should ponder the questions about these criteria, underlying aims, and consequences which are posed by the individual rights and the collective welfare models of justice. Hence, when a person is to make a preferential consideration in education or business, he might well start with the received standards of merit and ability. But, Edel argues, when a person considers these criteria as indicated above, he will find that they alone cannot provide a basis for just decisions in, say, hiring employees or admitting students.

Edel lays down a minimal and a maximal requirement for a preferential consideration remedying a major injustice in the distribution of society's goods. The minimal requirement is that no just preferential consideration is to result in the "sheer continuation of the injustice to the outs," and the maximal requirement is that the consideration result in "the actual achievement of an order that will bring the outs into the full participation of the society and its goods." In Edel's opinion, the *presently* desirable level of objective for affirmative action, in remedying the injustices against women and racial minority members in education and business, is that affirmative action achieve more than the minimal but less than the maximal. Briefly, it should achieve a "break-through" against "the Maginot line of discrimination." To do this, it does not have to rely upon quotas.

Professor Ruth Bader Ginsburg in her essay "Realizing the Equality Principle" is primarily concerned with what needs to be done to assure that women will have their fair share of the goods in education and business. She makes two proposals. One calls for affirmative action so that discrimination against women (and its after-effects) will be eliminated; the other calls for the elimination of the "home-work gap" so that women in their efforts to participate in business and education will not be unduly handicapped by domestic duties. Affirmative action, Ginsburg points out, presupposes a judicial "stop order" against a pattern of discrimination but it properly involves "forward motion, positive measures to correct accumulated consequences of the pattern enjoined." Moreover, it need yield ultimately neither a pattern of reverse discrimination nor abandonment of the merit principle. Of the various affirmative action remedies authorized by law and court, quotas present a problem of "particular sensitivity." Quotas, Ginsburg explains, seem necessary in some cases but not in others. Indeed, they are undesirable in some types of cases. "The "home-work gap," or the typical unequal apportionment to man and woman of responsibility for household management, is "the most stubborn obstacle to equal opportunity for women." This is especially true, Ginsburg argues, in the care (as opposed to the bearing) of children which poses "formidable psychological and logistical barriers for women who pursue and seek advancement in gainful employment." Ginsburg's proposal for the "home-work" problem is twofold: "Man must join woman at the center of family life, and government must step in to assist both of them during the years when they have small children."

In much of her discussion Ginsburg makes references to court cases concerning the equality of women but she makes no pretense at offering a theory of justice. Nevertheless, it seems that she has in mind certain views about justice in realizing the equality of women. First, she is plainly arguing that affirmative action is to be implemented and the "home-work" obstacle is to be removed not as compensations to women suffered by them but, rather, as ways for fairly allocating jobs and types of education. Like Professor Edel, therefore, she approaches her problem from the standpoint of distributive, not compensatory, justice. Second, by her references to equality, rights, and "the American ideal of freedom of choice for the individual," she suggests, but certainly does not imply, that she relies upon what Edel calls a "non-utilitarian" model of justice. By her considerations of ends to be attained by this or that remedy of affirmative action she indicates that she also relies somewhat upon what Edel calls a "utilitarian" model of justice. Indeed, one is tempted to regard Ginsburg's argument as resting on the kind of framework constituted by Edel's views on justice.

In his paper "Preferential Treatment: Some Reflections" Professor Dean Rusk vividly portrays the evils of racism and the progress made against it, with special reference to his experience in the Department of State. Equal opportunity for all, he argues, we must have, and our Constitution requires it. But he is quite wary of the notion of "group guilt" bandied around by many, by the reliance on class designation, and by "abuse by generalization" which may be entailed by very loose talk about compensation. When we speak of compensation, he insists, we must be clear about "who pays what compensation to whom for what."

The Constitution and the Fourteenth Amendment are living instruments, Professor Rusk insists. They must reflect and be applied to the society in which we live, and this requires, he suggests, realistic compensatory measures to overcome the results of past discrimination. That realism requires affirmative action at the door marked "entrance" in our educational system, not at the one marked "exit." In our quest for equality of opportunity we must search for new criteria of relevance for admitting students and critically re-examine the old ones. But we must insist that the high standards at the "exit" door be maintained, for no one gains if incompetent lawyers, doctors, and teachers are turned out by our educational institutions.

Professor Prince Wilson in his "Discrimination Against Blacks: A Historical Perspective" provides a historical perspective on the issue of compensatory justice for blacks with special reference to education. The current demand for compensation in the provision of educational opportunities, even for quotas in admission to institutions of higher education, is best seen, he argues, in the light of the long history of discrimination against blacks in education. The state of affairs concerning the education of blacks in three distinct historical periods is chronicled: Colonial America and Revolutionary America (1619–1770 and 1770–1800), the National and Civil War Reconstruction periods (1800–1875), and the Pre– and Post–World War II Eras (1880–1935 and 1945–1975). The systematic suppression of black education by both the state and private organizations and the intense deprivation of blacks and its concomitant crippling effects is clearly portrayed. This historical backdrop of institutionalized educational deprivation sheds great light on past and current claims of the intellectual inferiority of blacks in contrast to whites. Both the ups and the downs, the progress and the regression, of the education of blacks in the United States is vividly presented by Professor Wilson. A forceful conclusion emerges: 350 years of denying black citizens equal access to educational resources mandates that compensatory, affirmative action programs in education be instituted to rectify the sins of the past and current residual racism.

Professor Maxine Greene, the author of "Equality and Inviolability: An Approach to Compensatory Justice," endeavors to develop "an approach to equality and justice that rests upon a conception of individual inviolability and critical self-consciousness." While she allows that each person belongs to social groups and that there are objective arrangements created by this social system, she maintains that everybody, because he makes personal interpretations of what is shared, has a unique vantage point. Thus, the opportunities provided and withheld by a society have a special meaning to each member of that society. More specifically, equality in education and business means one thing to women and racial minority members; it means something else to white males. Justice, therefore, must be understood with reference to the inviolability of the individual.

Submitting that justice and kindred concepts cannot be clarified except within specific contexts, or "systems of relevance," Greene takes a hard look at a system of relevance long accepted in education and business, viz., meritocracy. She begins by challenging that meritocracy is necessarily relevant: Are such features of meritocracy as efficiency, interest, and achievement more important than self-development, respect for persons, and self-respect? Then, to present a framework within which to assess the fairness of meritocracy, she appeals to John Rawls's theory of justice, which she finds to accord with her view of the inviolability of the individual. A cardinal principle of this theory concerns individual freedom: no proper conception of justice can affirm that "the loss of freedom for some is made right by a greater good shared by others." Another principle concerns the distribution of goods: social and economic inequalities in a society must be so arranged that they benefit "the least advantaged" in the society. Accordingly, Greene (and Rawls, too) concludes meritocracy has been an unfair system for allocating the goods of education and business since "under meritocratic arrangements, equality of opportunity signifies an equal chance for the more fortunate to leave the less fortunate behind." Finally, Greene endeavors to rebut the points which Daniel Bell has made in favor of meritocracy and in criticism of Rawls's theory of justice and to examine affirmative action as it has been interpreted by defenders of meritocracy. In discussing the latter she agrees with the defenders that quotas and preferential treatment are unfair; but unlike meritocrats, she insists that they are so because each "violates some person's freedom or interferes with a choice of life."

For Greene certain conditions will help institute just arrangements in the educational and business sectors of society. Citizens as a group need more than externally imposed regulations; they need to become incensed over the injustices done to women and racial minority members. But before citizens can be expected to become upset over these injustices, they must change their perspectives toward differential economic rewards. That is, they must come to favor a smaller spread in economic rewards between the more and the less important jobs in our society for only then will they be able to appreciate the intrinsic worth of one another's undertakings as individual projects. In addition, specific changes in scholastic practices—pedagogical, curricular, and administrative —are requisite. Finally, the members of society must come to cherish foremost what is common to them all, viz., their equal inviolability.

Several observations about Greene's paper should be noted. While the paper explicitly mentions compensatory justice in its title, it seems to say as much, if not more, about distributive than about compensatory justice. Even though the essay has various references to equity, it does not dwell upon equity as Professor Banner's article does. And, by its strong reliance upon Rawls's theory of justice, the paper plainly favors what Professor Edel labels a "non-utilitarian" approach to justice.

As suggested by the title of his article "Compensatory Justice and the Meaning of Equity," Professor William Banner emphasizes the place of equity in compensatory justice and, thus, in rectifying the injuries suffered by minority groups in business and education. He begins by contending that compensatory justice, which seeks to compensate the individual member of society for what he has lost or otherwise suffered, involves equity, which seeks to correct the law, written or not, where it is defective. To be valid, Banner submits, a law must be reasonable, i.e., it must order actions and programs for free persons toward some good end; any law which is not reasonable needs correction. So, when a judge treats a case of compensatory justice, he must consider not only what the law is but also what the law should be. Where he finds the law unreasonable, he must rely upon the principle of reasonableness in deciding whether or not to extend compensation and what, if any, compensation is to be granted. Banner subsequently applies this interpretation of compensatory justice, which he buttresses with references to the literature of political thought, to personal injuries in modern times, which, for him, have arisen in major ways from economic exploitation and social status. According to Banner modern society has tolerated an unequal extension of the rewards of labor and an unequal extension of opportunity. In so doing it has adversely affected minority groups in particular. It is recognized by Banner that it is very difficult to compensate minority groups for their sufferings in business and education. For one thing, no person is fully compensated for an injury, perhaps, unless his life is made what it would have been had he never incurred the injury; and, while it seems possible, it certainly is not easy to amend a person's life in this way. For another thing, no compensation should be awarded an injured person which imposes another injury upon an innocent party; and it is often hard to formulate compensations for a minority group's members which injure no innocent member of the majority. These and other difficulties must be taken into account in any effort to compensate minority groups for their losses and other sufferings. However, it is clearly intended by Banner that, regardless of the difficulties to be overcome, judges must consider the grievances of minority groups and, in so doing, must consider not only what the law is but, in view of the demands of equity, what it should be.

WILLIAM T. BLACKSTONE
ROBERT D. HESLEP

The University and the Case for Preferential Treatment

RICHARD WASSERSTROM

DURING AT LEAST the past ten years three related proposals for change within the university have been made with regularity and persistence. In the early years the focus was almost exclusively upon race. More recently, it has been broadened to include sex and, to a lesser degree, economic and social class. The underlying complaint has been and still is that the university is too white, too middle class, and too male in respect to its student body, faculty, and curriculum. The three related remedial proposals have corresponded to the diagnosis of the evil: Change the composition of the student body, the faculty, and the curriculum so that each is now composed of or reflects racial, sexual, and class constituents of a more varied sort.

These proposals for change have been made at virtually every institution of higher learning in the United States. In just about every case each institution listened to and accepted these proposals to some degree or other. And while the degree of acceptance and implementation has varied substantially from institution to institution, the rationales for this acceptance and implementation have been substantially more varied still. Colleges and universities were, for example, a good deal more willing, on the whole, to change their admission policies in respect to blacks than they were able to formulate and articulate either a coherent program of admission for blacks or an ambiguous justification for the policies of the program.

There are several explanations for this discrepancy between the policies and their supporting justifications. One is that many academicians who favored the proposals for change did so for reasons quite extrinsic to the merits of the proposals. Such persons saw things in wholly strategic terms. There were, in their eyes, forces being brought to bear upon the university that required that some changes be made if any kind of peace were to prevail within the academy and if the business of the university were to continue at all. In addition, it was also understandable to these academicians why some of the groups involved were pressing so hard for these changes. Blacks, Chicanos, and American Indians, for instance, believed quite correctly that they had been treated quite badly by the world of which the university was one small part. To be sure, the contemporary institution of higher learning had really nothing to do with the way they had been treated in the past; nor did it have anything much to do with any contemporary injustices—at least, if the university in question maintained (as almost all universities now did) nondiscriminatory policies concerning student admission and faculty appointment to the university. As these academicians saw it, what had happened was that the university had become a readily identifiable, highly visible target for the anger, resentment, and youthful energy that ought really to have been directed elsewhere. The enthusiasms of youth combined with the injustices and corruptions of the world at large and with the inherent vulnerability of the university made it intelligible enough, but hardly justifiable, that these pressures should be directed so forcefully at the university. As these academicians saw it, too, it was essential that this energy be contained as much as possible. Hence the strategy of accommodation. They favored making those changes that would produce enough internal peace to permit the university to proceed pretty much as usual. They believed that most if not all of the changes would be counterproductive for all concerned. They believed that if unqualified minority students were to be admitted either the level of instruction would necessarily decline or the minority students would become still more frustrated, disillusioned and reinforced in their own sense of failure than they had been before. Still, they accepted some alterations in admission policy as the lesser of the evils at hand.

Of course, a number of academicians did not share this view. They thought that some if not all of the proposals were meritorious and deserved to be adopted and implemented for their own sake. But even here, a bewildering array of arguments and justifications were offered by different persons and groups in support of these recommended alterations in the composition of the population and curriculum of the university. It is these arguments that I concentrate upon in what follows. But my concern is that of the philosopher rather than that of the intellectual historian. That is to say, I am not interested in collecting those arguments and justifications that happen to have been given at any particular time or place in connection with any particular position or program. I am interested, instead, in possible arguments and justifications—those that most plausibly might have been advanced.

My own view is that these changes were and are desirable for fundamental reasons and not just on the strategic grounds outlined above. My ambition is to begin to persuade you of this, and in order to do so analysis is required more than rhetoric. For much of the intellectual problem in this whole area is that the issues are not all of a piece. Any informed assessment of the merits must, therefore, await a sorting out of the claims and arguments that are involved. In what follows I propose to concentrate upon some of those topics and issues which seem to me to be the most significant, the most deserving of careful consideration, and, typically, the most neglected.

The fundamental question I want to examine is whether the fact of minority membership is ever by itself a good reason for admitting a student to the university or appointing a person to a faculty position at the university. I hope that what I have to say will convince you that there are in fact sound and powerful arguments that ought to persuade reasonable persons of the appropriateness of taking minority group membership explicitly into account for purposes of admitting students to higher education or appointing persons to the faculty.

Before introducing these arguments, however, a few clarifying remarks must be made. To begin with, I want to say what I mean by minorities. I shall use the term "minority" to refer to Blacks, Chicanos, American Indians, women, and whites from a very low socioeconomic class background. I realize, of course, both that women are a numerical majority and that these categories are quite imprecise. I shall have a bit more to say about the latter point in the final portion of my paper. I do not think that the former one affects what I have to say in any way.

The second preliminary point I want to make is that it is important to distinguish my thesis from two others with which it might be, and often has been, confused. I think I can show that minority group membership is by itself a good reason for admitting a student or appointing a person to the faculty. And that is different from claiming either: (a) that minority membership is by itself a sufficient reason for admission or appointment, or (b) that a quota system or any other particular scheme of preferential treatment is a desirable means by which to take into account this fact of the relevance of minority group membership.

And third, I want to emphasize that my ambitions are modest in another respect as well. I shall be concerned in this paper with only a few of the variety of arguments that have been and that might be offered in connection with this question. I am not, for instance, going to say anything at all about the legal issues, about whether taking minority membership into account is constitutionally prohibited, required, or permitted. Nor do I make any claim to have explored all of the moral, prudential, or economic arguments that might merit analysis. I shall, as I have said, concentrate instead upon a few of those that seem to me especially interesting, persuasive, and somewhat less familiar.

II

It is obvious, I think, that those who wish to defend the relevance of minority membership have a variety of ways of proceeding open to them. Probably the first thing that it naturally occurs to them to do is to take on the problem of qualifications—the claim that the only relevant criteria for admission or appointment are, surely, those that distinguish among the individuals on grounds of competence. And competence, so the argument they must deal with goes, has nothing whatsoever to do with membership in any minority group. For instance, the skills required of faculty members are primarily those that relate to the ability to teach and to do research. Persons having those skills should be appointed to the faculty and retained within it. Attributes of sex, race, and class have as little to do with these academic qualifications as do eye color, food preferences, or political affiliation. Concomitantly, the abilities required of students are primarily those that relate to the intellectual capacity to comprehend, analyze, criticize, and communicate. Once again, what is significant is that whatever the appropriate specification of the qualifications may be, minority membership is just not seen to be at all connected with those qualifications. The general point is that wherever there is an identifiable skill, competence, or ability, it is that and that alone that is properly relevant. And because minority group membership is deemed to be in no way related to the identifiable skill, competence, or ability, it is never a relevant consideration or a good reason for admission or appointment.

Now, it is obvious, I believe, that those who wish to challenge this argument and to defend the relevance of minority membership have a variety of ways of proceeding open to them. They can, to begin with, accept, if they wish, the specific point about qualifications and yet claim that minority group membership is by itself connected in meaningful ways to the possession of the designated qualifications. On this view, minority group members are seen to possess those qualifications or attributes that the university avowedly seeks from its admittees and faculty members. This is a very significant argument; it is one to which I shall return in the latter part of this paper.

A second way of proceeding is to accept the general point about qualifications but to argue also that the customary *specification* of those qualifications or of the evidence for those qualifications is just that, namely, customary or conventional. If the presently favored criteria are not arbitrary, they are also not essentially linked to determining those most qualified for admission or appointment. That is to say, someone might argue like this: There is nothing wrong with law schools or universities generally seeking to admit those students who will be best able to do the work. And the way to decide who will be best able to do the work is to see who gets the highest scores on the LSAT or the SAT. But the problems here are twofold. On the one hand, the tests may be unknowingly biased in such a way that it is far harder for a minority member to get a good score than for a typical, white, middle-class male. This is certainly not surprising since the tests are made up almost exclusively by white, middle-class males. As Robert Havighurst is once supposed to have observed, if lions were to devise intelligence tests, lions would very likely turn out on those tests to be the smartest of the animals in the animal kingdom. On the other hand, it is equally plausible to call into question also what is to count as doing one's work well. Is it to be defined or described wholly in terms of doing the kind of work that has been done to date within the university? If so, there is at least the danger, if not the certainty, that the performances of white, middle-class males will unreflectively be taken to be the standards of excellence without much regard for the question of whether alternative, plausible standards or conceptions of excellence can be explored and developed—ones that will here, too, be free of irrelevant or unimportant cultural preferences.

These are, I take it, among the most familiar and conservative justifications that can be devised for minority programs. As a result, I want to move beyond them, to others that have been less commonly discussed and understood.

One way to do this is to attack the notion that the relevant qualifications for being a successful student or faculty member are all that ought to be relevant to the question of who shall be appointed to the faculty or admitted to the student body. For, it might be proposed, there are things that are appropriately considered that have nothing to do with qualifications for success— as success has traditionally been conceived. This argument is what leads some persons to argue quite plausibly that minority membership is relevant to teacher selection because minority teachers provide a significant, nontraditional value as role-models—both for minority students in the university and for minority persons in the world at large. But this is a somewhat familiar argument, too, and one which appeals at least to familiar pedagogical concerns.

A good deal less conventional is the claim that minority membership ought to be seen to be a relevant consideration just because of the benefits to be derived by minority group persons from admission to the university or appointment to the faculty. On this view, the case for a minority admission program rests upon the value to students in general of higher education. The first step in this argument consists in seeing that because higher education is something that is good for the students (and the good here can be conceived of in both economic and noneconomic terms), it is also good for minority group students. And the next step in the argument consists in establishing that upon some ground or other it is especially appropriate to make members of minority groups the recipients of this good. Among the more plausible, alternative grounds supporting this step in the argument are the following two:

a) the claim that present members of the minority group have for reparation owing to the wrongs suffered by other members of that group at another time, and

b) the fact that attendance will make a substantially greater positive difference in the lives of those members of the minority group who attend the university than it will in the lives of those from the majority group who would otherwise have attended the university but who as a result cannot now do so.

Analogous arguments can be developed in support of a policy which favors the appointment of minority group members to the faculty, for a faculty position—even more than a place within the student body—is a benefit to the holder of the position. On financial grounds alone, a professorial appointment is, relatively speaking, a good job. And when one adds to the financial picture the security, the prestige, the freedom to decide how to spend one's time, the setting, and so on, it is a very desirable situation indeed. Because that is so, it is certainly appropriate to argue that members of minority groups should be the recipients of this good, provided only that it can be shown that there is some reason which gives them a special claim to that good. Once again, the reason might plausibly be either one of the two reasons just enumerated in connection with the issue of minority admission.

It is an argument such as this that I imagine some, if not many, persons would think too outrageous and wrong. And they would, I suspect, want to reply in something like the following fashion. The only relevant and appropriate question to be asked about admission or appointment is the question of merit: Those persons who most fully possess those qualifications for successful university work—either as a student or as a teacher—are the persons who alone deserve to be admitted or appointed. Merit is the sole consideration, especially once its criteria have been corrected for possible bias. Reparations, needs, benefits to the individual are totally and properly beside the point—a misleading diversion and distraction which at best appeals to our sympathetic emotions instead of to our intellect.

I think it very important to see precisely what is and is not at stake in this objection to the relevance of minority memberships on the ground that, say, presence in the university might benefit minority members enormously more than majority ones. What is *not* at issue is any question of whether those who deserve to be admitted ought to be admitted. What *is* at issue is the question of whether merit, when measured in terms of past or projected performance, i.e., qualifications, is the sole or proper test for desert. It is clear that merit in this sense of qualification is, perhaps, the single most plausible criterion for determining who will be the most successful student or the most proficient academician (although, as I have indicated, it is certainly possible to challenge the conventional conception of qualifications). However, it is an enormous leap from that truth to any answers whatsoever to the question of desert. And it is the question of who deserves to be admitted to the university that was the force behind the objection we are presently considering.

It is essential to see, too, that the problem does not exist solely because attendance at the university, either as a student or as a faculty member, bestows a number of extrinsic, valuable benefits upon the participants. The gap between who is most qualified to perform a task and who deserves to be admitted or appointed would still be present even if higher education were merely an activity of inquiry—even if the university were simply and wholly a community of intellectuals who engaged in a variety of intellectual activities for their own sake. This is so because there is simply no necessary connection between academic merit or excellence and deserving to be a member of the university community. Suppose, for instance, that there is only one tennis court in the community. Is it clear that the two best tennis players ought to be the ones permitted to use it? Why not those who were there first? Or those who will enjoy playing the most? Or those who are the worst and therefore need the greatest opportunity to practice? Or those who have the chance to play least frequently?

Now, we might, of course, have a rule that says that the best tennis players get to use the court before the others. And if we did have such a rule, then in virtue of that rule, the best players would deserve the court more than the poorer ones. But that is just to push the inquiry back one stage. Is there any reason to think that good tennis players deserve to have such a rule? Indeed, the arguments that might be given for or against such a rule are many and varied. Few, if any, of those arguments that might support such a rule depend upon a connection between ability and desert.

But someone might reply that the most able students do deserve to be admitted to the university because all of their earlier schooling was a kind of competition with university admission being the prize awarded to those who came out the winners. They deserve to be admitted because that is what the rule of the competition provides. In addition, it would be unfair now to exclude them in favor of others, given the reasonable expectations they developed concerning the way in which their industry and their performance would be rewarded. Minority admission programs, which inevitably prefer some who are less qualified over some who are more qualified, all possess this flaw.

There are several problems with this way of thinking about things. And the most substantial of them is that it is an empirically implausible way to construe the world because most of what are regarded as the decisive ability characteristics for higher education have little to do with industry and a great deal to do with things over which the individual has neither control nor responsibility: I.Q., home environment, socioeconomic class of parents, and, of course, the quality of the primary and secondary schools attended. Since individuals as individuals do not deserve any of these things, they do not, for the most part, deserve whatever abilities or qualifications they have. This being the case they do not in any strong sense deserve to be admitted because of their abilities.

To be sure, if there is a rule which connects, say, performance in high school with admission to college, then there is a weak sense in which those who do well in high school deserve, for that reason alone, to be admitted to college. But then, as I have said, the merits of this rule need to be explored and defended. In addition, if persons have built up or relied upon their reasonable expectations concerning performance and admission, they have a claim to be admitted on this ground as well. But it is certainly not obvious to me that these claims of desert are any stronger or more compelling than competing claims based upon the needs of or advantages to minority group members.

Having said all of this, it is also necessary to acknowledge that qualifications are relevant in at least three other respects. In the first place, it is surely the case that there is some minimal set of qualifications without which the benefits of participation in higher education cannot be obtained by the individuals involved. In the second place, it is also the case that the qualifications of all of the individuals within the university will affect to some degree or other the benefits obtainable to anyone within it. And finally, the qualifications of all of the individuals within the university will also affect the way the university functions *vis-à-vis* the rest of the world. The university will do some things better and some things worse, depending upon the qualifications of those who make it up. But as I have said, all these considerations only establish that qualifications, in this sense, are relevant, not that they are decisive. And as such, this is wholly consistent with the claim that minority group membership is also a relevant but not decisive consideration when it comes to matters of admission and appointment.

III

The issues I have just considered concern the benefits obtainable by individuals from attendance at or appointment to the university. This may be an uncongenial way for some to think about the entire problem. I propose to turn, therefore, to a quite different way of looking at things. I want now to give an argument that is designed to show how the university, itself, is benefited from the presence within it of minority group students and teachers. I believe it is an argument that ought to appeal even to those whose ways of thinking about the university are especially conservative ones. The argument is this: Even the most traditional and unified conception of the university sees the search for truth as one of its essential functions. The addition of minority persons to the student body and the faculty will, *ceteris paribus*, increase substantially the likelihood that important truths, which would otherwise have gone undiscovered, will be discovered. Therefore, minority group membership is by itself a good reason for admitting a student or appointing a faculty member.

The crucial premise is the second one. The question, of course, is whether it is reasonable to suppose that minority group membership is connected in any significant way with the success of the university's ongoing search for truth.

One way to begin to see that it might be so connected is to see that in many, if not all, disciplines the ways in which the problems of that discipline get defined have a tremendous effect upon what eventually comes to be known and believed. Again, it is hardly a radical suggestion to observe that substantial progress in inquiry often occurs when someone succeeds in calling into question what was hithertofore deemed an obvious truth or what was not even previously seen to be an assumed fact. The link between minority group membership and meaningful inquiry is forged, on this argument, through the special likelihood that minority group persons (and especially minority group academicians) will tend to define conventional intellectual problems in new and different ways and will tend to perceive more easily unnoticed assumptions that would otherwise have gone unexamined and unchallenged.

The next step in the argument consists in making out the case that minority group persons would, within the university, tend to probe these intellectual problems and unnoticed assumptions. And here, it seems to me, the place to begin is with the claim that race and sex—at least within our culture—are sufficiently central features of experience so that they affect in quite fundamental ways how it is that individuals perceive, regard, and respond to the social and physical world. It need not be maintained that race and sex are the only two significant determinants; just that they are among the more significant ones. Because they are, however, persons who are members of minority groups will tend to look at the world and will tend to define problems quite differently from the way white, middle-class males will be inclined to.

I think that there is a good deal of truth to this claim and, consequently, a good deal of force to the argument on which it depends. In the two fields I know best, namely, law and philosophy, I think there is no question but that academicians look at a number of problems and issues differently because of the recent addition of minority group members to the student body and the faculty and because of the questions that have been raised about the previous composition of the university. A new awareness of the many and peculiar ways in which the legal system has treated the offense of rape is one example; a more critical recognition of the United States Supreme Court's dependence in *Brown* v. *The Board of Education* on a conception of the superiority of white, middle-class values is another; and a reassessment of the moral problems of abortion in terms of the claims of women to control their own bodies is still a third instance. The general claim seems to me more plausible in the case of the humanities and the social sciences than it does in the natural sciences. But even in the case of some of the natural sciences, I can imagine ways in which the claim might be both true and important.

The general point is an empirical one of sorts that falls, I take it, somewhere within the domain of the sociology of knowledge. It seems to me to be an important issue and one that deserves serious and sustained examination. It may be, of course, that this is a matter that has already been amply and convincingly explored and that I am simply ignorant of the conclusions that have been obtained. But if so, the results have certainly not been widely circulated in discussions of minorities and the university. I suspect, however, that there is little that is known in a systematic way on this point, and that it is, indeed, a difficult and complicated issue to explore in any kind of a thorough, convincing fashion. I lack, in any event, the training to provide an empirical approach. Yet what I can do I think is convey to you some of the grounds I have for believing this to be a plausible and important truth. Let me indicate two aspects of the problem which shed light both on the way it is to be approached and on some of the reasons for taking the underlying thesis seriously.

In the first place, it may be difficult to get the thesis taken seriously because part of the characteristic, white, middle-class point of view consists in the belief that reasonably well-educated, well-intentioned white, middle-class males possess the capacity to view both social and natural phenomena in a detached, objective, nondistorted fashion. Sometimes, of course, this view derives simply from a more general one concerning the comparable objectivity of all persons similarly situated. More often and more interestingly, however, the view is one that white, middle-class males tend to hold exclusively about themselves. That is to say, they are quite ready and eager to acknowledge that others— members of various racial groups, or women, or persons of other social classes—do look at the world, approach problems, define issues, etc., through particular, nonobjective points of view. But while this is something others do, it is not something that they do; for they possess the capacity and the detachment to look at things fairly, comprehensively, and completely—in short, to view things as they really are.

Such an attitude is reflected in the following tale. Once there was a case in which the plaintiff was black and the defendant was white. It was a contract case having nothing very much to do with race. The judge assigned to hear the case was himself black. Just before the trial was about to begin, the attorney for the white defendant, who was himself white, asked the judge if he could talk with him for a moment in chambers. The judge agreed and they repaired to the judge's chambers. The lawyer then asked the judge if he, the judge, didn't think that it would be better for all concerned if the judge disqualified himself from the case because it would be hard for him to be fair, given the fact that the plaintiff was black, too.

Now I do not think this is an especially instructive way to show that lots of whites believe that no black judge could be fair in judging a case between a black party and a white party. But I do think this is a useful way to make the other point—that an assumption of impartiality and objectivity is very often a part of the white, male, middle-class view of itself. I am not as interested in the lawyer's beliefs about black judges in this situation as I am about his uncritical assumption about white judges—his ready, unreflective recourse to the typical white judge as the person best able to look at the case in the way that justice and neutrality required.

If I am right that this is often a part of the white, middle-class, male outlook, then this creates a metaproblem at the outset. For among the assumptions of the white, male, middle-class point of view that it will be hardest to call into question is the assumption of the typical detachment, neutrality, and objectivity of the white, middle-class males in question—and they are the ones who in overwhelming numbers do make up the faculties of our universities.

In the second place, it is important to be clearer about how extensive the thesis is. Some might be inclined to accept it only because they interpret it in an unduly restrictive fashion, as the claim that the race or sex or class of the persons involved will make a substantial difference in the way issues get thought about only where the matters under consideration themselves directly involve race, sex, or class. That is to say, the thesis might be deemed plausible only in circumstances where one's interest as a member of a minority group is somehow directly relevant. I think, however, that this is an unnecessarily cramped conception of the general point (and, in fact, is probably a reflection of the white, male, middle-class point of view delineated above). A more ambitious interpretation of the thesis certainly seems to me to be both possible and plausible; it regards the race, sex, or class of the relevant individuals as affecting their points of view in respect to many matters that are not directly racial, sexual, or class-related.

Once again, an example drawn from the law can be instructive. Consider the question of whether it is important for different minorities to be present on juries and, if so, why it is important. One view which I take to be both dominant and overly simplistic thinks that minority representation is important only if, or because, all jurors will tend to act upon straightforward prejudices as jurors. White jurors will, for instance, tend to vote against black defendants and black jurors will tend to vote in favor of them—irrespective, to some degree, of the evidence. With this view minority representation makes sense as the way to cancel the unfair voting of other interests. I do not believe this is a very sensible way to think about the behavior of jurors, and I am not, therefore, surprised when judges act unsympathetically toward demands for minority representation on juries in cases in which the defendants are members of a minority. If this were all there were to the claim that white jurors cannot, say, give a black person a fair trial, it would be a rather unconvincing claim.

But the point is that this is not the only way to think about things. A black person may not be able to get a fair trial from a ☞

group of twelve white jurors, even though they are disposed to be fair and impartial, because the whites may simply bring with them into the jury box a general point of view which affects in very fundamental respects the way they look at the facts.

I was, for example, once involved in a case in which a young black male was charged with having thrown, without provocation, an empty coke bottle at a passing police car. As my client told it to me, however, nothing of the sort had occurred. Instead, he had been standing on the corner selling copies of the Black Panther newspaper when the police car drove by. The police slowed down and said: "Nigger, if we see you on the street with those papers again we will kill you." My client replied: "You mother fuckers can't scare me." The police stopped the car, chased and caught the youth, and took him to jail. They then charged him with throwing an object at a vehicle, a felony which carries in California a sentence of up to five years in the penitentiary. This was a tale the four officers in the car made up to justify the arrest. No bottle had been thrown by the youth or by anyone else. At the preliminary hearing when the officers told their story, they were insistent that they had made no mistake: they had seen the defendant clearly, he had thrown the bottle at their car, and he had done so with a pitching motion with his right hand. The magistrate held the defendant over for trial. Fortunately for the defendant he was left-handed, markedly so, and we also had a witness who had seen the incident and who was sure that no bottle had been thrown. The defendant had a jury trial before twelve white jurors. The police told the same story they told at the preliminary hearing, and we then put on our eyewitness together with a doctor who explained to the jury how he could tell that the defendant was left-handed. The jury then retired to deliberate and in a bit more than seven hours it returned with a verdict of acquittal.

Now someone might think that because the jury found the defendant not guilty, this shows how fair the jury was. But I do not think so. I think the interesting thing is that it took the jury more than seven hours to acquit the defendant. And I think the reason why it took so long is because the jurors were white and middle-class. I do not at all mean to suggest that they wanted to convict the defendant because they were white and he was black. Rather, I think that their general white, middle-class point of view made it hard for them to reach the correct decision. The problem was rooted in the difficulty the jurors had in convincing themselves that the police officers had deliberately fabricated a story about the defendant. I know that this was the problem I had with the case for a very long time. For there was simply nothing whatsoever in my experience with police that made it easy for me to entertain seriously the belief that they would be prepared to lie in so flagrant a fashion. I suspect, however, that the typical black experience is quite different. Many black persons, just because they are black, have had encounters with police in which the police were indifferent to the truth of what they said. And even more black persons have known a friend, relative, or associate who has had such an experience. If this is so, then one probable result is that a part of the typical black point of view consists in a quite different presumption about the credibility of police than that which is contained within the typical white, middle-class point of view. Thus, on this analysis the case for representational juries rests not upon the interest theory but upon the necessity of having different points of view of this sort reflected in the jury's deliberations, if trials are to be genuinely fair.

It is this same kind of argument, I believe, that prevails in respect to substantial minority presence in the student body and on the faculty. For if there are these distinctive points of view and if these points of view are typically connected with minority membership, then the case for the relevance of minority identity is in part the case for a useful and valuable type of intellectual pluralism which aids the university in the fulfillment of one of its most conventional and most important functions—the pursuit of knowledge.

The argument may not, of course, be a good one because I may be mistaken about the facts. It may be that it is not possible to formulate a coherent and meaningful account of the substance of these different points of view. Or it may be, instead, that these different points of view are not even typically connected with identifiable minority groups. These seem to me to be two of the more central, unresolved questions that remain about the issue of the relevance of minority membership for the university. It is also important to see, as well, that if the facts are as I suspect them to be then it is the university, too, that is benefited by the presence of minority persons and not just the members of the minorities.

Preferential Treatment in Admitting Racial Minority Students

ROBERT D. HESLEP

WITHIN THE PAST DECADE higher educational institutions whose student-bodies have been hitherto predominantly, if not exclusively, white have sought to increase their admissions of students from racial minorities. The policy for increasing such admissions which has had most attention may be dubbed the policy of "preferential treatment."[1] The policy has been employed by institutions in various parts of the nation. It has been subjected to public dispute and debate in various states. And it has been recently commented upon, at least implicitly, by members of the United States Supreme Court in their statements on the case of *DeFunis* v. *Odegaard*.[2]

To understand what the policy of preferential treatment is, one will find it helpful to note two sorts of standards immediately connected with admissions to colleges and universities. The first sort is the standards which function as indicators. Typical instances of standards of this kind are designated grade levels, given test score levels, graduation from an accredited institution, and a certain quality of personal recommendation. In everyday discourse standards of this sort are sometimes taken to be *the* standards of admissions; but they are neither the only kind nor logically the primary type. A second class of standards contains those matters of which the first are indicators. Sometimes such standards refer to knowledge, skills, and character habits which a student must have before he can be admitted; at other times they point to achievements which a student must be expected to attain during a given period if he were enrolled in the institution of concern. For convenience, the first type of admission standards will be called "indicator" standards and the second will be dubbed "substantive" standards.

The policy of preferential treatment addresses itself directly to indicator rather than substantive standards. Quite generally, the policy dictates that wherever feasible the admittance of racial minority students is preferable to the admittance of white students. More specifically, the policy assumes that an institution will measure both white and racial minority students by the same indicator standards. Furthermore, the policy, allowing for the limits set by a given desired increase in the admissions of racial minority students, says this: When a racial minority student and a white student have similar qualifications *vis-à-vis* the same indicator standards, the racial minority student will be admitted in preference to the white student. Accordingly, the two common guidelines of this policy stress indicator rather than substantive standards. The first guideline says that any racial minority student whose qualifications meet a set of indicator standards will be granted admittance in preference to any white student with similar qualifications. The second holds that any racial minority student whose record does not qualify him for admittance according to a set of indicator standards but whose record nearly qualifies him for admittance according to these standards will be admitted in preference to any white student with marginal or sub-marginal qualifications.[3]

Critics of this policy have characterized it as a policy of "racial discrimination" and "reverse discrimination," to cite only two of their epithets; thus, they have charged that it is a policy of preferential treatment in a bad sense.[4] It might seem, therefore, that the policy should be dismissed out of hand. Regardless of first impressions, however, a pair of plausible arguments can be made in favor of the policy. One argument appeals to compensatory justice while the other appeals to educational enrichment. If the former argument is not found to be satisfactory, the latter might be. If, however, the latter is not found to be acceptable, what other alternative is to be recommended?

II

The argument from compensatory justice may be initially stated briefly. Until recently the members of racial minorities in the United States, with exceptions, have been denied, relative to the nation's whites, equal educational opportunity. As a result, they have not been able to acquire on a par with whites the knowledge, skills, and dispositions (or whatever might be required) to meet the indicator standards of higher educational institutions. So they, generally speaking, have not been able to compete, and still cannot compete, with whites for entrance into higher educational institutions. Plainly, then, they should in the name of justice be compensated for the disadvantages in higher education which have been imposed upon them.[5] An obvious way for them to be compensated in this respect is for them to be given preferential treatment in college and university admissions as determined by indicator standards.[6]

To clarify this argument further, one will do well to inspect the concept of compensatory justice. Compensation, it has been noted by some philosophers, is one of the various modes of treatment which a person deserves.[7] To maintain that a person deserves a certain treatment is to allow that there is a specifiable condition pertinent to him by virtue of which he deserves the treatment. Thus, to hold that a person deserves compensation is to allow that there is a condition pertaining to him by virtue of which he deserves the compensation. The major types of conditions by virtue of which persons might be said to deserve compensation are injury and loss. By "injury" one does not here intend damage; rather, one intends the violation of a right. This, it will be recalled, is the etymological as well as a standard meaning of the word.[8] Any injury, of course, involves two parties, the injured and the injurer; and any injury is sufficient ground for the injured party to deserve a compensation. Typically, the involved injurer is liable to provide the compensation; but sometimes, as when the injurer is a minor, another is liable for the compensation (a case of the latter sort is an instance of what has been called "vicarious liability"). Regardless, an injury does include a party who is liable for the compensation.

By contrast, a loss, as intended here, is not a violation of a right. It might, yet need not, be one's own fault; but it never is another's fault. If a loss is one's own fault, it is sufficient ground for one's not deserving compensation (though it might be a condition for one's being a recipient of charity). Not every loss which is not one's own fault is a sufficient condition for deserving compensation. For instance, if a person accidentally loses his tobacco pipe, he does not thereby deserve compensation; and if he naturally loses his hair, he does not thereby deserve compensation (though he might if he loses it in an accident). The different kinds of no-fault losses which are sufficient conditions for compensation cannot be readily delimited, but a couple of candidates come to mind. One of them is a loss which impairs a person's functioning as a member of society. At least, this sort of no-fault loss seems to be at the bottom of compensation for the victims of floods and earthquakes, abandonment, and industrial accidents. The other sort is a loss suffered for a public's benefit. This seems to be the type at the bottom of veterans' benefits and unemployment compensation. It is also difficult to specify who is responsible for providing compensation to no-fault loss sufferers. Historically, the party typically has been family, church, guild, and government.

The receipt of compensation, whether for injury or loss, might well be associated with justice. As Aristotle observed, one type of justice is rectificatory and another is distributive.[9] There is rectificatory justice only when things are set aright, when amends are made, or, in a loftier phrasing, when the moral balance is restored. There is distributive justice only when one receives his fair share of money, honors, and other goods. Apparently, compensation for an injury might well be a case of rectificatory justice; and compensation for a loss might well be a case of distributive justice. Thus, when a court awards a plaintiff a sum for a grievance, it purports to correct a wrong done to the plaintiff and, in so doing, to compensate him for an injury. And when a government gives monetary allowances to the victims of an unemployment policy, it aims to help provide them with their rightful share of society's wealth and, thereby, to compensate them for being deprived of their means of livelihood. Nonetheless, it should not be concluded that every compensation is necessarily a matter of justice. That a person deserves compensation means, of course, that there is a good reason for his receiving the compensation; but this does not imply that it would be just for him to receive the compensation. First, the presence of merit is not always a guarantee of justice. Hence, a person who is worthy of an office cannot justly hold it if he does not satisfy all other qualifications for it. Second, some compensations, such as apologies for petty injuries, are arguably beyond the pale of justice. Third, it is dubious that compensation for a loss would be just if it were to violate the rights of another or endanger the public welfare. In sum, compensatory justice is not just any compensation; it is, rather, compensation which is a matter of rectificatory or distributive justice.

As originally presented, then, the argument from compensatory justice is ambiguous; for it pertains to two different sorts of compensatory justice and has a different meaning *vis-à-vis* each sort. To say that racial minority students should, in the name of justice, be compensated for the educational disadvantages which have been imposed upon them is to say both: (a) that they should, in the name of rectificatory justice, be compensated for an injury done them; and (b) that they should, in the name of distributive justice, be compensated for a loss suffered by them. To eliminate this ambiguity, let us reformulate the argument as it relates specifically (a) to rectificatory justice and compensation for injury and (b) to distributive justice and compensation for loss.

a) When directed toward compensation for injury and rectificatory justice, the argument intends that the educational opportunity which has been denied racial minority students is a violation of one of their cardinal rights, viz., the right to equal educational opportunity. Moreover, the argument purports that certain parties have been the violators of this right, namely, those whites who have denied equal educational opportunity to racial minority students. The argument, of course, does not mean that these individual whites are the parties responsible for compensating racial minority students by extending preferential treatment in admissions to higher education. Most of these whites are presumably dead now, and virtually none of the living among them is in a position to give preferential treatment of this type. What the argument intends is that the nation's formerly white colleges and universities are responsible for compensating racial minority students with preferential treatment in admissions. Such institutions are not thereby viewed as responsible by virtue of any guilt on their part, but they are regarded as vicariously responsible. By granting preferential treatment in the admissions of racial minority students, these institutions will help make amends for an injury done such students and, thus, will serve rectificatory justice.

b) When addressed to compensation for loss and distributive justice, the argument stresses that the denial of equal educational opportunity to racial minority students has resulted in losses for them, to wit, the knowledge, skills, dispositions, etc., needed to compete with whites for entrance into higher education. Furthermore, the argument regards these losses as deserving compensation; for they apparently will impair the functioning of racial minority students in the United States, where a higher education is frequently quite important for an individual's personal satisfaction as well as his social contributions. Formerly white colleges and universities, so the argument goes, can compensate racial minority students for these losses by extending them preferential treatment in admissions. And, insofar as they do give them such treatment and, thereby, help them obtain a higher education, they will help them gain their fair share of this society's goods, money, honors, services, etc., and consequently will serve distributive justice.

While it is the case that versions (a) and (b) of the argument from compensatory justice involve different sorts of compensation and different kinds of justice, it is also the case, it should be remembered, that they do share certain features. First, they make the same factual claims, for example: Racial minority members have historically been denied equal educational opportunity; they have not been able to gain, on a par with whites, the competencies needed to meet the indicator standards of higher educational institutions; and they have not been able to compete very well with whites for entrance into higher educational institutions. Second, they make the same general normative claims: Each insists that the preferential treatment of racial minority students in admissions to higher educational institutions is a matter of compensation, and each maintains that such treatment is a matter of justice. So, in an attempt to determine whether or not either version (a) or (b) is satisfactory, a person should inspect what (a) and (b) have in common as well as those points where they specifically differ.

There appears to be no difficulty with the factual claims taken severally within the argument from compensatory justice, but there is a trouble with them as they are related together within the argument. These facts are offered in two sets of cause-effect relations. In the first set, the fact that racial minority students in the United States have been historically deprived of equal educational opportunity is presented as the cause of the fact that such students have not been able to acquire, on a par with whites, the competencies required to meet the indicator standards of higher educational institutions. And in the second set, the latter fact is treated as the cause of the fact that racial minority students have not been able to compete very well with whites for entrance into higher educational institutions. There seems to be no sound reason to doubt the second cause-effect relation, but there is ground for questioning the first one. It might be that racial minority students have not gained, on a par with whites, the competencies needed to meet or exceed the indicator standards of higher educational institutions *because* they have been denied equal educational opportunity. Nevertheless, it might be that they have not acquired these competencies on a par with whites *because of* some other factor, e.g., genetic endowment.[10] The argument from compensatory justice, however, does not show why the fact of deprivation should be taken as the cause of the lack of competencies; it simply asks that it be taken as the cause itself. Unfortunately, the argument is asking too much. If the argument did not use the fact of deprivation as the cause of the lack of competencies, it would not have a basis for its references to compensation for injury and to rectificatory justice; and it would have a weakened foundation for its references to compensation for loss and to distributive justice. Thus, in asking that the fact of deprivation be taken as the cause of the lack of competencies, the argument is asking that a crucial premise be conceded. Presumably, a compelling case can be made to show that the fact of deprivation is the cause of the lack of competencies. But until the argument from compensatory justice makes that case, it must be regarded as faulty in its factual claims.

One of the normative claims common to versions (a) and (b) of the argument fares worse than the other. It might be that the general claim about preferential treatment's being a matter of justice has a flaw; but if there is one, it is not presently evident.

The case is different, however, with the general claim about preferential treatment's being a matter of compensation. Compensation, it will be recalled, is something deserved. Thus, when one maintains that the preferential treatment of racial minority students in admissions to higher educational institutions is a matter of compensation, one implies that racial minority students deserve such preferential treatment. But why do they merit such treatment? Why are they worthy of it? According to the argument from compensatory justice, they merit such preferential treatment because they have been deprived of an adequate opportunity to acquire the competencies needed to compete with whites for admissions to colleges and universities. This answer, though, apart from its cause-effect claim, harbors a problem.

When one says that X deserves, as compensation, preferential treatment in admission to higher educational institutions, one means, of course, that X deserves the preferential treatment by virtue of some injury or no-fault loss relevant to the admissions. In the case at hand, the injury is the deprivation of equal educational opportunity; and the loss is the lack of competencies needed to meet given indicator standards. But is this all that one means? Apparently not. Suppose a person had an injury or no-fault loss relevant to entrance into a college or university and could not perform well *à propos* the involved indicator standards. And suppose further that he could not satisfy the substantive standards of the given institution. Would one then be prepared to say that the person merits preferential treatment in admission to the institution? Normally one would not, and the reason why is plain. The function of an indicator standard, it will be recalled, is to determine whether or not a substantive standard will be satisfied. Thus, if an indicator standard is met by a person, there is a good reason to believe that he will satisfy a related substantive standard. Nevertheless, it must be emphasized, there might be reason to believe that a person might satisfy a substantive standard even though he cannot meet the relevant indicator standard (virtually all colleges and universities have admitted students who have failed to meet given indicator standards but who, even so, have been thought capable of satisfying the institutions' respective substantive standards). If a student does not meet an institution's indicator standards but can, regardless, satisfy its substantive standards, he still, insofar, merits entrance into the institution. If, however, he does not meet the indicator standards and cannot satisfy the substantive ones, he does not deserve admission to the institution. To say, therefore, that a student deserves, as compensation, preferential treatment in admissions to a college or university is to allow more than his having suffered an injury or no-fault loss. It is also to intend that there is reason to believe that he can satisfy the institution's substantive standards.

The argument from compensatory justice, accordingly, does not adequately answer the question of why racial minority students are worthy of preferential treatment. It is not enough for the argument to hold that such students have suffered injury or no-fault loss. It must also maintain that such students may be expected to satisfy the substantive standards of higher educational institutions. To be sure, the argument can be amended so that it states that preferential treatment is deserved by those racial minority students only who may be expected to satisfy the substantive standards of higher educational institutions. However, if it is modified in this way, it will not support the policy of preferential treatment as fully as one might otherwise hope. The policy, it will be remembered, has guidelines, one of which says that any racial minority student whose record does not qualify, but nearly qualifies, him for admittance according to a set of indicator standards will be admitted in preference to any white student with marginal or sub-marginal qualifications. This guideline, it is to be noticed, does not say that preferential treatment is to be given to only those racial minority students with sub-marginal qualifications (*vis-à-vis* indicator standards) who may be expected to satisfy substantive standards. And, because it does not say this, it would not be supported by the argument from compensatory justice if the latter were altered to state that preferential treatment is merited only by those racial minority students who may be expected to satisfy the substantive standards of higher educational institutions. The guideline, of course, could be amended to keep pace with the entertained change in the argument.

The respective special features of versions (a) and (b) of the argument from compensatory justice have more serious problems. In maintaining that preferential treatment in the admissions of racial minority students is a compensation which justly rectifies an injury suffered by such students, version (a) makes a claim that seems acceptable on at least two counts. First, racial minority students as a group have been subject to the violation of the right of equal educational opportunity. Second, the injury to which they have been subject is a grave one and needs correction. Even so, version (a) is troubling at a key spot. In holding that preferential treatment justly rectifies the wrong suffered, version (a) apparently means that such treatment, given the circumstances, is necessarily a matter of rectificatory justice; but it fails to show that such treatment, given the circumstances, is necessarily a matter of the sort. This is unfortunate; for it is doubtful that preferential treatment, even under the described circumstances, is necessarily an instance of rectificatory justice.

Preferential treatment, according to the specified circumstances, aims at rectifying a major wrong done to racial minority students, viz., a violation of their right of equal educational opportunity. If, however, preferential treatment in such circumstances were to violate the same right of white students, it would be unjust. Equal educational opportunity is as important a right for American white students as it is for American racial minority ones, for it is possessed by members of each group not as members of a racial group but as members of the class, American student. Thus, to violate the right belonging to one group of students is as unjust as it is to violate the right belonging to another group. That preferential treatment with the described circumstances will violate the equal educational opportunity of some white students is practically certain. When two students are equally qualified for entrance into a college or university and one of them is granted admission but the other is denied it, then the latter student is deprived of an equal educational opportunity. According to the policy of preferential treatment, a racial minority student with qualifications equal to a white student's will be awarded admission to a college or university in preference to the latter. Thus, in view of the necessarily limited enrollment openings in most higher educational institutions in the United States, the policy is quite likely to lead to denying entrance to some white students with qualifications equal to those of some racial minority students awarded entrance. Consequently, preferential treatment, as intended by version (a) of the argument from compensatory justice, should not be thought of necessarily as an instance of rectificatory justice. Indeed, it may be regarded as possibly an instance of injustice.[11]

Little reflection is required to see that a related problem pertains to version (b) of the argument from compensatory justice. According to this version of the argument, preferential treatment in the admissions of racial minority students will, as compensation, serve distributive justice by helping to give the students their due share of society's goods, money, services, etc. The obvious question here is whether or not such preferential treatment will necessarily serve distributive justice; and the apparent answer is that it will not. As previously explained, such preferential treatment might violate some white students' rights to equal educational opportunity; and, if it does so, it will create an injustice. Surely, however, that which makes an injustice in its distribution of society's goods, money, services, etc., cannot be properly said to distribute such matters duly. The same point may be advanced from a different direction. Possibly, preferential treatment in the admission of racial minority students will prevent some white students from entering colleges or universities who, without such treatment, would otherwise enroll in institutions of the sort. If preferential treatment does prevent such students from enrolling, it will, in effect, create for them a compensable loss whose remedy would be distributive justice. Certainly, an act which makes an unjust distribution of society's goods, money, services, etc., for one group of citizens cannot be fittingly described as serving distributive justice for another group.

III

The other plausible argument supporting the policy of preferential treatment appeals not to any sort of justice but to educational enrichment. According to this argument, the sources of a student's higher education are not limited to books and teachers. They also include his fellow students. Through interaction with other students, a person is in a position to thwart a tendency to view the world from the standpoint of just his particular interests or from those of his cultural and social group; for through such interaction he will have an opportunity to appreciate not only the individual differences and similarities among human beings but also the cultural and racial differences and similarities among them. This social source of education, the argument continues, is especially important for college and university students in the United States, where cultural and racial diversity is widespread. If entrance into higher education persists in being determined only or mainly by competition among students *vis-à-vis* indicator standards, as it often is nowadays, then many student-bodies are likely to remain predominantly white and, insofar, will remain impoverished sources of social education for their individual members. One way to help assure a significantly mixed student-body in a college or university is by using preferential treatment in the admission of racial minority students. Such preferential treatment, therefore, should be employed.[12]

The premises of this argument comprise some patently obvious truths. Culturally and racially diverse student-bodies in American colleges and universities are potentially beneficial, and preferential treatment would help secure culturally and racially variegated student-bodies. Indeed, one is inclined to embellish the argument with a couple of factual points. First, some of this nation's outstanding colleges and universities have long practiced preferential treatment in order to obtain a cultural balance within their respective student-bodies. Hence, educational enrichment as a reason for preferential treatment is nothing outlandish. Second, the courts have ruled that educational reasons may count as good reasons for practices that otherwise might be held illegal.[13] Consequently, there does not seem to be any legal basis for rejecting preferential treatment peremptorily when it is grounded on the argument from educational enrichment. Despite these considerations, however, the argument is beset by some enervating difficulties.

The least troublesome feature of the argument is the vagueness of the notion of a balanced student-body. There is general agreement that a student-body without any, or with only a few, blacks is not balanced; otherwise, though, there is much dispute. How many blacks should a student-body have? Must a student-body have Chicanos, Indians, Asiatics, and other racial minority members? If so, how many of each group? Moreover, will any collection of whites work in a balanced student-body; or should the whites also be culturally and racially balanced—a proper proportion of Anglo-Saxons, Welsh, Irish, Jews, Slavs, Italians, French, Basques, and so forth?[14] At first blush, one might lean toward answering that a balanced student-body is one which approximates the nation's citizen-body in its cultural and racial features. This suggestion will hardly do, however. It assumes that such a microcosmic student-body is generally available to each of the nation's colleges and universities, which is highly doubtful. And it imposes upon colleges and universities the arbitrary rigidity of quotas. All other things being equal, would Harvard's student-body be more balanced than Yale's if the former had the "correct" percentage of Chicanos and the latter had no Chicanos? The problem of determining what is a culturally and racially balanced student-body is not beyond resolution, presumably; but, until the problem is resolved, the argument from educational enrichment suffers.

A more serious trouble with the argument is that it poses a possible conflict with a social responsibility of the nation's higher educational institutions. With little doubt there is ample room to criticize some of the practices which these institutions have followed in grading and certifying their students for the private and public sectors of the United States,[15] but there is no question that the nation's colleges and universities are obligated to aim at turning out good students. These institutions have all been charged by society to provide well-educated citizens—not dullards or playboys; to furnish sound professional personnel—not hacks or immoral ones; to supply persons who excel in the pursuit of knowledge—not drones; to produce persons who are superior in artistic creation—not mediocrities; and so on. To be sure, America's colleges and universities have frequently failed to carry out this duty; but they are not thereby relieved of it. Indeed, they should not be freed of the responsibility; for they are the institutions most suitable for it. If, therefore, colleges and universities follow the policy of preferential treatment, they are likely to engender a situation at odds with their duty to turn out good students. In following the policy, they will probably enroll more sudents with marginal and submarginal qualifications than they otherwise would; and as a result they will probably have more students than they otherwise would, who will not do well with respect to the institutions' various substantive standards. In other and blunter words, the overall quality of the several student-bodies will probably drop. Despite the lowering of the caliber of their student-bodies, colleges and universities can endeavor, of course, to maintain the quality of their graduates by a firm enforcement of their substantive standards. But this attempt will mean an increase in their academic dismissal rate; and such an increase, in turn, will quite possibly lead to pressures to lower the substantive standards and, thus, the quality of the graduates. This problem will not materialize, of course, if there are only a relatively few students with marginal and submarginal qualifications to be enrolled or if the majority of such students who are enrolled do well *vis-à-vis* the given substantive standards. Nevertheless, the problem is present in the argument from educational enrichment.

The last and, perhaps, the most weighty objection to be raised against the argument is that preferential treatment is just as likely to hinder educational enrichment as it is to further it. According to the argument, the intent of preferential treatment is to help secure racially as well as culturally balanced student-bodies in higher education; and the point of having such student-bodies is that, thereby, white and minority students will learn, by interaction, about persons of different races and cultures. The policy of preferential treatment, however, seems destined to interfere adversely with what is learned. By virtue of the policy white students will learn that racial minority students generally cannot compete well with white students *vis-à-vis* indicator standards and can enter colleges and universities only through preferential treatment. To this extent white students will tend to believe that racial minority students generally are inferior to white ones. On the other side, racial minority students will learn that they generally cannot compete with white students *vis-à-vis* entrance requirements and usually can enroll in colleges and universities only by preferential treatment. Thus, they will tend to conclude that they are inferior to white students. Accordingly, the policy of preferential treatment might create invidious learning conditions comparable to the so-called "intangible" ones for which the policy of segregated schools was blamed by the United States Supreme Court in its decision on *Brown* v. *Board of Education, Topeka, Kansas*. The weight of this criticism can be significantly lightened, of course, under a certain condition. If racial minority students, after they are admitted to higher educational institutions, do as well as or better than white students, then they will learn that they are academically just as good as, if not better than, white students. As a result, the above objection will turn out to be a needless bother. Admittedly, racial minority students enrolled by preferential treatment might perform well in comparison with white students. Nevertheless, until a person knows that they are likely to do so, he should be quite concerned with the difficulty at hand.

IV

The present inquiry has examined two initially attractive arguments in favor of the policy of preferential treatment. Finding that each of the arguments has sundry flaws, the inquiry is compelled to conclude that neither of them satisfactorily supports the policy. It might be, of course, that there is an argument which quite adequately defends the policy; but it is not clear that one should search any further for it. If the policy of preferential treatment were the only one whereby the enrollment of racial minority students into American higher education could be increased, the policy would compel a person desirous of enlarging the enrollment to continue looking for a solid argument. The policy, however, is not the only one available.

One alternative, which will be called the policy of "appropriate indicator standards," is especially interesting.[16] This policy assumes that the prevalent indicator standards employed by American colleges and universities are biased toward white students and, therefore, are inappropriate for determining the admissions of racial minority students. Consequently, the policy proposes that the admissions of racial minority as well as white students be determined by indicator standards appropriate to each group.[17] According to this policy, there will be no preferential treatment in the admissions of racial minority or white students. To be sure, racial minority students will not be competing with white students *vis-à-vis* the same indicator standards; but the former will be competing with the latter with respect to the same substantive standards.

The evaluation of racial minority students according to their indicator standards will be matched, by equivalences, with the evaluation of white students according to their indicator standards. Thereby, there will be a common ranking of both racial minority and white students; and students are to be admitted in order of their individual rankings.

Why the policy of appropriate indicator standards looks worth pursuing may be quickly explained. For one thing, there exists a significant body of research which suggests that the indicator standards typically utilized in American higher education are biased toward white students.[18] Moreover, no one set of indicator standards seems to be essential to any American college or university; thus, different sets of indicator standards for each institution would not be necessarily bad. Finally, it has been well established that performance evaluations based on one set of indicator standards might be shown to be equivalent to performance evaluations based on another set of indicator standards.[19]

Of course, the fact that the policy appears to deserve serious consideration does not mean that it is free of all possible troubles. It does not seem, at least on first glance, to have damning faults; but it does have pitfalls. A few of them can be easily marked. One danger is to leave vague the sense in which any indicator standard will be appropriate to racial minority students.[20] Another obstacle is a failure to ascertain that a selected set of indicator standards deemed appropriate is reliable, i.e., that the standards do reliably predict performances with respect to an institution's substantive standards. Finally, there is the hazard that indicator standards applied to racial minority students will not have been determined as equivalent to those applied to white students. These pitfalls stand out for one reason. In its effort to increase its racial minority enrollment, a college or university following the policy of appropriate indicator standards will be tempted to take a course of expediency and ignore the questions to be asked about appropriateness, reliability, and equivalency. And, upon taking such a course, it will, in effect, pervert the policy of appropriate indicator standards into a strategy of disguised preferential treatment. If the policy of preferential treatment cannot be adequately justified on the ground of compensatory justice, then a strategy of preferential treatment certainly cannot be properly defended on the ground of expediency.

However, locating and marking the dangers connected with the policy of appropriate indicator standards is not the primary problem for an inquiry into the policy. The main problem is to develop an argument which will substantiate the policy satisfactorily. That task is a large one and must be undertaken at another time.

NOTES AND REFERENCES

1. The notoriety of the policy does not mean that it is the most frequently utilized one for enlarging the enrollment of racial minority students. Another policy often followed is that of remedial (compensatory) education. It has drawn strong criticism from some researchers and black educators. See Robert J. Panos, "Picking Winners or Developing Potential," *School Review*, 81 (1973), 440–42. Also, *The Atlanta Journal and Constitution*, May 26, 1974, p. 2–A.

2. 414 U.S. 1038. Excerpts from the Court's comments may be found in *The Chronicle of Higher Education*, April 29, 1974, pp. 6–8.

3. The second guideline is manifestly operative in *DeFunis* v. *Odegaard*. DeFunis had a marginal score of 76.23 *à propos* the indicator standards of the University of Washington Law School in 1971. He was denied admittance, but thirty-six racial minority students with scores below 76.23 were admitted.

4. For instance, in *DeFunis* v. *Odegaard* Associate Justice William O. Douglas refers to the University of Washington Law School's policy of preferential treatment as one of "racial preference" and as "working an invidious discrimination."

5. Cf. Charles Frankel, "Equality of Opportunity," *Ethics*, 81 (1971), 203–4: "If it seems unfair—an inequality of opportunity—that a man should not be able to take a test for a position he wants because he cannot afford to travel to the testing place—why is it not also unfair for a man to be deprived of the opportunity to prepare himself for such a test because he cannot get the necessary education? And if it is a mark of unequal opportunity to allow a man to be deprived of an education from which he would benefit when such an education is available to others, why is it not equally an example of unequal opportunity to leave him in an environment that deprives him even of the desire to seek such an education?"

6. For an article advocating the moral relevance of preferential treatment as compensatory justice, see Paul W. Taylor, "Reverse Discrimination and Compensatory Justice," *Analysis*, 33 (1973), 177–82.

7. For example, see Joel Feinberg, *Doing and Deserving* (Princeton, N.J.: Princeton University Press, 1970), pp. 74–76.

8. Cf. Thomas Hobbes, *Leviathan*, pt. 1, chap. 14; pt. 2, chap. 17.

9. Aristotle, *Nicomachean Ethics*, 1130b–1131a.

10. Cf. Arthur R. Jensen, "How Much Can We Boost IQ and Scholastic Achievement?", *Harvard Educational Review*, 39 (1969), 1–123.

11. According to *The Atlanta Journal and Constitution*, September 22, 1974, p. 20–A, this criticism has been rebuffed by Representative Andrew Young, fifth Congressional district of Georgia, in testimony before a subcommittee of the House Education and Labor Committee: " '[Injustice to some individual whites] . . . might be necessary in order to overcome an historic group injustice or series of group injustices.' A white person bumped off an admissions list by a black would have a multitude of other opportunities before him, whereas someone 'from the lower economic strata or some ethnic minority, or a woman,' would not." In response, one must be brief. The claim about the possible necessity of injustice to some individual whites apparently means this: The rectification of the historic injustices suffered by racial minorities (and women) might be secured only with injustice to some individual whites. Arguably, this possibility does not have to become an actuality (see *infra*, section IV). Moreover, the claim about the "multitude" of other opportunities before a white student bumped from an admissions list misses the point. If each college or university practices preferential treatment, it is doubtful that the student will have numerous other opportunities for admissions. And, even if he will have many other opportunities, he still has been treated unjustly with respect to his first opportunity.

12. An argument from educational enrichment has also been used by the AAUP's Council Commission on Discrimination to justify a policy of preferential treatment in faculty appointments. See "Affirmative Action in Higher Education: A Report by the Council Commission on Discrimination," *AAUP Bulletin*, 59 (1973), 178–83.

13. Cf. *Abington School District* v. *Schempp*, 374 US 203.

14. Associate Justice William O. Douglas raises similar questions in his comments on *DeFunis* v. *Odegaard*.

15. Cf. Clarence J. Karier, "Testing for Order and Control in the Corporate Liberal State," *Educational Theory*, 22 (1972), 154–80.

16. Another alternative, described as "selective placement," is proffered by Panos, *op. cit.*, 443ff.

17. This policy is advocated by Associate Justice William O. Douglas in his opinion on *DeFunis* v. *Odegaard*.

18. See, e.g., Alexander W. Astin, *Predicting Academic Performance in College* (New York: Free Press, 1971), pp. 13, 19; Edgar Epps, "Correlates of Academic Achievement among Northern and Southern Urban Negro Students," *Journal of Social Issues*, 25 (1969), 55–70; Julian Stanley and John R. Hills, "Easier Test Improves Prediction of Black Student's College Grades," *Journal of Negro Education*, 39 (1970), 390.

19. See, for instance, Robert L. Ebel, *Essentials of Educational Measurement* (Englewood Cliffs, N.J.: Prentice-Hall, 1972), 2d ed., chapter 19; Victor H. Noll and Dale P. Scannell, *Introduction to Educational Measurement* (Atlanta: Houghton Mifflin, 1972), 3d ed., chapter 4.

20. Hence, this warning by Frankel, p. 207: "even if we agree that many tests of school performance or ability are culturally biased, . . . this does not prove that individuals coming from different cultural backgrounds should not be measured by them. It is possible that they should be measured by them in their own interest."

Reverse Discrimination and Compensatory Justice

WILLIAM T. BLACKSTONE

IS REVERSE DISCRIMINATION justified as a policy of compensation or of preferential treatment for women and racial minorities?[1] That is, given the fact that women and racial minorities have been invidiously discriminated against in the past on the basis of the irrelevant characteristics of race and sex—are we now justified in discriminating in their favor on the basis of the same characteristics? This is a central ethical and legal question today, and it is one which is quite unresolved. Philosophers, jurists, legal scholars, and the man-in-the-street line up on both sides of this issue. These differences are plainly reflected (in the Supreme Court's majority opinion and Justice Douglas's dissent) in *DeFunis* v. *Odegaard*.[2] Declaring this particular case moot, the Supreme Court did nothing to resolve the issue legally. Of course, a legal resolution at this level may or may not be a moral resolution. In this paper I want to address this question from both the legal and moral perspectives (which, of course, overlap to the extent that laws and the Constitution reflect our moral commitments). That is, I want to address this question from the point of view of both (1) basic constitutional commitments and (2) basic moral commitments embedded in the egalitarian ethic.

I will argue that reverse discrimination is improper on both moral and constitutional grounds, though I focus more on moral grounds. However, I do this with considerable ambivalence, even "existential guilt." Several reasons lie behind that ambivalence. First, there are moral and constitutional arguments on both sides. The ethical waters are very muddy and I simply argue that the balance of the arguments are against a policy of reverse discrimination.[3] My ambivalence is further due not only to the fact that traditional racism is still a much larger problem than that of reverse discrimination but also because I am sympathetic to the *goals*

of those who strongly believe that reverse discrimin
policy is the means to overcome the debilitating effects of
justice. Compensation and remedy are most definitely required
by the facts and by our value commitments. But I do not thin
that reverse discrimination is the proper means of remedy or compensation. There are other modes of compensation and I will indicate those modes in the course of this paper.

II

Before we begin, we need a definition of compensatory justice,
since this is the main concept at stake. What do we mean by compensatory justice? Here we cannot attempt to distinguish ge-
nerically all of the various types of justice or to conceptually
delineate an entire theory of social justice. Let us simply observe
that political theorists as far back as Aristotle have spoken of
compensatory, or corrective, or rectificatory justice.[4] Two main
categories of justice which Aristotle discusses are distributive justice and corrective justice. The latter corresponds closest to what
we call compensatory justice. The former involves criteria for the
distributions of goods, offices, and honors among the citizens of
the state. Aristotle recognizes that there are different criteria of
distribution espoused by different people—democrats, oligarchs,
and his own theory, for example. Each would result in a different
distribution. Corrective justice, on the other hand, involves a
rectifying or reparatory transaction between one person or party
and another. Here the law and the judge attempt to restore a kind
of equality which existed prior to the injury of one party by the
other. The penalty imposed on the party who inflicted the injury
and the corresponding benefit bestowed on the injured party should
be proportional to the difference created by the injury. This proportion is no easy matter to ascertain even when it is restricted,
as Aristotle seems to do, to individuals.

Current demands for compensation include Aristotle's sense
of corrective justice but go well beyond the rectification of an injury wrongfully committed by one person on another. Reverse
discrimination as a species of that compensation insists on the
compensation of an entire class of persons (blacks, females, and

Justice
ation as a
past in-
both
k

ss or by society as a whole. It does not
or repair an injury which was directly
present society only but rather to repair
ties, or injustices which have resulted
ast generations are responsible. Thus
nsatory justice differs from corrective
important respects: (1) It involves
er indeterminate classes of persons as
tions between individuals. (2) It does
not require that wrongful injury has been committed by the party
obligated to pay the compensation. Also (3) reverse discrimination as a species of this current sense adds the appeal to class
characteristics—sex or race—as relevant grounds for compensatory action.[5]

The point of this brief definitional *caveat* is this: If we are to
be clear about what we are asking when we ask whether reverse
discrimination is justified, it is important that we keep in mind
the various components of this concept and the way(s) in which
it differs from the more classical sense(s) of compensatory justice.

III

I propose to begin by referring to the *DeFunis* case since it is
perhaps the best known legal case presumed by many to involve
reverse discrimination and since it brings to the fore a number of
the moral and constitutional issues involved in reverse discrimination. Marco DeFunis applied for admission to the University of
Washington Law School in 1971. He was denied admission to a
first-year law class which was restricted to 150 students and for
which there were 1600 applicants. He filed suit in a Washington
trial court, contesting that the Admissions Committee of the Law
School unfairly discriminated against him on the basis of race in
violation of the Fourteenth Amendment of the Constitution. A
mandatory injunction against the law school was granted at the
trial court and DeFunis was admitted. Subsequently, the trial court
judgment was reversed on appeal by the Washington Supreme
Court which held that the admissions policy of the law school did

not violate the Constitution. DeFunis then appealed to the U.S. Supreme Court which stayed the judgment of the Washington Supreme Court thereby permitting DeFunis to continue in law school. Since DeFunis was in his last quarter of law school when the court got around to his case, it was subsequently declared moot. The case was not a class action suit and DeFunis no longer needed remedy.

The constitutional and moral issue involved is the extent to which race figured in the admissions criteria and in the exclusion of DeFunis. The Washington Supreme Court said that the Admissions Committee had not violated the Equal Protection Clause. The U.S. Supreme Court refused to take a stand in declaring the case moot. For my purposes here, the undecided status of the DeFunis case at the highest level does not matter, and I would allow that the complexity of the case leaves room for doubt in both directions. Everything hangs on whether race was the dispositive factor in excluding DeFunis. Some of the facts of the case and the rationale given lead me to believe that this was not the case; some, that it was.

First, let me lay out three possible readings of the case in which reverse discrimination is not involved.

a) DeFunis was excluded but not arbitrarily or unjustly because the same criteria of merit for admission were applied to all applicants. But the indices of that merit—the evidence of the ability to do well in law school—were not uniform for all applicants. In the case of majority candidates, for whom there was no reason to think they had been handicapped by past injustices, the LSAT (Law School Admission Test) score and the PGPA (Predicted Grade Point Average) were virtually dispositive of the issue. But for minority candidates, for whom there was good reason to suspect that they had been handicapped by past injustices, other indices of ability were weighted stronger. Given those injustices and their impact, the LSAT itself may be biased against minority candidates. That is, the LSAT may itself reflect majority group values, background, and training, and hence not constitute a neutral instrument of measurement. These (possible) facts not only justify the separate treatment of minority candidates but fairness in competition also requires the recognition of the handicapping effect of past inequalities and the appeal to non-standard but relevant indices of ability and potential. On the basis of these non-standard indices, a number of minority candidates were admitted and some majority candidates excluded, including DeFunis, even though a number of the excluded majority students rated higher on the standard tests and criteria than the minority students. The admitted minority students were deemed as promising, or more so, as the majority students excluded on the basis of the same criteria of merit, even though the indices of the merit differed.

If this were the correct reading of the events, then the exclusion of DeFunis would be just. It would not involve reverse discrimination. Of course, the broadening of the criteria or indices of ability or potential has the effect, *in a sense*, of handicapping a DeFunis, since the old rules of the game of admission (the LSAT and PGPA emphasis) would have been to his advantage. He is handicapped as a result of the change in the rules of relevance in the admissions process. But if the change in the rules is reasonable, if the non-standard criteria are sound indices of ability, and if the rules are uniformly applied to all, the handicapping cannot be seen as unjust. In fact, if all this were true, we could speak of DeFunis as being handicapped only by reference to the probable different results for him under the new as opposed to the old rules. The statement, "DeFunis was handicapped or disadvantaged," under these conditions, is a *descriptive* judgment which points to the effects of the new rules in contrast to the old. It is not a moral condemnation of the treatment of DeFunis or of the expanded rules of relevance. In fact, if the new rules are reasonable and applied uniformly, then the change in the rules has the effect of helping overcome past invidious discrimination (the effects of which were perpetuated under the old rules whereby relevant criteria for assessing some candidates were excluded) and hence of assuring equality of treatment. The handicapping of a DeFunis in this descriptive sense is perfectly compatible with, in fact required by, the principle of equality. Viewed in this way, the exclusion of DeFunis would not be arbitrary or unjust; it would be the result of fair rules fairly applied.

b) Now I am not urging this interpretation of the events surrounding DeFunis. The expansion of the indices of ability was clearly involved, but so were other elements. Given these other reasons cited and the procedures employed by the Admissions Committee of the University of Washington Law School, a case could be argued that DeFunis's rights were violated when he was excluded, i.e., that he was arbitrarily disqualified or disadvantaged.

Why is this so? Not because separate treatment was given to candidates from racial minorities. It is perfectly consistent with fairness—in fact, fairness may require it—that race be used as a contingent characteristic enabling one to identify in general those candidates who were probably subject to past invidious discrimination and who need separate treatment in order to focus on other facts or criteria about them which are proper indices of their abilities and qualifications. To be aware that a group in general suffered past invidious discrimination which impairs their performance on normal test criteria (LSAT and PGPA) and not to look for other relevant criteria to assess their ability to perform in law school and to practice law—this is injustice. It simply continues unabated the results of past discrimination. Distributive justice requires this kind of compensatory action.

I have been speaking within a framework of our moral commitment to equality. Within a legal or constitutional framework the issue is complicated by the fact that the courts have declared that records based on race or ethnic origin cannot be maintained. This was done to protect minority groups from invidious discrimination. Undoubtedly the stand of the courts has had this effect in many cases, but the sword is two-edged. It can prevent the collection of pertinent information required for compensatory justice. Recently the Supreme Court has introduced important qualifications on the issue of racial or ethnic classification.[6] It has held that although racial distinctions are "highly suspect" and generally "irrelevant" to "constitutionally acceptable legislative purpose," still such classification may be permitted if there is "some overriding statutory purpose" which justified racial distinctions. In such cases racial classification is not deemed to violate the equal protection clause. On the contrary the equal protection clause may require such classification as a means of overcoming minority-group disadvantages. Thus, on neither moral nor constitutional

grounds can the separate classification of racial minority applicants serve as a basis for the claim that DeFunis was arbitrarily
excluded and that his rights under the Fourteenth Amendment
were violated.

But at least a substantial portion of the explanation of DeFunis's
exclusion by the University of Washington Law School and the
election of minority candidates as students indicates that race itself,
not alternative indices or measurements of abilities or potential
to perform in law school collected in part through racial classification devices, was the determining factor in admitting some
candidates and excluding others. Not mere race was the factor, of
course. The admissions procedure attempted to focus on indices
of abilities of racial minority students other than their results on
the LSAT and their PGPA. But the determining factor, officials conceded, in admitting a number of minority candidates and excluding
DeFunis, was race itself. The Admissions Committee admitted
that at least some minority applicants who were admitted as students were less promising than at least some of the majority applicants who were rejected. If those applicants had been white,
they would not have been admitted. This was done in order to
obtain a "reasonable representation" of racial minority candidates.
One way of reading the action of the Admissions Committee is
that it was an effort to balance two claims of justice—the uniform
treatment of all applicants and the obligation to correct past
injustices.

There is no doubt that DeFunis was fairly treated *vis-à-vis* all
other majority applicants. But *vis-à-vis* the minority applicants,
his exclusion appeared not to be racially neutral. On racial grounds
primarily he was effectively excluded from the competition for
admission for the limited seats set aside for minority students. The
result for DeFunis was that he found himself, *vis-à-vis* these
limited seats, in the same position today that many blacks and
racial minorities found themselves in the past, namely, excluded
on the basis of race.

c) The above is another rendering of the facts of the *DeFunis* case.
But there are yet additional complications and reasons which bear
on this case or which might bear on future *DeFunis*-like cases.
Suppose the Admissions Committee offered the following sorts of

reasons for its policy and the resultant exclusion of DeFunis: (1) The effort to obtain a "reasonable representation" of racial minority candidates was not to reach some racial quota but to enhance the legal education of all students in the law school. A more diverse student body results in broader educational experiences, in particular in the area of law where the plurality of values is continually manifest. (2) It is more likely that candidates from racial minorities will provide legal services in communities where such services are badly needed. (Cited as a relevant reason in Justice Douglas's dissenting opinion in the *DeFunis* case.) Surely this is one of the main reasons for the existence of law schools. (3) Furthermore, minority race lawyers may bring especially valuable perspectives on the law, its nature, and its functions in society. (4) Racism is one of our "most pressing national problem[s], and increasing the pool of black, brown, and red lawyers is an excellent way to address that problem."[7]

All of these reasons, some argue, support not only the conclusion that there is a "compelling state interest" in sustaining racial classifications, but also, as one legal scholar put it, a compelling state interest "adequate to justify the use of race as a basis for preferring minority applicants over non-minority students who come with better credentials."[8] In fact, Professor O'Neil argues that "the case for allowing special treatment in this sector seems so compelling that one is tempted to press it toward recognition of a constitutional right to preferential policies."[9]

It seems to me that the above sorts of reasons, some of which may have been present in the DeFunis case, are not irrelevant to admissions policies. Basically, they are consequential or utilitarian considerations underlying the *raison d'être* of the law itself and its sustenance and perpetuation. They need not conflict with justice or justice-regarding reasons in this case. The latter constitutes the framework of admissions procedures and criteria. The former constitute part of a set of goals for which the law, schools of law, and admission criteria are devised. As long as the goals are reasonable and the framework applied to all candidates, that is, as long as the consequential considerations are not invoked in an ad hoc or arbitrary fashion to the disadvantage of any one person or group, then there need be no conflict between justice-regarding and consequence-regarding reasons. However, it is possible for these consequence-regarding and justice-regarding reasons to conflict. John Stuart Mill clearly recognized this fact even though he refused to recognize it in theory. Since Mill a good number of ethical and political theorists have acknowledged the possible conflict of justice and utility. John Rawls's theory is the most recent fully developed one in which this is recognized.[10] The implications of this issue for the question of the justification of reverse discrimination is obvious: Even if reverse discrimination is unjust (and this is the central question we have yet to address in this paper), might it not be morally justifiable to practice it in some circumstances? That is, might not the moral weight of utilitarian reasons override that of injustice in such circumstances, thereby morally justifying injustice? This is in fact another way of reading the facts and the rationale of the DeFunis case. We will return to this issue later in this paper, after treating the more restricted issue of the justice of reverse discrimination.

IV

Let me now move from the DeFunis case to a somewhat more abstract level of argument on the issue of compensatory justice and, then, to the question of the justice of reverse discrimination. Let us assume that past invidious discrimination justifies and requires compensation and remedial action when possible in order to effect distributive justice. But compensation and distributive justice may require quite different action or policies in different contexts. Characteristics or conditions which are *relevant* to the differential treatment of persons or groups may hold in one context but not in another. Let me spell out this point, by reference both to the Equal Protection Clause of the Fourteenth Amendment and to the egalitarian ethic.

The Equal Protection Clause requires the elimination of invidious discrimination. It commands the elimination of irrelevant criteria for the differential treatment of persons. It does not require the identical treatment of persons if there are relevant grounds for treating them differently. If there are no relevant differences, then it does require substantially identical treatment. Now immediately the question arises: Which characteristics or criteria are relevant grounds for differential treatment and which are not? Race, sex, religion, national origin, and so on are generally taken as invidious grounds of discrimination, and I would agree that they are generally invidious and irrelevant. But are they always so? We have already observed that the courts have permitted racial classification for the purpose of overcoming past invidious discrimination. But race or racial characteristics may be relevant to differential treatment on other grounds. For example, race may be quite relevant to the choice of a candidate for a certain acting role in a movie. Restriction of candidates for such a role to a racial group we normally would not consider invidious discrimination. But such restriction in employing carpenters and bricklayers we would consider invidious. The same applies for sex. Sex and sexually associated characteristics may be irrelevant for a wide range of treatment but quite relevant in some contexts. Take, for example, the current issue of equal treatment for women in college athletics. There is little doubt that women as a class have been improperly discriminated against *vis-à-vis* athletic opportunities in colleges and universities. Funds for intercollegiate teams for women comparable to those for men have not been made available in cases in which the interest among women in such teams and competition has been high. A strong case might be made out for invidious class discrimination based on sex. Would this mean that equality of treatment or "equal protection" would be effected by permitting women to compete equally with men for positions on a single team? I would doubt this. In some sports, sex or sexual characteristics may be irrelevant to fair competition, and if a female wants to try to compete with males in a given sport, she surely should be given the opportunity. But if I am correct in certain factual assumptions about the general physical differences between men and women (allowing for wide individual variations, of course), then, if intercollegiate athletic teams simply were opened to women to compete for team positions along with the men, most teams would be entirely male. In this context it may well be that a "separate but equal doctrine" would best instantiate justice, providing sexually separate but equal opportunity for the intercollegiate competitive experience. A state-supported "separate but equal" doctrine in the context of general education, on the other hand, whether sexual or racial, would be invidious discrimination. It would not produce equal opportunity but quite the reverse.

Take another example involving race. If it were shown that a given race were particularly susceptible to a given disease, then equal treatment or distributive justice *vis-à-vis* medical services might require racial differentiation in public health policies.

The point of these examples is that the judgment that a given characteristic—sex, race, and/or racially or sexually associated characteristics—is relevant to differential treatment is in part a factual judgment about states-of-affairs in the world and their instrumental relationship to other states-of-affairs. In other words, part of the judgment that a given characteristic is relevant to the differential treatment of persons is fact-stating and descriptive. If this part of the judgment turns out to be false, then the facts cited are irrelevant in the factual sense, which denies that a given empirical, instrumental relationship exists. Also the rules of differential treatment which are constitutive of certain practices and which are based in part on such supposed empirical facts, are irrelevant in a second sense, namely, they are improper rules (an evaluative moral sense of "irrelevant," i.e., a claim that the rule is morally objectionable).

It must be granted, it seems to me, that this second sense of "relevant" or "irrelevant" presupposes a theory of justice or a set of general moral principles which define or specify criteria of relevance and, perhaps, a hierarchical ordering of those criteria. That is, the moral relevance or irrelevance of certain characteristics or conditions cannot be determined without some such framework of principles or commitments. This I take it is Jeremy Bentham's point in *The Principles of Morals and Legislation* when he says that "proof must have its commencement somewhere." I say this here not just to raise the question of whether there may be different commencement points, that is, different and conflicting theories of justice or moral principles, and hence the possibility of irreconcilable normative frameworks. Philosophers have had much to say about this possibility and I am not about to take on this issue here.[11] Rather I refresh our memories on Bentham's point in order to indicate as clearly as possible that the question of the justification of reverse discrimination can be resolved only

by reference to a theory of justice—distr
—and a set of moral principles. My interes
alternative theories of justice or morality but t
the question of the justification of reverse discr
the framework of our generally accepted principl
ments, those found in the Constitution and the egalit
I would not deny, of course, that there may be substant
ferent interpretations of those constitutional principles and
egalitarian ethic. Again, these are issues I cannot take on he
(See Appendix for discussion of emerging or developing conceptions of the egalitarian ethic and see "Developments in the Law:
Equal Protection," *Harvard Law Review* 82 (1969), 1065–1192,
for discussion of alternative interpretations and current developments of the Equal Protection Clause.) What I will do is invoke
one interpretation of that ethic and those principles and attempt
to resolve the question of the justification of reverse discrimination by reference to that base. That base will provide the normative sense of "relevant" invoked in this paper and I will spell it
out in a moment.

First, I want to indicate the importance of the factual sense of
"relevant" to the issue of compensatory justice. Constitutive rules
of many of our social practices have often been grounded on supposed facts which turn out not to be facts at all, or which turn
out to be simple prejudices. The "facts" are invented and the social
stereotype and their concomitant unjust practices come into existence. On the other hand, there are facts which really exist which
are relevant to differential treatment which we have not been per-
ceptive enough to see and which we have not instantiated into
rules of differential treatment in our social practices. The University of Washington Law School was trying to do this in its
admissions procedure and criteria. In fact, the history of the egalitarian ethic and the democratic concept of social justice has been
one of the gradual recognition and sloughing off of irrelevant
criteria for the differential treatment of persons and the adoption
of relevant ones. Much still needs to be done both in terms of
sloughing off and adding on; and major judicial decisions such as
Brown v. *Topeka, Harper* v. *Virginia Board of Education,* and
Griffin v. *Illinois,* in which an effort was made to assure equal access to public resources in education, voting rights, and criminal

butive and compensatory
here is not to discuss
attempt to answer
mination within
s or commit-
rian ethic.
ally dif-
f the
re.

2 These decisions and
ualities of two kinds—
es of one's birth, eco-
l in every sense), and
ious discrimination—
ive justice and equal
confront both types
treatment and social
the latter kind of in-
sense in which com-
re certain additional
ed in the next section.
ic as it has evolved
cluded this emphasis

on compensation (in both senses of compensation) as an essential part of a theory of distributive justice. Emphasis upon equality of opportunity and equal access to public resources, a fair chance to play the game and to compete within the same rules, is the core of that ethic. It has been clearly seen that without equality of opportunity, competition is unfair; that competition among those who do not have an equal chance of meeting the criteria of merit on the basis of which competition is conducted is unjust. A great deal of "competition" is stacked in just this way. It is unfair and violates the principle of equality of opportunity. It has only the surface appearance of being fair competition with uniform criteria applied to all. Beneath the surface there are gross inequalities in opportunities to compete. We cannot reasonably expect persons whose basic needs are unfulfilled or persons from deprived, poverty stricken backgrounds to compete equally on criteria of merit with those from affluent, highly advantaged backgrounds. As I have argued elsewhere,[13] social justice requires the moral priority of need-criteria as opposed to merit-criteria in the distribution of goods and services. It is not that merit-criteria are irrelevant in the distribution of goods and services. But distribution on the basis of merit is fair only if those who compete on that basis have an equal opportunity to acquire meritorious characteristics or abilities. If merit-criteria are given priority over need-criteria, many persons are effectively excluded from the competition as a result of circumstances and deficiencies over which they have no control. The result is invidious if the inability to compete on the basis of merit-criteria is due to unjust past discrimination by the social, political, and legal system.

The evolving egalitarian ethic to which I refer affirms these propositions: (1) that distribution of goods and services primarily on the basis of merit is unfair unless each has a fair chance to compete on the basis of those criteria; (2) that the use of merito-cratic criteria, without compensatory measures to permit those who suffer either from involuntary inequalities or from past invidious discrimination to improve their competitive position, simply per-petuates inequalities; and (3) that we must not only eliminate invidious discrimination but make "affirmative" efforts to assure equality of opportunity by adopting a variety of compensatory measures, such as special educational, training, and tutorial programs, apprenticeships, day-care centers, and the like, and by using non-standard but relevant criteria for assessing ability or potentiality.

Some would challenge the meritocratic conception (sometimes characterized as the "liberal" conception) of social justice even further. They insist not only upon the moral priority of need-criteria but they also challenge the justice of the distribution of goods and services on the basis of merit. This occurs on two levels. Some call merely for a reform of the system, arguing that the re-ward system does not distribute the proper proportion of economic and social benefits to those with certain talents and abilities—to statesmen, actors, professional athletes, teachers, bricklayers, and the like. Others challenge the entire system of distribution of benefits on the basis of talents or merit. Marx had at least this in mind when he said, "from each according to ability, to each ac-cording to need." John Rawls, Herbert Spiegelberg, and Thomas Nagel have all issued recent challenges to a meritocratic theory of distributive justice, to the thesis that differential talents dispensed by nature justify on justice-regarding grounds widely disparate economic benefits and social status. (See Appendix.) It is obvious that if the traditional meritocratic criteria of distribution are re-jected, then the question of the justification of policies of distribu-tion and compensation, including reverse discrimination is affected, for different rules for playing the game are invoked. We will see the importance of such a change of rules in the next section.

V

Let us now return to two lines of reasoning to which appeal might be made to justify reverse discrimination, both of which we suggested were present in the *DeFunis* case (b and c, III above): (1) the appeal to justice-regarding reasons, and (2) the appeal to social utility. We will consider (1) first.

The moral and constitutional (justice-regarding) grounds for characterizing reverse discrimination as unjust overlap to some extent. First, the Constitution requires racial and sexual neutrality, except in those rare cases where race or sex is actually relevant (see Section IV above). The egalitarian ethic does the same. But reverse discrimination is the opposite of racial or sexual neutrality. It is discrimination or preferential treatment on grounds of sex or race. If the preferential treatment were based on the fact of past injustice to a person and the current debilitating effects of that injustice, and if race or sex were simply used as helpful classification devices for isolating and identifying individuals who suffer from such past injustice, then compensatory action to such persons is not only consistent with but required by both the Constitution and the egalitarian ethic.[14] Such compensatory action, however, would not be reverse discrimination. Reverse discrimination insists on blanket preferential treatment for certain persons on the basis of sex or race itself, even if those persons do not suffer from past injustices.

If a case could be made that there is an invariable connection between being black or being female and suffering from past invidious discrimination, then perhaps a case could be made for blanket differential treatment for blacks or females. Such differential treatment some might call reverse discrimination, since, on the assumption of such an invariable connection, all that one needs to do is discern a person's sex or race and one then knows that differential, compensatory treatment is justified. Even on this assumption, however, race or sex is not the morally relevant feature justifying the special treatment. Rather it is the past invidious discrimination or injustice which is invariably (on this assumption) connected with a given race or sex.

But I would go further and argue that there is no invariable connection between a person's being black or female and suffering from past invidious discrimination. I do not intend to deny the obvious, namely, that social, political, and legal rules and practices have historically embodied criteria which discriminated brutally against blacks and females as classes. What I deny is that any given black or any given female in the here and now necessarily suffers from such past injustice. There are thousands of whites and males—as well as other minority group members—who also suffer from past invidious discrimination of one type or another, and there are many blacks and other minority group members who are highly advantaged, who are sons and daughters of well-educated, affluent lawyers, doctors, and industrialists. A policy of reverse discrimination would mean that such highly advantaged individuals would receive preferential treatment over the sons and daughters of disadvantaged whites or disadvantaged members of other minorities. I submit that such a situation is not social justice. It violates our basic commitment to equality, that is, it violates the principle that each person is to be judged on his own merit within a system in which each has an equal opportunity to compete.

Let me bring out this point in another way. If Aristotle is correct, corrective or compensatory justice requires compensation which is proportional to the degree of injury suffered. And the injury itself must be wrongfully perpetrated or at least caused by the compensator. There are two ways in which reverse discrimination violates these conditions. Preferential treatment on the basis of race or sex does not provide compensation which is proportional to injury. I am not here referring to the amount of compensation which an omniscient being alone perhaps could assess.[15] I am referring to the fact that compensatory justice requires that equality be given to compensatory claims. If Jones is white or male and Smith is black or female and each has been injured to the same extent, the principle of compensatory justice would require that each is entitled to equal compensation. But reverse discrimination endorses policies in which equal injuries are not entitled to equal compensation. As Professor Robert Simon puts it, under such policies "the basis on which compensation is awarded is independent of the basis on which it is owed, and so distribution is determined by application of principles which are irrelevant from the point of view of compensatory justice."[16] If a person or group has been injured more severely than others by injuries which prevent genuine equality of opportunity—and this is the case with many blacks—then both priority and higher proportionality in compensatory measures is justified. But the basis for that priority and proportionality would not be race but the extent of the injustice suffered and its debilitating effect.

In the same way in which reverse discrimination discriminates arbitrarily in favor of some who have suffered from past injustice and against others who have suffered, it also exacts compensation from persons in an arbitrary way. The young, white, male assistant-professor candidate, for example, who is displaced by a black or a female on a preferential hiring policy or a DeFunis who is displaced by a preferential admissions policy pays the price for injuries for which he most certainly cannot be held responsible and to which he may not have contributed one iota. He may have profited from such past injuries to others. His educational opportunities may have been enhanced in some way by past racism or sexism. But this is inadequate ground to exact the cost for such past injuries from him. And yet reverse discrimination distributes the corrective burden in just this arbitrary fashion. In fact, it is possible that the displaced white suffers from invidious past discrimination *of some type* to a greater extent than the preferred black or female.

Whatever benign intent lies behind acts of reverse discrimination, such acts have the effect of excluding whites, males, and others on the basis of their sex or race. But if the egalitarian ethic and the Constitution prohibit the exclusion of blacks on racial grounds, they surely prohibit the exclusion of whites on racial grounds. And if they prohibit the exclusion of women on grounds of sex, they surely prohibit the exclusion of men on grounds of sex.

The advocate of reverse discrimination might argue that his policy is not intended to disadvantage innocent persons, that he sees the obligation to pay reparations and compensation, not as one which any given majority person owes to injured minorities, but one which society as a whole owes to the classes of persons who are black or female, and that the disadvantaging of some majority innocents is an unfortunate consequence, indeed, a temporary injustice, of policies required to fulfill the collective responsibility of society to blacks and women. This response obviates the problem of holding individuals responsible for acts they did not commit, for it excludes guilt. But it does not obviate the arbitrary distribution of the cost of compensation nor the arbitrary distribution of benefits among the disadvantaged.

If the notion of collective responsibility is taken as implying the collective guilt of white males or of society in general, something is amiss—and some black (and feminist) rhetoric does speak of the guilt of the white man (or of men). Surely whites, like anyone else, are guilty of injustices as individuals, and I would add, blacks or females suffer injustices as individuals. As Professor Joel Feinberg argues, "Liability can transfer but not agency, causation or fault (the components of 'contributory fault') and certainly not guilt."[17] This is not to deny that there is or has been institutionalized injustice which applied uniformly to a class or to classes; nor is it to deny that injustice was the fault principally of white men. It is to emphasize that the results cannot be attributed to all white males collectively, and that fault cannot be transferred *simpliciter* across generations.

I am not advocating that we throw out the notion of collective responsibility. Only that it be properly conceptualized so that it is consistent with an acceptable theory of responsibility and of justice. We properly can speak of collective responsibility in such a way that the notion of guilt, criminal or moral, is *not* involved. Collective responsibility can mean overall societal liability or corporate liability not where the question of guilt and punitive reparations are at stake but where compensation is seen as owed.[18] In the case of racism or sexism, the liability of different members of the corpus may be of different degrees, depending on their roles. Mere passive acceptance of a system in which racism or sexism exists may be seen as a kind of contributory fault even if one does not actively participate in racist or sexist acts or policies.[19] Though a sin of omission, this is certainly not racism. As Professor Graham Hughes argues, "If white people are not active enough in doing something about the social injustice suffered by black people, neither are black people active enough in helping the American Indian or the mentally ill or the starving Biafrans. We are most of us indolent most of the time, and it is very proper that we should be reminded that this is a failing, but it is also proper to point out that it is not equivalent to the offense of racism."[20] Still, corporate liability or collective responsibility, construed within these limitations, not only makes sense; it is the proper stance of a nation committed to social justice which recognizes its own past institutionalized injustice and the current effects of that injustice.[21]

Thus far the reasons cited have weighed against reverse discrimination. But there is another side to this picture, indicated by the (b) reading of the *DeFunis* case above. We can put this case this way: Our current system of distributive justice presupposes the acceptance of some form of the meritocratic conception of equality or social justice (meritocratic standards of access to positions and of the distribution of goods and services). If, however, all meritocratic rules of distribution of goods and services are rejected, or if it is maintained that some such rules are acceptable (say, that differential effort justifies differential reward even though differential natural abilities do not) but that our operative rules of distribution are grossly unfair, then justice-regarding arguments for policies of compensation, and, perhaps reverse discrimination, are affected. If the meritocratic system or its current instantiation is itself unjust, then economic and social benefits are being distributed unjustly. This means that those who happen not to meet the merit-criteria suffer economic injustice through no fault of their own. It might be argued that the alleviation of this kind of injustice under such a system might justify inequalities in the distribution of education and employment opportunities. That is, the justice-regarding reason calling for economic justice might override the justice-regarding reason calling for equality in the distribution of educational and employment opportunities. As Professor Thomas Nagel puts it, "It may then be necessary to decide that justice in the distribution of one advantage has priority over justice in the distribution of another that automatically goes with it."[22] Under such circumstances, as Nagel argues, those with better qualifications to succeed in a certain position "cannot claim that justice requires the allocations of positions on the basis of ability, because the result of such allocation, in the present system, is serious injustice of a different kind."[23]

This argument which pits one justice-regarding reason against another has been taken to be an argument for reverse discrimination. But it is not. If sound, the argument supports compensatory action *vis-à-vis* educational and employment opportunities for anyone, regardless of sex or race, who has been disadvantaged unjustly and who suffers economic injustice because he has never been accorded genuine equality of opportunity. Even taken in this more general way, it is very difficult to assess an argument for the priority of the right to compensation over the right to the equal application of meritocratic rules for access to positions. On the one hand there is great injustice in the present meritocratic system of rewards. Reform is needed with a priority emphasis on those need-criteria required for genuine equality of opportunity. (Nagel is correct in saying that "some of the worst aspects of what we now perceive as racial or sexual injustice are merely conspicuous manifestations of the great social injustice of differential reward."[24]) On the other hand, ad hoc violations of the meritocratic rules governing access to positions also results in great injustice, as we have argued above. It is no easy matter to balance these demands on justice-regarding grounds alone. I have strong doubts, also, on utilitarian grounds that the means of compensation and remedy for past injustice should violate the meritocratic rules governing access to positions. Imagine the consequences if those rules were systematically violated! Perhaps the answer is retention of meritocratic rules of access but a broadening of the indices of merit (ability or potential) and a lessening of the differential rewards between those who successfully gain access and those who do not. This would lessen, if not overcome, the conflict between economic justice and the uniform application of meritocratic rules of access to positions.

In any case, few of us have a clear-cut hierarchy of justice-regarding reasons and much depends on facts surrounding individual cases. It is for this reason that many who consider the question of compensatory justice and reverse discrimination turn to consequential or utilitarian considerations as moral grounds for resolution. We will turn to these considerations in the next section. With reference to justice-regarding reasons alone the weight of the arguments lead me to the conclusion that compensatory policies should be racially and sexually neutral.

VI

Let us now turn to the possibility of a utilitarian justification of reverse discrimination and to the possible conflict of justice-regarding reasons and those of social utility on this issue. The category of morally relevant reasons is broader, in my opinion, than reasons related to the norm of justice. It is broader than those related to the norm of utility. Also it seems to me that the norms of justice and utility are not reducible one to the other. We cannot argue these points of ethical theory here.[25] But, if these assumptions are correct, then it is at least possible to morally justify injustice or invidious discrimination in some contexts. A case would have to be made that such injustice, though regrettable, will produce the best consequences for society and that this fact is an overriding or weightier moral reason than the temporary injustice. Some arguments for reverse discrimination have taken this line. Professor Thomas Nagel argues that such discrimination is justifiable as long as it is "clearly contributing to the eradication of great social evils."[26] Professor Graham Hughes *appears* to argue similarly: "We must acknowledge that the large institutional changes which will be necessary in order to achieve rectification of major social injustices can only be accomplished at the cost of some individual injustice . . ." and that ". . . techniques of discrimination in reverse ought to be regarded as a short-term measure for meeting a crisis of thundering urgency."[27]

Another example of what I would call a utilitarian argument for reverse discrimination was recently set forth by Congressman Andrew Young of Georgia. Speaking specifically of reverse discrimination in the context of education, he stated: "While that may give minorities a little edge in some instances, and you may run into the danger of what we now commonly call reverse discrimination, I think the educational system needs this. Society needs this as much as the people we are trying to help . . . a society working toward affirmative action and inclusiveness is going to be a stronger and more relevant society than one that accepts the limited concepts of objectivity. . . . I would admit that it is perhaps an individual injustice. But it might be necessary in order to overcome an historic group injustice or series of group injustices."[28] Congressman Young's basic justifying grounds for reverse discrimination, which he recognizes as individual injustice, are the results which he thinks it will produce: a stronger and more relevant education system and society, and one which is more just overall. His argument may involve pitting some justice-regarding reasons (the right of women and racial minorities to be compensated for past injustices) against others (the right of the majority to the uniform application of the same standards of merit to all). But a major thrust of his argument also seems to be utilitarian.

Just as there are justice-regarding arguments on both sides of the issue of reverse discrimination, so also there are utilitarian arguments on both sides. In a nutshell, the utilitarian argument in favor runs like this: Our society contains large groups of persons who suffer from past institutionalized injustice. As a result, the possibilities of social discord and disorder are high indeed. If short-term reverse discrimination were to be effective in overcoming the effects of past institutionalized injustice and if this policy could alleviate the causes of disorder and bring a higher quality of life to millions of persons, then society as a whole would benefit.

There are moments in which I am nearly convinced by this argument, but the conclusion that such a policy would have negative utility on the whole wins out. For although reverse discrimination might appear to have the effect of getting more persons who have been disadvantaged by past inequities into the mainstream quicker, that is, into jobs, schools, and practices from which they have been excluded, the cost would be invidious discrimination against majority group members of society. I do not think that majority members of society would find this acceptable, i.e., the disadvantaging of themselves for past inequities which they did not control and for which they are not responsible. If such policies were put into effect by government, I would predict wholesale rejection or non-cooperation, the result of which would be negative not only for those who have suffered past inequities but also for the justice-regarding institutions of society. Claims and counter-claims would obviously be raised by other ethnic or racial minorities—by Chinese, Chicanos, American Indians, Puerto Ricans—and by orphans, illegitimate children, ghetto residents, and so on. Literally thousands of types or groups could, on similar grounds as blacks or women, claim that reverse discrimination is justified on their behalf. What would happen if government attempted policies of reverse discrimination for all such groups? It would mean the arbitrary exclusion or discrimination against all others relative to a given purpose and a given group. Such a policy would itself create an injustice for which those newly excluded persons could then, themselves, properly claim the need for reverse discrimination to offset the injustice to them. The circle is plainly a vicious one. Such policies are simply self-destructive. In place of the ideal of equality and distributive justice based on relevant criteria, we would be left with the special pleading of self-interested power groups, groups who gear criteria for the distribution of goods, services, and opportunities to their special needs and situations, primarily. Such policies would be those of special privilege, not the appeal to objective criteria which apply to all.[29] They would lead to social chaos, not social justice.

Furthermore, in cases in which reverse discrimination results in a lowering of quality, the consequences for society, indeed for minority victims of injustice for which reverse discrimination is designed to help, may be quite bad. It is no easy matter to calculate this, but the recent report sponsored by the Carnegie Commission on Higher Education points to such deleterious consequences.[30] If the quality of instruction in higher education, for example, is lowered through a policy of primary attention to race or sex as opposed to ability and training, everyone—including victims of past injustice—suffers. Even if such policies are clearly seen as temporary with quite definite deadlines for termination, I am sceptical about their utilitarian value.

It is for similar reasons that I do not believe that the constitutional escape clause which might permit reverse discrimination in theory would permit it in practice. I am referring here to the appeal to a "compelling state interest" which was utilized in 1944 in *Korematsu* v. *United States*[31] whereby the government imposed evacuation and detention orders upon citizens of Japanese descent who lived in the western part of the country. Chief Justice Burger has argued that no state law has ever "satisfied this seemingly insurmountable standard."[32] It is also an insurmountable standard, I believe, for a federal policy of reverse discrimination.

VII

The inappropriateness of reverse discrimination, both on utilitarian and justice-regarding grounds, in no way means that compensation for past injustices is inappropriate. It does not mean that those who have suffered past injustices and who have been disadvantaged by them are not entitled to compensation or that they have no moral right to remedy. It may be difficult in different contexts to translate that moral right to remedy into practice or into legislation. When has a disadvantaged person or group been compensated enough? What sort of allocation of resources will compensate without creating additional inequities or deleterious consequences? There is no easy answer to these questions. Decisions must be made in particular contexts. Furthermore, it may be the case that the effects of past injustices are so severe (poverty, malnutrition, and the denial of educational opportunities) that genuine compensation—the balancing of the scales—is impossible. The effects of malnutrition or the lack of education are often non-reversible (and would be so even under a policy of reverse discrimination). This is one of the tragedies of injustice. But if reverse discrimination is inappropriate as a means of compensation and if (as I have argued) it is unjust to make persons who are not responsible for the suffering and disadvantaging of others to suffer for those past injuries, then other means must be employed unless overriding moral considerations of another type (utilitarian) can be clearly demonstrated. That compensation must take a form which is consistent with our constitutional principles and with reasonable principles of justice. Now it seems to me that the Federal Government's Equal Opportunity and Affirmative Action Programs are consistent with these principles, that they are not only not committed to reverse discrimination but rather absolutely forbid it.[33] However, it also seems to me that some officials authorized or required to implement these compensatory efforts have resorted to reverse discrimination and hence have violated the basic principles of justice embodied in these programs. I now want to argue both of these points: first, that these federal programs reject reverse discrimination in their basic principles; secondly, that some implementers of these programs have violated their own principles.

Obviously our country has not always been committed constitutionally to equality. We need no review of our social and political heritage to document this. But with the Fourteenth Amendment, equality as a principle was given constitutional status. Subsequently, social, political, and legal practices changed radically and they will continue to do so. The Fourteenth Amendment declares that states are forbidden to deny any person life, liberty, or property without due process of law or to deny to any person the equal protection of the laws. In my opinion the principles of the Equal Opportunity and Affirmative Action Programs reflect faithfully this constitutional commitment. I am more familiar with those programs as reflected in universities. In this context they require that employers "recruit, hire, train, and promote persons in all job classifications without regard to race, color, religion, sex or national origin, except where sex is a bona fide occupational qualification."[34] They state explicitly that "goals may not be rigid and inflexible quotas which must be met, but must be targets reasonably attainable by means of good faith effort."[35] They require the active recruitment of women and racial minorities where they are "underutilized," this being defined as a context in which there are "fewer minorities or women in a particular job classification than would reasonably be expected by their availability."[36] This is sometimes difficult to determine; but some relevant facts do exist and hence the meaning of a "good faith" effort is not entirely fluid. In any event the Affirmative Action Program in universities requires that "goals, timetables and affirmative action commitment, must be designed to correct any identifiable deficiencies," with separate goals and timetables for minorities and women.[37] It recognizes that there has been blatant discrimination against women and racial minorities in universities and elsewhere, and it assumes that there are "identifiable deficiencies." But it does not require that blacks be employed because they are black or women employed because they are women; that is, it does not require reverse discrimination with rigid quotas to correct the past. It requires a good faith effort in the present based on data on the availability of qualified women and racial minorities in various disciplines and other relevant facts. (Similar requirements hold, of course, for non-academic employment at colleges and universities.) It does not mandate the hiring of the unqualified or a lowering of standards; it mandates only equality of opportunity for all which, given the history of discrimination against women and racial minorities, requires affirmative action in recruitment.

Now if this affirmative action in recruitment, which is not only consistent with but required by our commitment to equality and social justice, is translated into rigid quotas and reverse discrimination by those who implement equal opportunity and affirmative action programs in the effort to get results immediately—and there is no doubt in my mind that this has occurred—then such action violates the principles of those programs.

This violation—this inconsistency of principle and practice—occurs, it seems to me, when employers hire with *priority emphasis* on race, sex, or minority-group status. This move effectively eliminates others from the competition. It is like pretending that everyone is in the game from the beginning while all the while certain persons are systematically excluded. This is exactly what happened recently when a judge declared that a certain quota or number of women were to be employed by a given agency regardless of their qualifications for the job,[38] when some public school officials fired a white coach in order to hire a black one,[39] when a DeFunis is excluded from law school on racial grounds, and when colleges or universities announce that normal academic openings will give preference to female candidates or those from racial minorities.

If reverse discrimination is prohibited by our constitutional and ethical commitments, what means of remedy and compensation are available? Obviously, those means which are consistent with those commitments. Our commitments assure the right to remedy to those who have been treated unjustly, but our government has not done enough to bring this right to meaningful fruition in practice. Sound progress has been made in recent years, especially since the Equal Employment Opportunity Act of 1972 and the establishment of the Equal Employment Opportunities Commission. This Act and other laws have extended anti-discrimination protection to over 60% of the population.[40] The Commission is now authorized to enforce anti-discrimination orders in court and, according to one report, it has negotiated out-of-court settlements which brought 44,000 minority workers over 46 million dollars in back-pay.[41] Undoubtedly this merely scratches the surface. But now the framework exists for translating the right to remedy into practice, not just for sloughing off race and sex as irrelevant criteria of differential treatment but other irrelevant criteria as well—age, religion, the size of hips (I am thinking of airline stewardesses), the length of nose, and so on.

Adequate remedy to overcome the sins of the past, not to speak of the present, would require the expenditure of vast sums for compensatory programs for those disadvantaged by past injustice in order to assure equal access. Such programs should be racially and sexually neutral, benefiting the disadvantaged of *whatever sex or race*. Such neutral compensatory programs would have a high proportion of blacks and other minorities as recipients, for they as members of these groups suffer more from the injustices of the past. But the basis of the compensation would be that fact, not sex or race. Neutral compensatory policies have definite theoretical and practical advantages in contrast to policies of reverse discrimination: Theoretical advantages, in that they are consistent with our basic constitutional and ethical commitments whereas reverse discrimination is not; practical advantages, in that their consistency, indeed their requirement by our constitutional and ethical commitments, means that they can marshall united support in overcoming inequalities whereas reverse discrimination, in my opinion, can not.

APPENDIX:
COMPENSATION AND NATURAL INEQUALITIES

We have said little about compensation for natural inequalities. When the inability to compete is not due to invidious past discrimination of the social system but to natural inequalities, the accident of birth, the luck of the draw—however one wishes to put this—what is required by the egalitarian commitment to equal rights? There are importantly different answers to this question among egalitarians, with important differences for policies of compensatory justice. In the long run the answer to this question may be far more significant for social justice than the answer to the question of compensation for past invidious discrimination. Earlier we stressed that the egalitarian is committed to the moral priority of need-criteria in contrast to merit-criteria in the distribution of goods and services. Thomas Nagel goes further and argues that "people with different talents do not thereby deserve different economic and social rewards, even though they deserve the opportunities to develop and use those talents."[1] (Nagel does allow that differential effort may deserve differential reward.) Some egalitarian theorists go further and argue that "the more fortunate owe to those less fortunate a compensation in proportion to their handicaps."[2] Spiegelberg stresses that none of us have a "moral title to whatever accidental, non-essential position we find ourselves and others to be in, be it economic plight, sex or skin color."[3] In fact, there is "something like a moral unbalance if people sharing similar situations are subject to a 'discrimination' which favors those more 'fortunate' by the mere 'happenstance' of 'good luck,' and disfavors the 'unfortunate' victims of 'bad luck'."[4] If I read Professor Spiegelberg correctly, he is insisting that inequalities due to nature create a moral imbalance, that this imbalance exists prior to any voluntary action by persons or by the state, and that those favored by the accident of birth (those who have unearned advantages) owe those who were disfavored (those who have unearned disadvantages). If this debt is translated into a moral right to redress, in contrast to an obligation in which there is no right, and I believe this is what he intends, then the social and political implications of Spiegelberg's rendering of the egalitarian ethic is tremendous.

Equally far-reaching implications follow from John Rawls's rendering of the egalitarian ethic which is similar to that of Spiegelberg but explicated in far greater detail. Rawls, too, rejects a theory of distributive justice based primarily on "desert," for no one deserves the arbitrary advantages or disadvantages of inherited wealth or inherited poverty, of inherited intelligence or inherited imbecility, of inherited health or invalidity and so on; and yet if the basic criterion of distribution is desert, and if fulfillment of desert-criteria is heavily determined by arbitrary natural inequalities, then distributive justice is not possible under a basically meritocratic system. These natural inequalities, Rawls insists, "are to be somehow compensated for."[5] Rawls does not suggest a complete leveling process or that all distinctions of wealth and power based on greater natural and inherited capacities be eliminated. Rather he proposes the "difference principle" which he characterizes in this way: "The difference principle represents, in effect, an agreement to regard the distribution of natural talents as a common asset and to share in the benefits of this distribution whatever it turns out to be. Those who have been favored by nature, whoever they are, may gain from their good fortune only on terms that improve the situation of those who have lost out."[6]

This is Rawls's basic principle for redress of inequalities. If put into effect in social and political policies, it would have far-reaching results (quite independently of any attempt to compensate for past invidious discrimination). What those results would be *vis-à-vis* redress in the employment of women or racial minorities I would hesitate to say largely because Rawls's total theory is quite complicated with his lexical ordering of the difference principle and the principle of fair equality of opportunity *within* a broader lexical ordering of the principle of equal liberty. This lexical ordering requires the complete satisfaction of the principle of equal liberty before considerations bearing on the principle of fair equality of opportunity and the difference principle come into play. This ordering would preclude the denial of anyone's basic liberties on the grounds of redress of inequalities. Although the implications of Rawls's theory for a policy of compensation for women and racial minorities are not entirely clear (it could justify wide inequalities), it is clear that the theory would have very important implications for policies of compensation.

NOTES AND REFERENCES

1. There are wide differences between the kinds and degrees of injustice suffered by blacks and by women. Women have not literally been slaves. But these differences are not my concern here. Primarily I am concerned with any possible grounds for reverse discrimination, and women and blacks are the classes for whom such treatment is generally pressed. Also this question could be broken down into two distinct ones: (1) Is reverse discrimination justified as a policy of compensation? (2) Is reverse discrimination justified as a policy of preferential treatment? One could answer affirmatively to (2) without answering affirmatively to (1), seeing preferential treatment as a means of assuring social justice but not as a mode of compensation in the strict sense of "compensation."

2. 94 S.CT. 1704 (1974).

3. I hasten to add a qualification—more ambivalence!—resulting from discussion with Tom Beauchamp of Georgetown University. In cases of extreme recalcitrance to equal employment by certain institutions or businesses some quota requirement (reverse discrimination) may be justified. I regard this as distinct from a general policy of reverse discrimination.

4. Aristotle treats the various subdivisions of justice in Book Five of his *Nicomachean Ethics*.

5. A current sense of compensatory justice, which also goes well beyond what Aristotle meant by corrective justice, calls for the overcoming of natural inequalities which are the result of the accident of birth. This sense of compensation differs from reverse discrimination in that it does not appeal to race, sex, or ethnic origin as a relevant basis for differential treatment, whereas reverse discrimination does. Also it differs in that the compensation is totally for involuntary conditions whereas reverse discrimination emphasizes *past* voluntary acts of discrimination and their results as a basis for compensation. Compensation for natural inequalities is an important aspect of the (emerging) egalitarian ethic. I will say little about it in this paper, but I will try to indicate its directional significance for the egalitarian ethic and for compensatory policies. (See Appendix.)

6. For discussion of Supreme Court decisions on racial classification, see Norman Vieira, "Racial Imbalance, Black Separatism, and Permissible Classification by Race," *Michigan Law Review* 67 (1969), 1553–1600; also Robert M. O'Neil, "Preferential Admissions: Equalizing Access to Legal Education," *University of Toledo Law Review* (1970), 281–320.

7. Sanford J. Rosen, "Equalizing Access to Legal Education: Special Programs for Law Students Who Are Not Admissible by Traditional Criteria," *Toledo Law Review* (1970), 364.

8. See O'Neil, pp. 309, 294.

9. *Ibid.*, p. 309.

10. *A Theory of Justice* (Cambridge, Mass.: Harvard University Press, 1971).

11. See, for example, Richard Hare's *The Language of Morals* (Oxford, 1953) and Paul Taylor's *Normative Discourse* (Englewood Cliffs, N.J., 1961).

12. 347 U.S. 483 (1954); 383 U.S. 663 (1966); 351 U.S. 12 (1956).

13. See "Equality and Human Rights," *The Monist*, 52 (1968); also William Frankena's *Some Beliefs About Justice*, The Lindley Lecture, University of Kansas (Lawrence, Kansas, 1966).

14. For discussion of constitutional grounds for and against preferential treatment or reverse discrimination, see Vieira, *supra;* O'Neil, *supra*, especially 284–94. In the context of education one author says this about the constitutional requirement of compensation: "school districts must recognize unequal preparation of students and provide programs which are 'unequal' in their treatment in order to meet the requirements of equal protection" (Note, "Equality of Educational Opportunity: Are 'Compensatory Programs' Constitutionally Required?", *Southern California Law Review*, 42 [1968], 149).

15. The fact that no exact criteria exist for measuring injuries or allocating compensation is not a good reason, in my opinion, for not having some sort of compensatory policy. For discussion, see Hugo Bedau, "Compensatory Justice and the Black Manifesto," *The Monist*, 56 (1972).

16. Robert Simon, "Preferential Hiring: A Reply to Judith Jarvis Thompson," *Philosophy and Public Affairs*, 3 (1974), 316. Simon denies further that reverse discrimination which benefits individuals constitutes compensation to a class: "...although compensation is owed to the group, preferential hiring policies award compensation to an arbitrarily selected segment of the group; namely, those who have the ability and qualifications to be seriously considered for the jobs available. Surely, it is far more plausible to think that collective compensation ought to be equally available to all group members, or at least to all kinds of group members. . . . either compensation is to be made on an individual basis, in which case the fact that one is black or a woman is irrelevant to whether one ought to receive special treatment, or it is made on a group basis, in which case it is far from clear that preferential hiring policies are acceptable compensatory instruments." (*Ibid.*, 315.) Professor Graham Hughes, on the other hand, argues that this is "a legitimate way of pursuing objectives for a group." (Graham Hughes, "Reparations for Blacks," *New York University Law Review*, 43, pt. 2 [1968], 1073.)

17. See Joel Feinberg's "Collective Responsibility," in his *Doing and Deserving* (Princeton: Princeton University Press, 1970), p. 233.

18. *Ibid.*, pp. 230–34, 246–51.

19. See Dwight MacDonald, *Memoirs of a Revolutionist* (New York: Meridian, 1958), p. 45, cited by Feinberg.

20. Graham Hughes, "Reparations for Blacks," p. 1070.

21. Professor Feinberg prefers the phrase "representational attributability" for this kind of responsibility (p. 251).

22. Thomas Nagel, "Equal Treatment and Compensatory Discrimination," *Philosophy and Public Affairs*, 2 (1973), 356.

23. *Ibid.*, p. 359.

24. *Ibid.*, p. 353.

25. For discussion, see William Frankena, *Ethics* (Englewood Cliffs, N.J., 1963).

26. *New York University Law Review*, 43, pt. 2 (1968).

27. Graham Hughes, "Reparations for Blacks," pp. 1072–73. I cite Professor Hughes because his argument, at first blush, is one justifying reverse discrimination on utilitarian grounds. The oncoming of a "crisis of thundering urgency" seems to be a consequence which justifies some individual injustice. However, his further remarks make clear that he conceives his argument as one in which some justice-regarding reasons override others (long-term social justice overrides temporary injustice), for he agrees with John Rawls that justice-regarding reasons always take precedence over consequence-regarding reasons in the hierarchy of moral reasons. Hughes states that even if utilitarian reasons are "conclusively ranked against large-scale remedial intervention, utilitarian considerations would have to yield here to the demands of justice." (Hughes, p. 1065.) The inference to be drawn is that, for Professor Hughes, there can be no utilitarian justification of temporary injustice.

Full-fledged utilitarians, of course, reduce all considerations of justice to those of utility because they conceive rules of justice as rule-utilitarian devices. By no means do I want to force Hughes or anyone else into this mold. It does seem to me that reasons which bear on the enforcement of the entire practice of justice, of justice-regarding institutions, or of social justice generally are different from justice-regarding reasons which are constitutive of certain practices or rules. Still, this does not mean that obligations involving the former are based merely on consequential considerations. One is involved in a conceptual oddity when one says, as Hughes must, that unjust acts (in the sense of violations of rules constitutive of certain accepted and just practices) are justified on grounds of justice (on the basis of higher-order justice-regarding reasons). The linguistic oddity can be explained, however, by reference to a hierarchy of justice-regarding reasons. The hierarchy would make it plain that violation of a constitutive rule of a just practice need not be unjust overall. Neither a contradiction nor a lapse into utilitarianism need be involved.

28. *The Atlanta Journal and Constitution*, Sept. 22, 1974, p. 20–A.

29. For similar arguments see Lisa Newton, "Reverse Discrimination as Unjustified," *Ethics*, 83 (1973).

30. Richard A. Lester, *Antibias Regulation of Universities* (New York, 1974); discussed in *Newsweek*, July 15, 1974, p. 78.

31. 323 U.S. 214.

32. In his dissent in *Dunn* v. *Blumstein* (405 U.S. 330, 363–4, 1972).

33. See The Civil Rights Act of 1964, especially Title VII (which created the Equal Employment Opportunity Commission), amended by The Equal Employment Opportunity Act of 1972, found in *ABC's of The Equal Employment Opportunity Act*, prepared by The Editorial Staff of The Bureau of National Affairs, Inc., 1972. Affirmative Action Programs came into existence with Executive Order 11246. Requirements for affirmative action are found in the rules and regulations 41-CFR Part 60-2, Order #4 (Affirmative Action Programs) generally known as Executive Order #4 and Revised Order #4 41-CFR 60-2 B. For discussion see Paul Brownstein, "Affirmative Action Programs," in *Equal Employment Opportunities Compliance*, Practising Law Institute, New York City (1972), pp. 73–111.

34. See Brownstein, "Affirmative Action Programs" and, for example, *The University of Georgia Affirmative Action Plan*, Athens, Ga., 1973–4, viii, pp. 133, 67.

35. Brownstein and *The University of Georgia Affirmative Action Plan*, Athens, Ga., 1973–4, p. 71.

36. *Ibid.*, p. 69.

37. *Ibid.*, p. 71.

38. See the *Atlanta Journal and Constitution*, June 9, 1974, p. 26-D.

39. See *Atlanta Constitution*, June 7, 1974, p. 13-B.

40. *Newsweek*, June 17, 1974, p. 75.

41. *Ibid.*, p. 75.

APPENDIX NOTES AND REFERENCES

1. Thomas Nagel, "Equal Treatment and Compensatory Discrimination," *Philosophy and Public Affairs*, 2 (Summer 1974), 355.

2. Herbert Spiegelberg, "Albert Schweitzer's 'Other Thought', Fortune Obligates," in *Africa: Thought and Praxis*, 1 (1974). See also Spiegelberg's essay, "A Defense of Human Equality," *Philosophical Review*, 53 (1944), 113. Reprinted in W. T. Blackstone (ed.), *The Concept of Equality* (Minneapolis, Minn.: Burgess Publishing Co., 1969).

3. Herbert Spiegelberg, "Ethics for Fellows in the Fate of Existence," in Peter Bertocci (ed.), *Mid-Twentieth Century American Philosophy* (New York: Humanities Press, 1974), p. 199.

4. *Ibid.*, p. 202.

5. John Rawls, *A Theory of Justice* (Cambridge, Mass.: Harvard University Press, 1971) p. 100, n. 1.

6. *Ibid.*, p. 100.

The Justification of Reverse Discrimination

TOM L. BEAUCHAMP

IN RECENT YEARS government policies intended to ensure fairer employment and educational opportunities for women and minority groups have engendered alarm. Target goals, timetables, and quotas seem to many citizens to discriminate against more talented applicants who are excluded, yet would be accepted on their merits were it not for the preferential advancement of others. Such government policies are said to create a situation of "reverse discrimination." By balancing or compensating for past discrimination against persons on the basis of morally irrelevant characteristics (race, sex, nationality, and religion), these policies now require discrimination in favor of such persons and therefore against the members of other previously favored classes. These policies seem unfairly discriminatory to some because they violate basic principles of justice and equal protection. I believe this conclusion to be reasonable but incorrect, and in this paper I argue that some government policies which would result in reverse discrimination are appropriate and justifiable.[1]

Most all published discussions on this subject known to me are opposed to public policies which would permit reverse discrimination. Among those writers who would permit policies of reverse discrimination, a fairly standard approach is taken: They attempt to justify reverse discrimination by showing that under certain conditions compensation owed for *past* wrongs justifies (for varying reasons) *present* policies productive of reverse discrimination.[2] *This is not my argument;* and it is important to see that it is not. I draw only weak obligations from the claims of compensatory justice; I contend only that because of past wrongs to classes of persons we have *special and strong* obligations to see that these wrongs do not continue. My argument differs from more usual ones since I hold that reverse discrimination is permitted and even required in order that we might eliminate *present* discriminatory practices against classes of persons. I adduce factual evidence for this claim of present, continuing discrimination.

As will become apparent, I construe the issue of reverse discrimination as *primarily* a factual one, and as only secondarily an ethical one. My factual argument is based on factual evidence which establishes the following: There exist discriminatory social attitudes and selection procedures so deeply entrenched in contemporary society that they are almost certainly ineradicable by good faith measures in an acceptable period of time. My ethical contention is that because these crippling conditions exist, policies producing reverse discrimination are justified. These policies are morally *permitted* because they are social measures necessary for the protection of those harmed by invidious social attitudes and selection procedures.[3] A stronger thesis is that such policies are morally *required* and not merely morally permitted. I also support this stronger contention on grounds that past discriminatory practices have created a special and strong obligation to erase invidious discrimination and ensure equal protection of the law. Hence these policies are morally required (by compensatory justice) under the kind of incorrigible social conditions I discuss in my factual arguments.

I proceed by first establishing a principled framework for resolving moral issues about the justifiability of reverse discrimination (I). I then discuss the factual evidence of present discriminatory practices and the difficulties which attend weak attempts to offset or overcome such bias (II). Finally, I apply the result of the arguments in the first two sections to present government policies of affirmative action, which I criticize as insufficiently stringent (III).

I

My moral argument is intended to show that policies productive of reverse discrimination are compatible with basic principles of justice and utility. This is not to say that no injustices result from the occurrence of reverse discrimination, but it is to say that these injustices can be justified.

For moral philosophy the main issues of reverse discrimination may be formulated as follows: Under what conditions, if any, are policies resulting in reverse discrimination justified? Can basic ethical principles of justice and utility be successfully employed for the justification of reverse discrimination? Conceivably other ethical principles, such as beneficence, might be invoked. But since justice and utility are universally recognized as the most directly relevant principles, I shall confine my discussion to them, beginning with justice.

An initial difficulty must be faced in any appeal to principles of justice. Since there are different theories of justice, and different kinds of justice recognized within the different theories, it might be thought that a comprehensive theory of justice must be defended before problems of reverse discrimination can be intelligently discussed. Fortunately, for our purposes, this difficulty may be largely ignored for two reasons. First, we can without prejudicing the arguments successfully operate with two rather minimal principles of justice, both of which derive from Aristotle and both of which receive wide acceptance as at least necessary, even if not sufficient, conditions of justice. The first is the principle of *formal equality*. It says that equals must be treated equally and unequals unequally; or, more fully stated, it says that "No person should be treated unequally, despite all differences with other persons, until such time as it has been shown that there is a difference between them relevant to the treatment at stake." One demand of the principle is the egalitarian ideal of equal consideration of persons: Every person is to be evaluated on his or her merit when there is equal opportunity to compete. The problem with the principle is notoriously more in its abstractness than in any deficiency of content. That equals ought to be treated equally, by law and elsewhere, is not likely to stir disagreement. But who is equal and who unequal? Presumably all citizens should have equal political rights, equal access to public services, and should receive equal treatment under the law. But almost all would allow that distinctions based on experience, merit, and position do sometimes introduce criteria justifying differential treatment. Whether race, sex, and religion similarly justify differential treatment under some conditions is more controversial. This issue of the appropriate *application* of the principle of formal equality is one that we shall be considering.

The second principle of justice deserving explicit statement is the principle of *compensatory justice*. It says that whenever an injustice has been committed, just compensation or reparation is owed the injured parties. The idea is to restore, so far as possible, the state of affairs prior to the injury or injustice which created the need for compensation, and also to benefit the injured parties in a manner proportional to the injury or loss suffered. The compensation might be to groups or to individuals, but in either case the same justifying principle is used. It is now a widespread view that groups invidiously discriminated against in the proximate and remote past, including women, blacks, North American Indians, and French Canadians, should be recompensed for these injustices by compensatory policies, at least in those cases where injury is traceable to particular persons. I shall be discussing not merely whether some form of compensation is deserved, but the more controversial question whether such compensation might justifiably result in reverse discrimination. I shall not, however, argue that compensatory claims by themselves justify direct monetary reparations or quota allotments to classes of persons. My account is weaker: Compensatory justice both (1) demands that we make an especially vigorous attempt to discover *present* discrimination against classes of persons discriminated against in the past and (2) creates a *special* obligation to eliminate such present discriminatory treatment wherever it is found. I will take for granted that this weakened claim about obligations generated by compensatory justice is reasonable, and that any society which fails to act on this obligation is an unjust society, whether or not this failure is intentional.

Recently a rather large literature has emerged in which the attempt is made to show that policies causing reverse discrimination violate the above (and perhaps other) principles of justice. It is argued in this literature that since reverse discriminatory policies create injustices they cannot be justified. The most widely circulated form of the argument makes a direct appeal to the principle of formal equality. The following is a typical example of this basic argument:

Now, if justice (Aristotle's justice in the political sense) is equal treatment under the law for all citizens, what is injustice? Clearly, injustice is the violation of that equality, discriminating for or against a group of citizens, favoring them with special immunities and privileges or depriving them of those guaranteed to the others. . . . But, of course, when the employers and the schools *favor* women and blacks, the same injustice is done. Just as the previous discrimination did, this reverse discrimination violates the public equality which defines citizenship and destroys the rule of law for the areas in which these favors are granted. To the extent that we adopt a program of discrimination, reverse or otherwise, justice in the political sense is destroyed, . . . [and] the ideal of equality is undermined, for it has content only where justice obtains. . . . [Reverse discrimination] destroys justice, law, equality, and citizenship itself, and replaces them with power struggles and popularity contests.[4]

Among reasons proposed as supplementary to this primary argument are the following: (1) Some who are innocent of and not responsible for the past invidious discrimination pay the price (e.g., qualified young white males); but this treatment is discriminatory because such persons are penalized solely on the basis of their race. (2) Male members of minority groups such as Poles, Irish, and Italians—themselves discriminated against in the past —will bear a heavy burden of the cost of compensating women and minority groups such as blacks. (3) Many members of the *class* selected for preferential treatment will have never themselves been unjustly treated and will not deserve preferential policies. (4) There are some relevant differences between the sexes which justify differential expectations and treatment (men are naturally better at some things, women at others). (5) Compensation can be provided to *individuals* treated unfairly in the past without resort to reverse discrimination, which is the result of blanket treatment for groups. The last reason (5) is presumably not only a reason against reverse discrimination, but an alternative *policy*, as well.

These arguments have a great deal of plausibility. Policies which would cause reverse discrimination in present North American society have a heavy presumption against them, for both justice-regarding and utilitarian reasons: The introduction of such preferential treatment on a large scale could well produce a series of injustices, economic advantages to some who do not deserve them, protracted court battles, jockeying for favored position by other minorities, congressional lobbying by power groups, a lowering of admission and work standards in vital institutions, reduced social and economic efficiency, increased racial hostility, and continued suspicion that well-placed women and minority group members received their positions purely on the basis of quotas. Conjointly these reasons constitute a powerful case against the enactment of policies productive of reverse discrimination.

I find these reasons against allowing reverse discrimination to occur both thoughtful and tempting, and I want to concede from the outset that policies of reverse discrimination can create serious and perhaps even tragic injustices. One must be careful, however, not to draw an overzealous conclusion from this admission. Those who argue that reverse discrimination creates injustices often say that, because of the injustice, such policies are *unjust*. I think by this use of "unjust" they generally mean "not justified" (rather than "not sanctioned by justice"). But this conclusion does not follow merely from the arguments thus far mentioned. A policy can create and even perpetuate injustices, as violations of the principle of formal equality, and yet be justified by other reasons. It would be an injustice in this sense to fire either one of two assistant professors with exactly similar professional credentials, while retaining the other of the two; yet the financial condition of the university or compensation owed the person retained might provide compelling reasons which justify the action. The first reason supporting the dismissal is utilitarian in character, and the other derives from the principle of compensatory justice. This shows both that there can be conflicts between different justice-regarding reasons and also that violations of the principle of formal equality are not in themselves sufficient to render an action unjustifiable.

A proper conclusion, then—and one which I accept—is that all discrimination, including reverse discrimination, is *prima facie* immoral, because a basic principle of justice creates a *prima facie* duty to abstain from such treatment of persons. But no absolute duty is created come what may, for we might have conflicting duties of sufficient weight to justify such injustices. The latter is the larger thesis I wish to defend: Considerations of compensatory justice and utility are conjointly of sufficient weight in contemporary society to neutralize and overcome the quite proper presumption of immorality in the case of some policies productive of reverse discrimination.

II

I now turn away from moral considerations to factual ones. It is difficult to avoid accepting two important claims: (a) that the law ought never to sanction any discriminatory practices (whether plain old unadorned discrimination or reverse discrimination), and (b) that such practices can be eradicated by bringing the full weight of the law down on those who engage in discriminatory practices. The first claim is a moral one, the second a factual one. I contend in this section that it is unrealistic to believe, as *b* suggests, that in contemporary society discriminatory practices *can* be eradicated by legal measures which do not permit reverse discrimination. And because they cannot be eradicated, I think we ought to relax our otherwise unimpeachably sound reservations (as recorded in *a* and discussed in the first section) against allowing any discriminatory practices whatever.

My argument is motivated by the belief that racial, sexual, and no doubt other forms of discrimination are not antique relics but are living patterns which continue to warp selection and ranking procedures. In my view the difference between the present and the past is that discriminatory treatment is today less widespread and considerably less blatant. But its reduction has produced apathy; its subtleness has made it less visible and considerably more difficult to detect. Largely because of the reduced visibility of racism and sexism, I suggest, reverse discrimination now strikes us as all too harsh and unfair. After all, quotas and preferential treatment have no appeal if one assumes a just, primarily nondiscriminatory society. Since the presence or absence of seriously discriminatory conditions in our society is a factual matter, empirical evidence must be adduced to show that the set of discriminatory attitudes and selection procedures I have alleged to exist do in fact exist. The data I shall mention derive primarily from historical, linguistic, sociological, and legal sources.

STATISTICAL EVIDENCE. Statistical imbalances in employment and admission are often discounted because so many variables can be hypothesized to explain why, for non-discriminatory reasons, an imbalance exists. We can all think of plausible non-discriminatory reasons why 22% of Harvard's graduate students in 1969 were women but its tenured Arts and Sciences Faculty in the Graduate School consisted of 411 males and 0 females.[5] But sometimes we are able to discover evidence which supports the claim that skewed statistics are the result of discrimination. Quantities of such discriminatory findings, in turn, raise serious questions about the real reasons for suspicious statistics in those cases where we have *not* been able to determine these reasons—perhaps because they are so subtle and unnoticed. I shall discuss each factor in turn: (a) statistics which constitute prima facie but indecisive evidence of discrimination; (b) findings concerning discriminatory reasons for some of these statistics; and (c) cases where the discrimination is probably undetectable because of its subtleness, and yet the statistical evidence is overwhelming.

a) A massive body of statistics constituting *prima facie* evidence of discrimination has been assembled in recent years. Here is a tiny but diverse fragment of some of these statistical findings.[6] (1) Women college teachers with identical credentials in terms of publications and experience are promoted at almost exactly one-half the rate of their male counterparts. (2) In the United States women graduates of medical schools in 1965 stood at 7%, as compared with 36% in Germany. The gap in the number of women physicians was similar. (3) Of 3,000 leading law firms surveyed in 1957 only 32 reported a woman partner, and even these women were paid much less (increasingly so for every year of employment) than their male counterparts. (4) 40% of the white-collar positions in the United States are presently held by women, but only 10% of the management positions are held by women, and their pay again is significantly less (70% of clerical workers are women). (5) 8,000 workers were employed in May 1967 in the construction of BART (Bay Area Rapid Transit), but not a single electrician, ironworker, or plumber was black. (6) In the population as a whole in the United States, 3 out of 7 employees hold white-collar positions, but only 1 of 7 blacks holds such a position, and these latter jobs are clustered in professions which have the fewest jobs to offer in top-paying positions.

b) I concede that such statistics are far from decisive indicators of discrimination. But when further evidence concerning the reasons for the statistics is uncovered, they are put in a perspective affording them greater power—clinching power in my view. Consider (3)—the statistics on the lack of women lawyers. A survey of Harvard Law School alumnae in 1970 provided evidence about male lawyers' attitudes.[7] It showed that business and legal firms do not generally expect the women they hire to become lawyers, that they believe women cannot become good litigators, and that they believe only limited numbers of women should be hired since clients generally prefer male lawyers. Surveys of women applicants for legal positions indicate they are frequently either told that a woman will not be hired, or are warned that "senior partners" will likely object, or are told that women will be hired to do only probate, trust, and estate work. (Other statistics confirm that these are the sorts of tasks dominantly given to women.) Consider also (5)—a particular but typical case of hiring in non-white-collar positions. Innumerable studies have shown that most of these positions are filled by word-of-mouth recruitment policies conducted by all-white interviewers (usually all-male as well). In a number of decisions of the Equal Employment Opportunity Commission, it has been shown that the interviewers have racially biased attitudes and that the applications of blacks and women are systematically handled in unusual ways, such as never even being filed. So serious and consistent have such violations been that the EEOC has publicly stated its belief that word-of-mouth recruitment policies without demonstrable supplementary and simultaneous recruitment in minority group communities is in itself a "prima facie violation of Title VII."[8] Gertrude Erorsky has argued, convincingly I believe, that this pattern of "special ties" is no less present in professional white collar hiring, which is neither less discriminatory nor more sensitive to hiring strictly on the basis of merit.[9]

c) Consider, finally, (1)—statistics pertaining to the treatment of women college teachers. The Carnegie Commission and others have assembled statistical evidence to show that in even the most favorable construal of relevant variables, women teachers have been discriminated against in hiring, tenuring, and ranking. But instead of summarizing this mountain of material, I wish here to take a particular case in order to illustrate the difficulty in determining, on the basis of statistics and similar empirical data, whether discrimination is occurring even where courts have been forced to find satisfactory evidence of discrimination. In December 1974 a decision was reached by the Commission against Discrimination of the Executive Department of the State of Massachusetts regarding a case at Smith College where the two complainants were women who were denied tenure and dismissed by the English Department.[10] The women claimed sex discrimination and based their case on the following: (1) Women at the full professor level in the college declined from 54% in 1958 to 21%, and in the English department from 57% in 1960 to 11% in 1972. These statistics compare unfavorably at all levels with Mt. Holyoke's, a comparable institution (since both have an all female student body and are located in Western Massachusetts). (2) Thirteen of the department's fifteen associate and full professorships at Smith belonged to men. (3) The two tenured women had obtained tenure under "distinctly peculiar experiences" including a stipulation that one be only part-time and that the other not be promoted when given tenure. (4) The department's faculty members conceded that tenure standards were applied subjectively, were vague, and lacked the kind of precision which would avoid discriminatory application. (5) The women denied tenure were at no time given advance warning that their work was deficient. Rather, they were given favorable evaluations of their teaching and were encouraged to believe they would receive tenure. (6) Some stated reasons for the dismissals were later demonstrated to be rationalizations, and one letter from a senior member to the tenure and promotion committee contradicted his own appraisal of teaching ability filed with the department. (7) The court accepted expert testimony that any deficiencies in the women candidates were also found in male candidates promoted and given tenure during this same period, and that the women's positive credentials were at least as good as the men's.

The commissioner's opinion found that "the Complainants properly used statistics to demonstrate that the Respondents' practices operate with a discriminatory effect." Citing *Parham* v. *Southwestern Bell Telephone Co.*,[11] the commissioner argued that "in such cases extreme statistics may establish discrimination as a matter of law, without additional supportive evidence." But in this case the commissioner found abundant additional evidence in the form of "the historical absence of women," "word-of-mouth recruitment policies" which operate discriminatorily, and a number of "subtle and not so subtle, societal patterns" existing at Smith.[12] On December 30, 1974 the commissioner ordered the two women reinstated with tenure and ordered the department to submit an affirmative action program within 60 days.

This case is interesting because there is little in the way of clinching proof that the members of the English Department actually held discriminatory attitudes. Yet so consistent a pattern of *apparently* discriminatory treatment must be regarded, according to this decision, as *de facto* discrimination. The commissioner's ruling and other laws are quite explicit that "intent or lack thereof is of no consequence." If a procedure constitutes discriminatory treatment, then the parties discriminated against must be recompensed. Here we have a case where irresistible statistics and other sociological evidence of "social exclusion" and "subtle societal patterns" provide convincing evidence that strong, court backed measures must be taken because nothing short of such measures is sufficiently strong to overcome the discriminatory pattern, as the Respondents' testimony in the case verifies.[13]

Some understanding of the attitudes underlying the statistical evidence thus far surveyed can be gained by consideration of some linguistic evidence now to be mentioned. It further supports the charge of widespread discrimination in the case of women and of the difficulty in changing discriminatory attitudes.

LINGUISTIC EVIDENCE. Robert Baker has assembled some impressive linguistic evidence which indicates that our language is male-slanted, perhaps male chauvinistic, and that language about women relates something of fundamental importance concerning the males' most fundamental conceptions of women.[14] Baker argues that as the term "boy" once expressed a paternalistic and dominating attitude toward blacks (and was replaced in our conceptual structure because of this denigrating association), so are there other English terms which serve similar functions in regard to women (but are not replaced because not considered by men as in need of replacement). Baker assembles evidence both from the language itself and from surveys of users of the language to show the following.

a) *Substitutions for "Woman."* The term "woman" is broadly substitutable for and frequently interchanged in English sentences such as "Who is that ————— over there?" by terms such as those in the following divisions:

A. *Neutral Categories*	B. *Animal Categories*	C. *Plaything Categories*	D. *Gender Categories*	E. *Sexual Categories*
lady	chick	babe	skirt	snatch
gal	bird	doll	hem	cunt
girl	fox	cuddly thing		ass
broad	vixen			twat
(sister)	filly			piece
	bitch			lay
				pussy

Baker notes that (1) while there are differences in the frequency of usage, all of these terms are standard enough to be recognizable at least by most male users of the language; (2) women do not typically identify themselves in sexual categories; and (3) typically only males use the non-neutral categories (B-E). He takes this to be evidence—and I agree—that the male conception of women differs significantly from the female conception and that the categories used by the male in classifying women are "prima facie denigrating." He then argues that it is clearly and not merely prima facie denigrating when categories such as C and E are used, as they are either derived from playboy male images or are outright vulgarities. Baker argues that it is most likely that B and D are similarly used in denigrating ways. His arguments center on the metaphorical associations of these terms, but the evidence cannot be further pursued here.

Although Baker does not remark that women do not have a similar language for men, it seems to me important to notice this fact. Generally, any negative categories used by women to refer to men are as frequently or more frequently used by men to apply to women. This asymmetrical relation does not hold, of course, for the language used by whites and blacks for denigrating reference. This fact perhaps says something about how blacks have caught onto the impact of the language as a tool of denigrating identification in a way women have yet to do, at least in equal numbers. It may also say something about the image of submissiveness which many women still bear about themselves—an image blacks are no longer willing to accept.

b) *The Language of Sexual Intercourse.* Baker argues that the conception of sexual intercourse in our culture depicts women more as objects of sexual exploitation than as persons with the same entitlements as males. He analyzes the many terms that are synonymously used with "had sexual intercourse with" ("screwed," "layed," "fucked," "balled," "humped," "diddled with," etc.). He shows—again quite convincingly in my view—that: (1) Male names are the subjects of sentences with active constructions, while names for females require passive constructions. That is, we conceive of the male as doing the action and the female as the recipient, and therefore conceive of the two as having different sexual roles. (2) This linguistic difference cannot be explained merely in terms of the sexual differences in physiology (as "screw," e.g., suggests), since many other words could be chosen ("engulfing," e.g.) but never are. (3) Most of the terms used to portray the male's action are also terms used to indicate that a person is harming another person ("screwed," "had," and "fucked," e.g.) and that the language itself would indicate that we see the woman as "being taken advantage of." (4) Similarly terms such as "prick" used expressly to refer to the male are words in our language for one who hurts or is abusive or brutalizing.

Baker concludes from his linguistic studies that "sexual discrimination permeates our conceptual structure. Such discrimination is clearly inimical to any movement toward sexual egalitarianism and virtually defeats its purpose at the outset." [15] His conclusion may somewhat overreach his premises, but when combined with the corroborating statistical evidence previously adduced, it seems apt. Linguistic dispositions lead us to categorize persons and events in discriminatory ways which are sometimes glaringly obvious to the categorized but accepted as "objective" by the categorizer. My contention, derived from Baker's and to be supported as we proceed, is that cautious, good faith movements toward egalitarianism such as affirmative action guidelines *cannot* succeed short of fundamental conceptual and ethical revisions. And since the probability of such revisions approximates zero (because discriminatory attitudes are covertly embedded in language and cultural habit), radical expedients are required to bring about the desired egalitarian results, expedients which may result in reverse discrimination.

CONCLUSIONS. Irving Thalberg has argued, correctly I believe, that the gravest contemporary problems with racism stem from its "protectively camouflaged" status, which he calls "visceral." Thalberg skillfully points to a number of attitudes held by those whites normally classified as unprejudiced which indicate that racism still colors their conception of social facts.[16] John Stuart Mill argued a similar thesis in the nineteenth century about sexism.[17] Virginia Held has recently argued the additional thesis that under present, legally acceptable policies and programs of "gradual improvement" in the hiring of women and nonwhites, it will take decades to achieve equality of occupational opportunity.[18] My alliance with such positions ought to be obvious by now. But my overall intentions and conclusions are somewhat different. I hold that because of the peculiarly concealed nature of the protective camouflage under which sexism and racism have so long thrived, it is not a reasonable expectation that the lightweight programs now administered under the heading of affirmative action will succeed in overcoming discriminatory treatment. I turn now directly to this topic.

III

The rawest nerve of the social and political controversy concerning reverse discrimination is exposed by the following question: What government policies are permissible and required in order to bring about a society where equal treatment of persons is the rule rather than the exception? Fair-minded opponents of any government policy which might produce reverse discrimination—

Carl Cohen and William Blackstone, for example—seem to me
to oppose them largely because and perhaps only because of their
factual belief that present government policies not causing reverse
discrimination will, if seriously and sincerely pursued, prove sufficient to achieve the goal of equal consideration of persons. Cohen
seems plainly to agree when he says: "This controversy is not between good guys and bad guys, but between very sophisticated
parties who differ about what, in the effort to achieve a very pressing and very difficult end, we may rightly use as a means."[19]

Once again a significant factual disagreement has emerged:
what means are not only fair but also sufficient? I must again support my contentions by adducing factual data to show that my
pessimism is sustained by the weight of the evidence. The evidence
comes from two sources: (1) history, (2) government data concerning affirmative action programs. I begin with historical evidence in order to show directly how utterly hollow optimism
about removing racial prejudice has proven to be in the past, even
when extremely tough laws and practices prevailed. From this
direct evidence I infer that optimism in the present about the use
of affirmative action guidelines is similarly unwarranted. Or, more
precisely stated, the historical evidence shows that progress in
eliminating injustices occurs only when extraordinarily tough
policies are enacted, from which I infer that extraordinary policies
are also presently in order. I shall then discuss the affirmative
action program in order to show that on the basis of present government guidelines (which, to my knowledge, are the best either
in law or proposed as law by those who oppose reverse discrimination), discriminatory business as usual will surely prevail.

HISTORICAL EVIDENCE. It is widely believed that the history
of racial and sexual struggles for equality in the United States has
been an uphill but nonetheless continuously progressive battle.
Included is the belief that this progress has been made by the
legal enforcement of crucial national legislation and by court decisions. As this history is applied to blacks in the United States
(the only class I shall here consider), the following are thought
to be crucial features in the historical landscape of continuing and
toughening progress: The Emancipation Proclamation, Reconstruction and the Civil War Amendments, the integration of the

armed services, Truman's Executive Order 9908, the *Brown* v. *Bd. of Education* decision, Lyndon Johnson's Executive Order 11246 (affirmative action), and the Civil and Voting Rights Acts of the 1960s. This continual progression interpretation has been either explicitly or implicitly the standard textbook account of the history of blacks in the United States. Accordingly, some of us are surprised to discover that historians who write as specialists about the history of blacks provide narratives that stand in stark contrast to this interpretation; and this is so whether they be black or white historians.

These historians[20] see this history not as an uphill, progressive battle but rather as analogous to a roller coaster, with peaks of progress followed by steep grades of regression. Some of the more prominent regressive landmarks in this history are the following: In 1667 the colony of Virginia repealed an earlier statute enfranchising all blacks who had converted to Christianity. Between 1807 annd 1838, four northern states (Connecticut, New Jersey, New York, Pennsylvania) passed laws which either disenfranchised, or abridged the voting rights of blacks, who were then migrating in large numbers from the South. In 1857, though they had secured innumerable rights in many states, blacks were faced with the Dred Scott Decision (*Scott* v. *Sanford*[21]), which held slavery a valid enterprise nationally and which boldly proclaimed that blacks were "so far inferior" that they had "no rights which the white man was bound to respect." In 1865 much promised progress resulting from the Civil War was damaged by the issuance of "Black Codes" in several Southern States and then destroyed by President Hayes's compromise in the close 1876 election. In 1873 the enormous promise of the 13th–15th Amendments seemed virtually erased, within three years of passage, when the Supreme Court ruled, in the Slaughterhouse cases, that the "due process" clause provides protection of national rights, but not of states' rights. In 1875 Congress had enacted a strong Civil Rights Act guaranteeing equal treatment to blacks in hotels, transportation facilities, and amusement centers—partially in response to Black Codes—but in 1883 the Supreme Court struck down those sections of this act which prohibited discrimination in public places. By 1885 the South was again almost completely resegregated. This downhill ride was crowned in 1896 with the "separate but equal" dictum in *Plessy* v. *Ferguson*; and thereby virtually all the progress made in the period of Reconstruction seemed to be eliminated or legally eliminable. Hostilities continued to grow and lynchings increased annually for many years. In 1941 President Roosevelt issued an Executive Order (8802) which established a supposedly rigorous Fair Employment Practices Commission, and President Truman's Executive Order (9908) in 1946 buttressed and extended Roosevelt's order. Truman expressed outrage at the lack of progress and insisted that violations be promptly reported. In 1948 he created a Fair Employment Practice Board; but in 1955 President Eisenhower replaced this board with a weaker one not required to report violations to the President. Actual findings of discrimination were noticeably sparse—less than 12 per year in the entire country. In 1957 and 1960 two Civil Rights Acts were passed; they were thought to be powerful and sufficient measures to ensure at least basic rights, such as the right to vote. But by 1965, President Johnson and most members of Congress admitted that these Acts had been almost totally inefficacious in insuring the right to vote and that they required stringent reinforcement. In 1968, after a series of violent disorders widely believed to be outbreaks of lawlessness, the *Report of the National Advisory Commission on Civil Disorders* was given to President Johnson and released to the public. It argued that (1) de facto segregation and unequal treatment were increasing, not decreasing, in the United States, (2) that the major cause (whatever the contributing causes) of urban disorders was institutionalized racism, and (3) that only massive governmental measures could resolve the problem. These measures were not forthcoming, and the report was largely ignored, though widely discussed for a short period of time.

Gunnar Myrdal is a notable exception to those who interpret recent American history in this manner. In the first edition of *An American Dilemma* (1944) he confidently predicted rapid progress. Twenty years later in the second edition he claimed that his prediction had been proven accurate: There had been, he said, unanticipatedly rapid and virtually continuous progress. He and his associate Arnold Rose again predicted continued progress, including the total elimination of unequal treatment by roughly 1990.[22] But even Myrdal and Rose's optimism is tinged with a constant insistence that "the Negro's 'place' in American society has been precarious, uncertain and changing . . . [and] the conflicting and vacillating valuations of the white majority have been decisive, whether the issue was segregation in the schools, discrimination with reference to public facilities, equal justice and protection under the laws, enjoyment of the franchise, or the freedom to enter a vocation and earn an honest living."[23] This is small comfort to those with an optimistic outlook. As even Myrdal's study indicates, progress comes only on occasions of rigorous national enforcement.

It is not irrelevant to note, in concluding this discussion of historical evidence, that the historical judgments I have supported are similar to the ones accepted by the Supreme Court of Washington in the *DeFunis* case. The Court determined that twenty years after Brown was long enough to reach racial balance. But since this had not occurred in schools below the law school level, they reasoned, it was acceptable to conclude that the only measure strong enough to work now is a preferential admission policy. They even concluded that this stringent policy is *necessary to fulfill a compelling and overriding state interest.*[24]

The history of blacks and other minority groups hardly demonstrates that government programs not permitting reverse discrimination will prove insufficient. But it does give valuable perspective to such policies, and much similar historical evidence could be added in areas such as the denial of access to educational facilities. In the past fair-minded Americans have believed that emancipation policies and Supreme Court decisions were measures sufficient for the elimination of discriminatory practices. The historical facts surveyed above provide evidence that in virtually all cases where such expectations abounded, the means adopted were not sufficient means to their envisioned ends. They proved insufficient because they were always without teeth, or at least not stringently enforced. Now again, in assessing the efficacy of present affirmative action policies, we seem to be struggling with the same question of necessary means. Whatever the deficiencies in the above historical sketch, it helps us see (when reviewing the result of present affirmative action programs) why stronger measures, such as quotas, are probably necessary for an acceptable rate of progress, even if they may not be fully sufficient.

AFFIRMATIVE ACTION. Some contemporary government programs are conceived as compensatory programs, whereas others are construed as non-compensatory legal means of ensuring equal treatment. I am not concerned with this distinction, except that where the programs are expressly compensatory I construe government intent as that of providing compensatory programs which do not permit reverse discrimination. This is the stated intent of those who administer such programs in the United States, and I believe this statement of intent is generally consistent with their practice. There has, however, been considerable confusion over the meaning and content of various government "regulations" and "guidelines" for enforcing federal laws, and a moment must be spent on this interpretative problem.

These rules are interpreted as having various levels of strength. Gertrude Ezorsky, numerous congressmen, and the columnist William Raspberry, who favor strong action, interpret them as resolute government documents requiring vigorous action, in the form of statistical goals, timetables, and perhaps even quotas.[25] So do those, such as Sidney Hook, who regard the guidelines as major threats to merit hiring.[26] While I agree with Ezorsky and Raspberry (contra Blackstone and Cohen) that the government *ought* to regard its affirmative action programs as permitting such measures, the plain fact remains that the relevant governmental officials *do not* so interpret them (as Blackstone and Cohen correctly notice). Consequently, when I speak of "affirmative action programs," I shall mean for our purposes what those who administer affirmative action guidelines say they permit and require. I make this stipulation only in order to clarify how I use the term, not to score a point in argument.

For further clarification, I mention a sample of the affirmative action guidelines, as understood by those who administer them. I use the example of HEW guidelines for educational institutions receiving federal financial aid. These guidelines cover three areas: admission, treatment of students, and employment. A sample of the sorts of requirements universities are under includes: (1) They may not advertise vacant positions as open only to or preferentially to a particular race or sex, except where sex is a legitimate occupational requirement. (2) The university sets standards and criteria for employment, but if these effectively work to exclude women or minorities as a class, the university must justify the job requirements. (3) An institution may not set different standards of admission for one sex, race, etc. (4) There must be active recruitment where there is an under-representation of women and minorities, as gauged by the availability of qualified members of these classes. However, the relevant government officials have from time to time made it clear that (1) quotas are unacceptable, either for admission or employment, though target goals and timetables intended to correct deficiencies are acceptable and to be encouraged. (2) A university is never under any obligation to dilute legitimate standards, and hence there is no conflict with merit hiring. (3) Reserving positions for members of a minority group (and presumably for the female sex) is "an outrageous and illegal form of reverse bias" (as one former director of the program wrote).[27] By affirmative action requirements I mean this latter interpretation and nothing stronger (though I have given only a sample set of qualifications, of course).

The question I am currently asking is whether these guidelines, assuming they will be vigorously pursued, can reasonably be expected to bring about their goal, which is the social circumstance of non-discriminatory treatment of persons. If they *are* strong enough, then Cohen, Blackstone, and others are right: Reverse discrimination is not under such circumstances justified. Unfortunately the statistical and linguistic evidence previously adduced indicates otherwise. The *Smith College* case is paradigmatic of the concealed yet serious discrimination which occurs through the network of subtle distortions, old-boy procedures, and prejudices we have accumulated. Only when the statistics become egregiously out of proportion is action taken or a finding of mistreatment possible. And that is one reason why it seems unlikely that substantial progress can be made, in any realistic sense of "can," by current government measures not productive of reverse discrimination. According to Peter Holmes, currently the Director of HEW's Office for Civil Rights and in charge of interpreting affirmative action guidelines: "It has been our policy that it is the institutions' responsibility to determine non-discriminatory qualifications in the first instance, and that such qualifications, in conjunction with other affirmative action steps, should yield results."[28] This is the received HEW view, but the last sentence contains an ambiguous use of the word "should." If the "should" in this statement is a moral "should," none will disagree. But if it is an empirical, predictive "should," as I take Mr. Holmes to intend, we are back to the core of the difficulty. I now turn to a consideration of how deficient such affirmative action steps have proven to be.

GOVERNMENT DATA. The January 1975 Report of the United States Commission on Civil Rights contains a section on "compliance reviews" of various universities. These are government assessments of university compliance with Executive Orders pertaining to affirmative action plans. The report contains a stern indictment of the Higher Education Division (HED) of HEW— the division in charge of overseeing all HEW civil rights enforcement activities in the area of higher education. It concludes that "HED has, in large part, failed to follow the procedures required of compliance agencies under the Executive order regulations."[29] But more interesting than this mere failure to enforce the law is the report's discussion of how very difficult it is to obtain compliance even when there is a routine attempt to enforce the law. The Commission reviewed four major campuses in the United States (Harvard, University of Michigan, University of Washington, Berkeley). They concluded that there is a pattern of inadequate compliance reviews, inordinate delays, and inexcusable failures to take enforcement action where there were clear violations of the Executive order regulations.[30]

Consider the example of the "case history of compliance contacts" at the University of California at Berkeley. According to HED's own staff a "conciliation agreement" with this university "is now being used as a model for compliance activities with other campuses." When the Office for Civil Rights of HEW determined to investigate Berkeley (April 1971), after several complaints, including a class action sex discrimination complaint, the university refused to permit access to its personnel files and refused to permit the interviewing of faculty members without an administrator present. Both refusals are, as the report points out, "direct violations of the Executive order's equal opportunity clause," under which Berkeley held contracts. Despite this clear violation of the law, no enforcement action was taken. A year and one-half later, after negotiations and more complaints, the university was instructed to develop a written affirmative action plan to correct "documented deficiencies" of "pervasive discrimination." The plan was to include target goals and timetables wherever job under-utilization had been identified.[31]

In January 1973 the university, in a letter from Chancellor Albert H. Bowker, submitted a draft affirmative action plan which was judged "totally unacceptable." Throughout 1973 Berkeley received "extensive technical assistance" from the government to aid it in developing a better plan. No such plan emerged, and OCR at the end of the year began to question "the university's commitment to comply with the executive order." The university submitted other unacceptable plans, and finally in March 1974 "a conciliation agreement was reached." However, "the document suffered from such extreme vagueness that, as of August 1974, the university and OCR were in substantial disagreement on the meaning of a number of its provisions," and "the agreement specifically violated OFCC regulations in a number of ways." These are extensive and serious, and the report characterizes one part as "outrageous." Four years after this "model" compliance case began, it is unresolved and no enforcement proceedings have been taken against the university. The report concludes: "In its Title VI reviews of colleges and universities, HEW routinely finds noncompliance, but it almost never imposes sanctions; instead HEW responds by making vague recommendations. Moreover, HEW does not routinely require the submission of progress reports or conduct sufficient followup to determine if its recommendations have been followed."

It is not to be forgotten that all in the above paragraphs comes from a government commission report on a government department.

IV

No one could be happy about the conclusions I have reached or about the depressing and disturbing facts on which they are based. But I do take it to be a *factual* and not an *evaluative* conclusion both (1) that the camouflaged attitudes I have discussed exist and affect the social position of minority groups and women and (2) that they will in all likelihood continue to have this influence. It is, of course, an evaluative conclusion that we are morally permitted and even required to remedy this situation by the imposition of quotas, target goals, and timetables. But anyone who accepts my *interpretation* of the facts bears a heavy burden of moral argument to show that we ought not to use such means to that end upon which I take it we all agree, viz., the equal consideration of persons irrespective of race, sex, religion, or nationality.

By way of conclusion, it is important to set my arguments in the framework of a distinction between real reverse discrimination and merely apparent reverse discrimination. My evidence demonstrates present, ongoing barriers to the removal of discriminatory practices.[32] My contentions set the stage for showing that *because* of the existence of what Thalberg calls "visceral racism," and because of visceral sexism as well, there will be many occasions on which we can only avoid inevitable discrimination by policies productive of reverse discrimination. Sometimes, however, persons will be hired or admitted—on a quota basis, for example—who appear to be displacing better applicants, but the appearance is the result of visceral discriminatory perceptions of the person's qualifications. In this case there will certainly appear to the visceral racist or sexist to be reverse discrimination, and this impression will be reinforced by knowledge that quotas were used; yet the allegation of reverse discrimination will be a mistaken one. On other occasions there will be genuine reverse discrimination, and on many occasions it will be impossible to determine whether or not this consequence is occurring. The evidence I have adduced is, of course, intended to support the contention that real and not merely apparent reverse discrimination is justified. But it is justified only as a means to the end of ensuring genuinely non-discriminatory treatment of all persons.

APPENDIX: ON IMPROPER UNDERSTANDINGS OF THE NATURE OF REVERSE DISCRIMINATION

Writers on the subject of reverse discrimination often engage in mere verbal battles because they use different meanings of the term "reverse discrimination." At a minimum this term means discrimination by one person or set of persons P_1 at the expense of another set of persons P_2, where P_2 formerly had discriminated against P_1. It is usually said that, by definition, the discrimination favoring P_2 must be on the basis of the *same* morally irrelevant characteristic(s) (race, sex, nationality, religion) that P_1 formerly used to discriminate against P_2. While I think discrimination might be reversed on the basis of *different* characteristics, I shall not pursue this peripheral matter here. But I would like to challenge other widespread assumptions.

It is often asserted or assumed that, by definition, reverse discrimination occurs only as a result of policies involving blanket preferential treatment on the basis of sex or race for whole groups of persons who are members of those classes. This is mistaken on at least two counts. First, properties other than race or sex may be used. Religion and nationality are obvious candidate properties. Second, and much more importantly, there is no reason why (by definition) a policy of compensation resulting in reverse discrimination must apply in a blanket indiscriminatory way to whole groups and not in a more restricted way to a limited number of individuals who are members of those groups. Suppose one adopted a preferential policy which competitively advantaged the job applications of all blacks earning less than $10,000/year (and which discriminated against competitive whites earning equivalent amounts) but did not advantage blacks who earned more than that figure. This would certainly be reverse discrimination based on race, but the entire racial group has not been given blanket preferential treatment.

This seemingly trivial observation is important because debating points are easily, but fallaciously scored in discussions of reverse discrimination by using the emotional argument that affluent women and minority group members would be advantaged and disadvantaged poor whites or males discriminated against. It is true that some authors—Graham Hughes,[1] for example—have argued that "the mere fact of a person's being black in the United States is a sufficient reason for providing compensatory techniques even though that person may in some ways appear fortunate in his personal background." But this is a particular thesis about the justifiability of reverse discrimination; it is not part of the term's definition, as Hughes would agree. Hence, one can advocate even radical policies of compensation resulting in reverse discrimination and at the same time advocate non-blanket, perhaps highly restrictive policies of preferential treatment. Scholarship programs in universities often have this character—whether justifiably or not.

These clarifying points seem to me of the highest importance. If we cannot agree on the nature of reverse discrimination, we will as a consequence be fruitlessly arguing over the justifiability or unjustifiability of different public policies. I think we should give the concept the kind of latitude I have suggested, largely because the proposals in contemporary society favoring preferential consideration vary greatly in scope and restricting conditions. None ought to be analytically excluded without argument. In sum, I have not attempted an analysis of reverse discrimination which sets forth necessary and sufficient conditions for proper use of the term, but I have argued the following: At a minimum, reverse discrimination is a discriminatory action or practice based on a (normally) morally irrelevant property; policies resulting in reverse discrimination may also apply to individual persons and/or groups and need not involve unqualified blanket preferential treatment; and, finally, any morally irrelevant property could be used—not simply race and sex, though these are at present the most interesting properties.

NOTES AND REFERENCES

1. Nuances concerning the concept of reverse discrimination and how it is often misused are discussed in an Appendix.

2. The best argument of this more standard form known to me is Louis Katzner, "Is the Favoring of Women and Blacks in Employment and Educational Opportunities Justified?," in Joel Feinberg and Hyman Gross, eds., *Philosophy of Law* (Encino, California: Dickenson Publishing Company, 1975), pp. 291–96.

3. I do not claim that policies productive of reverse discrimination are necessary for the elimination of every particular case of invidious discriminatory treatment. Obviously some non-reverse discriminatory measures will on some occasions suffice. My claim is that without such policies the problems of intractable discriminatory treatment in society at large cannot be resolved.

4. Lisa H. Newton, "Reverse Discrimination as Unjustified," *Ethics*, 83 (1973), 310, 312. Also reprinted in Wasserstrom.

5. From "Statement of Dr. Bernice Sandler," *Discrimination Against Women: Congressional Hearings on Equal Rights in Education and Employment,* ed. Catharine R. Stimpson (New York: R. R. Bowker Company, 1973), pp. 61, 415. Hereafter *Discrimination Against Women.*

6. All of the statistics and quotations cited are taken from the compilations of data in the following sources: (1) Kenneth M. Davidson, Ruth B. Ginsburg, and Herma H. Kay, eds., *Sex-Based Discrimination: Text, Cases, and Materials* (Minneapolis: West Publishing Company, 1974), esp. ch. 3. Hereafter *Sex-Based Discrimination.* (2) *Discrimination Against Women,* esp. pp. 397–441 and 449–502. (3) Alfred W. Blumrosen, *Black Employment and the Law* (New Brunswick, New Jersey: Rutgers University Press, 1971), esp. pp. 107, 122f. (4) *The Federal Civil Rights Enforcement Effort—1971,* A Report of the United States Commission on Civil Rights.

7. *Discrimination Against Women,* pp. 505f.

8. *Sex-Based Discrimination,* p. 516.

9. "The Fight Over University Women," *The New York Review of Books,* May 16, 1974, pp. 32–39.

10. *Maurianne Adams and Mary Schroeder* v. *Smith College,* Mas-

sachusetts Commission Against Discrimination, Nos. 72–S–53, 72–S–54 (December 30, 1974). Hereafter *The Smith College Case.*

11. 433 F.2d 421, 426 (8 Cir. 1970).

12. *The Smith College Case*, pp. 23, 26.

13. *Ibid.*, pp. 26f.

14. Robert Baker, " 'Pricks' and 'Chicks': A Plea for Persons," in Richard Wasserstrom, ed., *Today's Moral Problems* (New York: Macmillan Publishing Company, 1975), pp. 152–70.

15. *Ibid.*, p. 170.

16. "Visceral Racism," *The Monist*, 56 (1972), 43–63, and reprinted in Wasserstrom.

17. *On the Subjection of Women* (London: Longmans, Green, Reades, and Dyer, 1869), and especially as partially reprinted in Tom L. Beauchamp, ed., *Ethics and Public Policy* (Englewood Cliffs, N.J.: Prentice-Hall, 1975), pp. 11–19.

18. "Reasonable Progress and Self-Respect," *The Monist*, 57 (1973), 12–27, and reprinted in Beauchamp.

19. Carl Cohen, "The DeFunis Case: Race and the Constitution," *The Nation*, Feb. 8, 1975, p. 137.

20. A classic source is John Hope Franklin, *From Slavery to Freedom*, 3d ed. (New York: Alfred A. Knopf, 1969). A more abbreviated and popularized source is Eric Lincoln, *The Negro Pilgrimage in America* (New York: Frederick A. Praeger, 1969), rev. ed. Basic documents are arranged in historical sequence in Henry Steele Commager, ed., *The Struggle for Racial Equality: A Documentary Record* (Gloucester, Mass.: Peter Smith, 1972), a much expanded documentary account based on his earlier *Living Ideas in America*, chap. 14.

21. 60 U.S. 392 (1857) [Justice Taney].

22. New York: Harper and Row, 1962. Cf. esp. the statement by Rose on p. xliv.

23. As quoted in Commager, p. 2.

24. *DeFunis* v. *Odegaard*, 82 Wash. 2d 11, 507 P 2d 1169 (1974); cert. denied 94 S.CT. 1704 (1974).

25. Ezorsky, *passim*. Raspberry published a series of articles in *The Washington Post* (1974–75).

26. "Discrimination Against the Qualified?," *New York Times*, Nov. 5, 1971, p. 43.

27. J. Stanley Pottinger, "Race, Sex, and Jobs: The Drive Towards Equality," *Change Magazine*, 4 (Oct. 1972), 24–29.

28. Peter E. Holmes, "HEW Guidelines and 'Affirmative Action,'" *The Washington Post*, Feb. 15, 1975.

29. *The Federal Civil Rights Enforcement Effort—1974*, 3: 276.

30. *Ibid.*, p. 281.

31. *Ibid.*, all subsequent references are from pp. 281–86.

32. The evidence I have adduced is only a brief introduction to the kind of evidence for this thesis that could be mentioned—not only in the

three areas in which I have concentrated, but in others as well. For example there is significant *economic evidence* which shows that women are routinely paid much less for the same work and with the same credentials; and Virginia Held (*op. cit.*) has shown how the use of some plans for efficient economic allocation of job positions inevitably results in an unacceptably slow rate of progress toward equality. There is *psychological evidence* to indicate that women and minority group members are systematically downgraded by secondary school teachers (and graded higher when the race or sex is unknown to the grader), that women are routinely counselled to go only into majors and careers which have little or no market value (literature, arts, and home economics——but never engineering), and that a woman's name on an assigned paper leads students to rate it lower than the same paper with a man's name on it.

NOTE TO APPENDIX

1. "Reparations for Blacks?," *New York University Law Review*, 43 (1968), 1073. Reprinted in Beauchamp, p. 29.

Preferential Consideration and Justice

ABRAHAM EDEL

THE UNDERLYING problem context of our Conference is, I take it, how to increase participation of women and racial minorities in education and business in ways compatible with our conception of justice. This particular direction of query is made necessary not only by difficulties and controversies in the application of affirmative action—that is, specific programs involving governmental regulation and use of sanctions—but by a growing number of legal cases of which the DeFunis case was almost paradigmatic. This paper is devoted to some general theoretical aspects of the problem, chiefly relating preferential consideration to our concepts of justice. It falls into six parts:

I: The meaning and scope of preferential consideration
II: Conceptions of justice
III: How we operate with principles of justice
IV: The objectives of affirmative action
V: Issues about quotas
VI: An epilogue on basic directions.

I

I use the term "preferential consideration" in preference to either "compensatory justice" or "reverse discrimination." "Compensatory justice" contains already a full answer: It formulates the situation as one of preference to compensate for some, usually past, injustice. It certainly fits some types of cases, such as giving compensation to Indian groups for past forcible seizure of their lands. But it narrows the pathways of justification where one might want to argue preferential consideration for refugees or victims of some natural disaster or even preference on grounds of some sound national interest. "Reverse discrimination" already labels as discrimination and is thus somewhat pejorative. It seems to speak almost as if whites or men, having discriminated hitherto against blacks or women, should now be at the other end of the stick. In any case it passes too lightly over the question of deciding where helping A for a good and strong reason, though it uses limited resources and so shuts out B, is to be regarded as discrimination against B, and where as an unfortunate consequence of limited resources. "Preferential consideration," on the other hand, is a term that simply describes a phenomenon. The ethical question, whether a given preferential consideration is just, is thus separated and transferred to the grounds for giving a go-ahead signal to a preference and for the direction of that preference.

The phenomenon is common enough. We have veterans' preference in some forms of employment whether this is to be construed as an expression of gratitude, a recognition of alternative forms of experience credit, or compensation for time out for a social purpose of overwhelming importance. In college admission athletic skill has often been a ground of preference not reckoned unjust in choosing between two students of equal academic record; familiar too is the selection of a student with high athletic ability and normal academic record over one with only a high academic record (musical ability rarely counts in the profile). The draft in war-time raised many questions of preferential consideration both in acceptance and in exemption. Finer tuning of criteria might have used older men for some jobs in which experience would be more helpful than youth, and it could have exempted youths of higher ability who had not had a chance to go to college as well as those who happened to be already in college. The point is simply that to find and formulate the grounds for preferential consideration in any area carries us into a broader and deeper inquiry. We need to explore the criteria used in the light of underlying aims, usually institutional or social. We have to understand the structure of the situation, the complex conditions under which the selection is being made. We have to predict to some extent the consequences of action along the lines of those criteria, with respect to those aims and under those conditions. Anything less than such a full exploration in deciding the justice of the modes of preferential consideration embodied in affirmative action programs is likely to distort the problem and the issues.

Is there anything novel in the fact of preferential consideration as it occurs in affirmative action programs? In general, or on a macroscopic view, almost any decision of policy or any permitted drift in social life means a loss to some and a gain to others. To allow car travel in a large city is to deny the streets to pedestrians and people who do not own cars. (Would it be unjust now to limit car-driving to certain hours or make a mall out of certain streets for certain periods, just as some squares in older European cities serve as markets in the morning and parking-places in the afternoon?) The claim for prescriptive or traditional rights need not be decisive. For example, we are only beginning to realize the rights of non-smokers, even though these may cut down the rights of smokers in certain contexts. Comparable decisions will now have to be made in many areas of newly discovered pollution and health hazards. (Should the need for a safe water supply in Duluth be preferred to the rights of the copper industry to pour its waste into Lake Superior? If it should be, should compensation go to the industry or to the workers who become unemployed?) To wage a war is to bring death to some part of the civilian population nowadays. (Would it be unjust to have free insurance at public expense for civilians killed or hurt in bombing, as we have had for soldiers?) As property law takes one form or another, so are the chances of some enhanced or diminished against others. (Should a medical school have to pay royalties if it xeroxes articles on recent medical discoveries to circulate to doctors to keep them up-to-date?) In general, those who have—whether property, money, jobs—are constantly being assessed for many purposes through taxation and through inflation (it is perhaps clearer in the former than in the latter where the money goes). In short, we live in an atmosphere of constant redistribution with preferential effects, often unintended, and the built-in patterns of redistribution are quite literally patterns of preference. They may become explicit and when we are conscious of them we may make them the subject for definite social policy. What then are to be the criteria for considering one redistributive pattern just, another unjust?

II

The theory of justice is itself highly controversial today. There are two chief paths. One sets its formulae of justice in reference to the kind of life that action according to the formulae will make possible. Older utilitarian theories spoke of the formulae that under the existing conditions of life yielded "the greatest happiness of the greatest number." More recently, theories in this vein talk of the quality of life made possible by the arrangements taken to be just. The second path looks for an independent or autonomous structure of justice inherent in human life and personal relations, antecedent to any pursuit of the good and setting limits on the direction the latter may take. It is usually cast in terms of a theory of individual human rights. Though compatible with a variety of underlying philosophies it is often associated in our tradition with a contractualism that takes obligation to emanate from the individual's will and social obligations from the meeting or consensus of wills.

The two paths reflect an old conflict in the history of moral philosophy—the struggle for primacy between the good and the right. To give primacy to the good means that moral laws, principles, virtues, policies, and proposed rights must all pass the bar of evaluation in the light of their consequences for the good. In the complex conditions of modern life it means room for uncertainties, use of probabilities, greater relativity of answers under differing conditions. To give primacy to the right puts in the forefront stern principles and absolute rights, a greater demand for explicit conformity, narrower scope for excuses, a moral rigidity rather than a moral flexibility. If the primacy of the good sometimes invites opportunism, it may also invite a more sophisticated moral sense and a sensitivity to changing conditions. If the primacy of right sometimes invites dogmatism and a legalism that narrows equity, it may also invite principled sincerity that makes great sacrifices in the name of morality and an unbending resistance to oppression. In the 19th century, the contrast would have been formulated as Bentham vs. Kant. At the moment, in technical moral philosophy, it happens to be the bout of utilitarianism vs. a Rawlsian contractarianism.

I shall not engage in these controversies here. There are too many straw men, too much shadow-boxing, and too sharp a contrast which cannot, I think, bear up under analysis. On the whole, the first seems to me to be a more realistic philosophy in its understanding of the panoramic procession of concepts of justice over the ages. And it is not incapable of the stiffening of moral fiber that our contemporary world badly needs. But I shall not pursue it here, nor argue from its acceptance.

The fact is that whichever path is taken, the massive pressure of our contemporary world problems and the basic demands of the peoples of the globe—both their needs and aspirations—will force their way through either framework. They will simply find different paths of entry. Absolute property rights will not help much where taxation is justified, where collective bargaining is accepted, and where prices may be freely moved about or manipulated. Tax decisions, wage structures, and price structures do the redistributing. Similarly, when ideals and basic goods are translated into institutions, the latter take on an inertial life of their own. Still, the theoretical issue may be important in determining the readiness to change redistributive patterns in pursuit of definite goals. The utilitarian will ask whether property laws or laws governing conditions of employment or public expenditure should be changed to yield greater well-being. The individual rights position will filter the question of change through that of determining what rights are to be allowed or are relevant, or if the list is closed, what are to be the interpretations in applying the ones that are already recognized. For example, does the right to property include a right to any property, as the capitalist world has claimed with an eye to property for production, or is it limited to personal property? (In the latter case society could grant or withdraw rights to property for production as it thought best at a given period.) This was a serious issue in the debates that preceded the adoption of the United Nations Declaration of Human Rights. The practical consequence at issue was clearly that where productive property constituted a human right it could not be lightly socialized. In any case, the Declaration widely expanded the number and types of rights, thereby broadening the area of social justice. At least on the theoretical level, individual rights theory has often today been as aggressive as utilitarian theory in seeking to expand human well-being.

I propose therefore that instead of thinking in terms of opposing theories, we think of two models—briefly, the individual rights model and the collective welfare model—and ask in which areas of social life it is desirable to use the one model, in which the other. To take extremes: In the domain of criminal justice certainly no man should be punished for what he has not himself done or willed. Here long experience of humanity has established the individual rights model. But in war a man is drafted whether he wills it or not, and that is suffering if not punishment. Obviously, without raising the question here of the merits of defensive wars, we would feel we ought to use the collective model, with some reservations about conscientious objectors. Now the domain in which affirmative action enters—employment and education—is an intermediate one. What kind of argument can we employ to decide which model should annex it or to what extent?

Lest you think I am begging the question on a higher level by using a kind of utilitarian ground for deciding where to use which model, let me note that in the current controversy over utilitarianism and justice the same thing is happening on both sides. I see a growing convergence on the view that the greatest happiness of the greatest number is not enough; for there is always the minority —the rest of the people. William James with his usual sensitivity early offered a counter-instance to this utilitarian formula: If some god offered us all perpetual happiness provided only one lost soul were condemned to suffer endless torment, we would be outraged. The bizarre speculations of one generation of philosophers usually become the practical problems of a subsequent generation. Is it right that 80% of the population enjoy a high standard of living and 20% bear the burdens or be thrust out of the society's functioning? The point has been reached where an outraged minority will be driven in despair to rock the whole social foundation and so compel an attention that morally should have come long ago. The liberation movements of recent years have shown that the well-being of the majority is not enough. Interestingly, in questions of intellectual and political liberty we recognized long ago that the right of the minority, even (in J. S. Mill's formulation) of one man against all mankind, should be protected. In the area of economic opportunity and social participation, minorities need also to be protected, even against "the greatest happiness of the greatest number."

In the individualist model the same conclusion can be built quite directly into the theory of justice. This is clear in John Rawls's currently much discussed conception. Without entering into presently raging controversies about this theory and its proclamation of the independent priority of the right, we may note that the "difference principle" which is its central moral claim ties the formula of justice to the view that no change in distribution is justified which does not improve the lot of the least advantaged. So, whatever the framework, everybody is worried about the disadvantaged.

We may stop speaking of minorities at this point, a formulation induced in part by the utilitarian reference to the greatest happiness of the greatest number, as well as conditions in the United States. Aristotle pointed out, in defining democracy and oligarchy, that number is not of the essence. Suppose the oligarchs were a majority; it would still be at bottom a question of the rich and the poor. In the United States, blacks are a minority, but women are not. In South Africa blacks are a majority. It is therefore a question of the disadvantaged, not the few.

III

Let us now turn to actual formulae of justice. They will specify the ground for apportionment: burdens to be distributed according to property X, gains or goods according to property Y. Here are some of the criteria-candidates: ability, merit, work done, need, class position, chance acquisition, wealth, poverty, social contribution, aggressiveness, lack of aggressiveness, tendency of the formula to encourage socially desirable character, tendency to promote survival or a higher standard of living, intelligence, strength, moral worth, and so on. Whatever one's type of theory of justice, there will be a plurality of principles. The utilitarians will ask us to decide which it is desirable to use in what area under what conditions and with what aims. The nonutilitarians will answer all these questions indirectly by selecting and balancing principles, whether by hierarchical order, fixing priorities, determining relevance, distinguishing jurisdictions, balancing according to weight, fashioning compromises, or enduring the tragedies of conflict. Once again, I expect that social necessities and realities will break through either procedure.

Let us explore the problem of selection of principles from the field of our present concern. The criteria in employment and education have usually been merit and ability, not always distinguished. How do we decide whether these are appropriate criteria, and if they are, how do we interpret and apply them? And where can preferential considerations be allowed to enter?

First, as to merit or desert, let us pay respect to the old quip: "If we got what we deserved, then God help us all." And as for ability, it is well to recall that absolutist governments have often been tolerable only because of the inefficiency of their agents. If we were asked for a criterion for appointment to government offices in such states we might recommend inability as the most desirable property.

Though to invoke such extremes is close to caricature, still it shows that the use of meritocratic criteria is relative to the kind of job and the ends for which that kind of job exists and the conditions of its operation. For example, for each job there is a level of competence that is necessary; only for some jobs need it be the highest competence attainable. For a job of unskilled labor in a mechanical assembly-line, working with a machine at a fixed pace, only an ordinary competence is needed. For the surgeon or the mathematician in advanced research, the highest competence is desirable. Why is that? Because the surgeon's business is a risky one for the patients, and in the mathematician's case there is always the feeling that a higher ability increases the possibilities of richer discoveries. Now in the types of jobs that require only a given level of competence, there may be considerable room for other considerations to enter into employment. For example, it may very well be that for certain jobs preferential consideration should be given to mentally retarded persons who can just manage to do them, precisely because these may be the only kinds of jobs they would be capable of doing. Similar considerations arise for the physically handicapped. If a private employer adopted such a policy he might very likely be praised for his humanitarian attitude. If the government adopted such a policy for jobs under its control, would this be denying equal protection of the laws to the brilliant, particularly if we were in the midst of a recession? And what if the government, finding itself spending large sums for assistance to the mentally retarded, passed a law reserving a certain proportion of jobs in interstate commerce for such persons? It might add the further argument that instead of spending money for them, the taxpayers would be getting taxes in return! No doubt many further considerations would enter into the decision about preference, but it is hard to see it as ruled out in principle in advance.

Let us turn back to the doctor or the lawyer or the teacher. If each of these had the kind of pure essence that angels were thought to possess, then meritocratic criteria could be readily applied. But human aims in the professions are complex and mixed, and the criteria for the best practitioner and the most promising student—for employment and for admission to schools—are more problematic than the use of a one-word name for the profession would suggest. Take, for example, the relation of teaching and research in higher education. Some countries will separate the research institute from the teaching university. Others keep them together hoping that research will fructify teaching. They are then faced with the questions of choosing in appointment between the candidate excellent in research and poor in teaching and the one excellent in teaching but only moderate in research. Similarly, medical selection might have to choose between average medical competence but greater appreciation of psychological problems and interpersonal relations and high specialty skill without the other abilities. In such situations, one begins to ask about the conditions of practice. If the surgeon will only be called in to operate, then of course there is no question about the criteria.

Two linguistic formulations are possible about preferential consideration in such complex cases. If the grounds are to be found within the description of aims, then it need not be considered preferential consideration at all; rather the problem is weighting the components in a pattern of complex aims. If the grounds are not contained within the aims, then the problem is one of outside weighty considerations that may or may not prove overriding. The questions are now whether the considerations are legitimate and what weight they have. Even which formulation is to be used may be a difficult issue in cases where the aims of the profession are undergoing change or the conception of a capable member of the profession is being transformed by increased knowledge or major social reconstruction. Many of the current problems about the need for role models in the case of women and blacks—or for that matter, men in elementary and nursery schools—are of this sort.[1] In general, as the educational level of a society goes up, the proportion of jobs to be assigned on merit alone may be considerably reduced, since the needed level of competence may be widespread for many types of jobs. In certain areas it may well be that the effective principle should be decision by lot in some areas, rotation in others.

The general conditions that most affect the principles of justice, adjusting degrees of relevance among them, are the extent of scarcity and abundance. David Hume, who argued for a purely instrumental value to justice, pointed this out by taking the extreme cases. Given complete abundance, there is no need of distributive rules, given complete scarcity they lose all effectiveness. He paralleled this with a consideration of human attitudes toward one another: Given complete affiliative concern for fellow humans there is no need of justice; given complete rapaciousness and aggressiveness there is no room for it. The instrumental value of justice becomes clear in the intermediate zones. But there it is precisely where the principles become most controversial if there is no fine tuning to public well-being. In our present concern—jobs in business and places in education—the state of the economy and the extent of educational opportunity have obvious relevance. In educational opportunity open admissions is a recent institution that makes the problem of affirmative action less relevant in that area, provided services within the educational institutions are adequate. A DeFunis case has meaning only when openings are limited. Similarly, given full employment, the problem of affirmative action would not arise, except insofar as there were discriminatory practices in wages, types of position, promotion, conditions of work. As for good will, I do not think its strength and prevalence in our society should be underestimated. It was especially evident during the rise of the liberation movements. But it is not the attitude fostered by our competitive economy and our competitive life, and it has to function constantly against the tide. It is particularly prone to become isolated and minimal in effect when scarcity advances.

Two cautions are requisite in considering the selection of principles of justice and their application. The first is that the formula for distribution need not be the same for burdens and gains. To say "from each according to his abilities" need not entail "to each according to his abilities." Each formula, its place, its scope, and so on, has to be justified separately. In ancient Athens when the city needed ships for the navy, the rich were assigned the care of individual vessels because they were rich; similarly, they were assigned the production of plays for the festivals. In return they got honor, especially if their play won or their ship did well. In contemporary times the armaments are part of the defense budget, and the cultural life is encouraged by the National Endowment for the Humanities. Both come from tax funds, and the principles of justice and injustice here lie in the formulae of the tax budget and the derivation of internal revenue.

The second caution is that the complex character of principles of justice and of preferential consideration has to be matched with a clear view of the whole of the resultant social processes, not by looking simply at one favored sector of what is going on. Let me illustrate this briefly by a paradox. Suppose the body of possible workers in a field is 1000, for whom there are 900 jobs, and the 900 hold on keeping the 100 at bay. By refusing any accommodation, they are in effect subsidizing them through the tax fund for relief, unemployment insurance, etc. Therefore the 900 work more than they have to, for if the other 100 shared the work they would have to work less. Of course in a planless situation they may gain more than they would have in a wider distribution of work, but certainly not without some actual cost. Some unions today, in fields that are closed and well-organized, have in fact been meeting the present recession by such procedures of sharing the work. There may, of course, be many different kinds of formulae which would yield equitable solutions for different fields and their special conditions.

What happens when a society becomes conscious of a great injustice to a part of its population, when it is realized that women's potentialities are thwarted by all sorts of built-in discriminations, that blacks suffer through unemployment, lack of education, segregation, and so on? The moral problem and the legal problem and the practical problem step out on the scene and decision and action come on the agenda of social life. But what is to be done becomes the center of controversy. Naturally, those who are entrenched feel that their position will be endangered where a vast expansion of resources is not available; profits will go down and standards of living be reduced if the injustices are remedied. Counter-principles of justice tend to be invoked in defense, principles recognized as intuitively acceptable or socially useful—for example, seniority rights, prescriptive rights, need to keep initiative and motivation at a high level for production, and so on. There may even be dire warnings of unavoidable strikes or backlash as more ominous than the acts of disruption and despair from the disadvantaged. Or more constructively, there may be alternative proposals for remedying the situation, or specific procedures for seeking remedies. The one absolutely basic criterion in evaluating all the proposals from the point of view of justice is that they cannot be such as to result in the sheer continuation of the injustice to the outs. This is the *minimal* requirement. The *maximal* requirement is the actual achievement of an order that will bring the outs into the full participation of the society and its goods. The task of affirmative action, as I see it, is to guarantee the minimum and move toward the maximum, as fast and effectively as possible.

IV

Affirmative action can span a range of objectives from the minimum to the maximum just indicated, and it can employ a range of instruments. It makes considerable difference where it sets its objective and what instruments it employs. Maximally, it could impose directly some formulae of distribution, as in the use of quotas. Less maximally, it could set goals and longer range strategies for diminishing injustices. Minimally, it could engage in mediation, keeping the problem alive and spurring action. In method, maximally it could use strong sanctions for enforcement; less maximally it could call to account where progress is too slow or is thwarted; minimally it could engage in educational campaigns (or in the economic parallel what has been called "to jaw-bone"). Such a variety of objectives and methods is familiar enough in other sectors of our life—for example, the critical economic problem of keeping prices and wages from advancing in an inflationary spiral. What objective one sets and what methods one uses depend on how critical the situation is and what the analysis of the forces at work is. In the case of discrimination against blacks the situation was recognized as most critical after the violent upsurge in the cities a few years ago.

In the light of the heated controversies there have been over affirmative action it would be useful to look at parallels in our national and international life in which the same sort of thing was done and quite accepted. I choose a national one where in effect we used a super-maximal objective and compulsion as the means and an international one in which less maximal objectives and almost minimal means were used with perhaps retrospective regret.

The national example is the development of compulsory public schooling. The principle of a just distribution of basic education was quite simple—equal educational opportunity for everyone. We used the super-maximal solution of public education, education nationalized as it were, not something less such as supporting private schools or giving every child a grant to attend private schools. As to method, we use the truant officer to ensure attendance; and at the present moment our courts, as in New Jersey, are using judicial power to compel a revision of mode of financing for the schools to ensure a greater equality. To see that all this is a type of affirmative action we have only to look back to the situation that existed before the public schools arose—one in which only a few had educational opportunities and enjoyed all the advantages that education brought.

For the international parallel look to what happened to many of the former colonies after World War II. The old imperial power was often the one left with a mandate. The mandatory power, according to the Trusteeship Council of the UN, had the obligation to bring the former colony up to the point of freedom, and then it would be set free. But periodically the mandatory power had to report on the progress that was being made and show that it was rapid enough to give freedom by a set date. As objective and method, this fell rather far below the maximum. We can, of course, look back on this procedure and see where it worked and why, and where it produced the kind of situation that was found later in the then-called Belgian Congo, though there may also be other reasons why such catastrophes developed. It does not require much hindsight to recognize that if stronger measures had been possible—even moderate ones such as requiring a specific budget for education in the former colonies and checking periodically that it was properly distributed—some great evils might have been minimized. More realistically, it is hard to avoid the conclusion that the weak type of affirmative action employed there simply reflected the readiness of the mandatory powers to cloak their continued exploitation of the colonies under new titles. And, I may add, a comparable conclusion would be inevitable if present pressures to hamstring affirmative action against discrimination are successful.

What level of objectives affirmative action should set today and what methods it should employ are thus policies dependent on analysis of conditions, feasible means, urgency, and so forth. Since conditions of groups may vary, the policy need not be uniform with respect to all groups. For example, if we had a policy of affirmative action in employment for the physically handicapped, it would probably have to be less strong today than a few years ago since sensitivity to discrimination has become greater and we are quicker to see it in groups whose suffering has been hitherto insufficiently noticed. If we had a policy of affirmative action in employment for persons who have gone through a period of psychiatric institutionalization, it would have to be quite strong to counter the prejudice that still is paramount. Again, to remove discrimination against some ethnic groups has simply required legal weapons, in other cases a strong executive action. In the case of blacks and women the habits of discrimination are built into our culture so deeply that only a rude shock may wake us up. The advantages that the established power groups have as a consequence of the discrimination are regarded as rights not to be touched. In practice delaying tactics, obfuscating tactics, even shock tactics, are employed constantly. Whether the problem is one of intentional obstruction or deep-seated bad habits is not our present concern. The important point is that something strong has to be done to prevent the greater evils of nothing being done, or, of injustice being overcome so slowly as to condemn several generations of the disadvantaged to despair and suffering.

I would suggest therefore that the desirable level of objective for affirmative action be reached by thinking in terms of a *breakthrough*—to use a military metaphor explicitly—against the Maginot Line of discrimination. Of course it will have to judge both strategy and tactics wisely, but to tie its hands as to means would be like saying that the line should be broken without tanks, or without planes, or without surprise in timing and attacks. There is always the grim reminder that if it loses it will have to be replaced by a strategy on a stronger level, just as in the opposite direction strategies can become milder if conditions become better—if peace is secured in the military example or full employment in our present problem.

One consequence of using the break-through notion might be setting a limited time perspective for the experiment. One could conjecture that a quarter of a century may be needed to change our national ways in habits of discrimination—just as ten years may be required for developing new energy sources. On the other hand, it is possible that some permanent regulation would be required, as in the case of compulsory public education. So we shall have to wait for the outcome of our present experiment in affirmative action to see where to go from there.

Another consequence of the break-through notion as a defining objective for affirmative action would be that we make no attempt to specify a hoped-for final state to determine a formula for a permanent just distribution. For one thing, we cannot quite foresee all the changes in our institutional structures that a breakthrough and associated economic and social changes would bring. This raises, however, the heated problem of quotas.

V

Are quotas in affirmative action a matter of injustice, folly, or unavoidable necessity? There are all sorts of quotas—loose quotas, tight quotas, unjust quotas, reasonable quotas. The term has largely become associated with unjust quotas of exclusion, as a means of keeping out racial and ethnic groups and women from desirable participation and control. Jews have suffered particularly in our history from quotas that aimed to exclude.

There are two questions about quotas which are currently discussed as matters of principle, as involving principles of justice. They fall, equitably, on opposing sides. On the one side it is argued that any attempts at quotas to remove discrimination would have to be stated in terms of race or sex and would constitute unjust and unequal treatment, defective both in morals and in law. In short, it is assumed that preferential consideration of A on grounds of race or sex is *ipso facto* reverse discrimination *against* B on grounds of race or sex. On the other side, it is argued as a question of *right* that if women are 50% of the population they should have 50% of the jobs. I think that the use of both these arguments in a somewhat a priori fashion obstructs an effective understanding of the pros and cons of quotas.

The use of a race or sex label is certainly invidious when its purpose is to exploit, oppress, or exclude the designated group from participation and social benefits. It is not invidious when its purpose is to liberate, bring into participation, open the area of benefits. The group has to be designated by the race or sex label because the oppression exists or existed against the group as so labelled. In the recent negotiations to allow more Jews to emigrate from the Soviet Union, no one raised the question whether this was discriminating against other groups that might want to emigrate from the Soviet Union. There are many areas in which a loose quota has been readily considered just and reasonable. If Hawaii had a law that every Board of Education should have at least one Chinese member, one Japanese member, one native Hawaiian member, the ground for it would be quite apparent from the history of the different groups to win a place against discrimination. Perhaps one might object on the ground that it did not also have a Samoan member! This need not be a permanent policy; it would depend on the state of the problem of discrimination. In New York politics it was long a practice to have a political ticket with one Catholic, one Protestant, one Jew, and later on, one Black and one Italian. This was a "practical" not a "principled" matter; no one in the political clubs would have accused the district leaders of imposing quotas. (In the long run one would hope this would give way to the "best person" principle; but perhaps probability of being elected is one of the criteria of "best." I do not recall the quota charge having been raised when the courts insisted, in effect, that blacks be on jury lists; the reason was too transparent in the light of the grim behavior of all-white juries. Whey then is the quota charge raised when affirmative action calls for women on police forces? Or for blacks in law schools?)

The argument for numerical representation as an inherent right has no clear basis. There is no inherent relation between being a woman or black and the criteria for specific job occupancy. If there are in some jobs, then maybe women should have 75% of some jobs and 20% of others. More likely numerical representation is being invoked as the only way to be sure there is no discrimination. But affirmative action does not need the lack of proportionality to investigate. There should be no bar to its investigating on complaint or even at random as the Internal Revenue office does. (Its reason is the same: to check for error or because it is operating in a domain where the tendency to avoid obligations is strong and widespread!) What it investigates for is progress in overcoming discrimination and habits of discrimination. Even if all jobs were filled by randomizing devices there would be no guarantee of proportions in each enterprise, though it would surely guarantee no discrimination.

The fear—often expressed in caricature—that every group that can fashion an identity will therefore demand representation is not well-grounded. Not every shoe of esoteric style pinches, and if it does it might be settled by a little stretching. Complaints have to be well-grounded and serious and a good complaint department will treat according to the case; it will not stop business because it has had enough complaints! For example, should left-handed people demand a quota? It all depends on what is going on in the society. If left-handed people are being compelled to turn right-handed to get jobs, and if this produces a distortion of personality with far-ranging consequences, and if the dominant right-handed community consistently discriminates in education, in the production of toys and tools that favor right-handedness, and if there cannot be ready solutions—then perhaps it is time for left-handed people to demand representation on Boards of Education at least! Is there any doubt about the complaints of the handicapped in employment? Recent history and the proliferation of liberation movements has encouraged complaints about ever fresh categories of discrimination. A humanistic society can only welcome this and look at each on its merits. Representation demands and loose quota demands are the crop of the oppressed and the loud sigh of the neglected. It is well to recall at the time of the bicentennial that "no taxation without representation" was the first demand of this type.

There is a great deal to be said against quotas as an instrument of affirmative action. They are drastic, possibly dangerous, and likely to be extremely disruptive. But they could be effective in breaking through. Recently, I heard a law professor defend them as the milder alternative. The most obvious, and most revolutionary, and most disruptive thing to do when we discover a basic injustice in the distribution of jobs, he said, would be to fire everybody and start afresh! Quotas at least would be only partially disruptive. The crucial point, however, was his further assumption that nothing less than quotas has worked or were likely to work under present conditions. Now whether this is a good general argument or not, it clearly has some domains of application. One of the most serious in the recession and/or depression we are undergoing is that seniority rules will mean that the disadvantaged, as most recently hired, will be first fired. Hence the demand has arisen for two lists in seniority, with firing from both but so as to maintain some kind of proportion not less than presently existing. It is hard to see this as unreasonable, unless a better solution is offered. Again, there are domains in which even the more extreme procedure of starting afresh might be quite applicable. I recall a case—though not in sufficient detail—of a longshoremen's union that had hiring halls but was dominated by its officers who kept favorites in established jobs. When the union was democratized, it instituted a rotation system: Everyone who finished a job went to the bottom of the waiting-list and had his turn. There was no seniority. In such a situation a disadvantaged group had only to be among the members to be fully equal; good and bad times were equally shared. Of course this type of solution is possible only under certain conditions such as: a closed or limited number, with careful control of entry much as in the old guilds; a strong union with a thoroughly democratic outlook; union control over job assignment; probably also effective unemployment insurance; some degree of constancy in jobs. There would be sociological consequences too, such as the union rather than the job center becoming the functioning community. And probably the type of job would have to be one that any representative member of the group could do competently.

In many contexts, then, we can get behind the question of quotas to a very complex set of different mechanisms; there the concrete question will always be which mechanism to use and what results it would secure. There is no gainsaying the widespread objection today that is found to numerical quotas as a general policy. I shall not enter here into the grounds for this common judgment; they range from the historical passions roused by past use of discriminatory quotas to the recognition that in practice they would yield an over-rigidity and engender collateral injustices. But note that such reasoning is not based on any intrinsic injustice in the conception of loose quotas as an instrument of break-through. There is instead the assumption (or the hope) that other ways will be found to remedy the injustices for which quotas have been invoked.

Let us finally look at the charge so current today that affirmative action is just a devious way of imposing quotas, that no tenable distinction can be drawn. The Health, Education and Welfare Department generally draws a distinction, and so did the Democratic mini-convention when it settled on the idea of affirmative action to keep peace between the old and the new forces. On the other hand, some labor leaders, especially in education, have constantly expressed suspicion of affirmative action. Such instances reflect clearly the position of the "haves" who are entrenched. But equally, the distinction may reflect the dilemma of interests caught between the haves and the have-nots and grasping at straws to prevent a break. We must therefore attempt dispassionately to analyze the possible differences. By "quotas" we mean in this context the use of numerical proportions and by "affirmative action" we mean programs to break up discrimination in a general sense, abstracting from the means adopted. The issue is whether there can be a viable affirmative action which is not tied with quotas.

There are a number of differences suggested by theoretical distinctions that have a long history in moral philosophy. They may be indicated briefly:

1. Quotas rest on formulae or recipes, affirmative action on more general methods or principles operating as ways of analyzing a situation rather than as fixed directives for action.

2. Insofar as anything is measured in affirmative action, it is degree of success in the effort to solve a problem that counts; in quotas the numerical relations at the end are measured. In affirmative action results may be looked at to get an inquiry started.

3. Excuses have a greater scope in affirmative action than in quotas.

4. In affirmative action there is greater particularization and differentiation of means than in quotas. There is recognition of stages, processes attempted, closer attunement to types of problems, and greater credit for progress and attempts at progress.

5. In quotas exact results are a mark of success; in affirmative action they may even be a ground for suspicion!

6. Affirmative action stimulates or engenders purposive efforts and inventiveness in solving problems. Quotas allow only one path.

Clearly then there is no logical difficulty in the conception of affirmative action without quotas.

The action of the Democratic mini-convention was in many respects a paradigm of the whole situation. Though determined by pressures and threats of withdrawal, it was held together by the realization that unless some solution were achieved there were great losses for all in losing the next election. It acknowledged the aim of wider participation and called on everyone to take action to secure it. It opposed mandatory quotas, but allowed challenges to delegates where affirmative action performance was inadequate. It ruled out proportion in results as the sole basis of challenge. And there was the further guarantee that where an exact equality appeared between men and women it should not be seen as a violation of the previous conditions! (There was a battle over a proposed clause about burden of proof based on the composition of results, but this was dropped so that there is no mandatory burden of proof.) In our society as a whole all have as much to lose, as vast a stake in removing discrimination and healing our society as the Democrats had in their hope of election success. The detail of the pattern could fit equally well for investigations about discriminatory practices in employment and education. Any use of proportions could only be as starting-points for inquiry. The main force of the program is to make sure that something is being done, that effort is directed to removing the injustices, that a plan of action is on its way. That it requires sanctions in order to make the break-through is an unfortunate fact of our culture. It would, of course, be much better if we internalized the sense of injustice and the pressure to remedy it. But as a people we have been very blind in these moral matters, in spite of our humanitarianism. The story is now very likely to be repeated on the international scene if we do not quickly appreciate in action as well as in thought and feeling that we are using a tremendous part of the world's energy and resources for our own consumption while a great part of the rest of the world is in a deprived state. The questions of justice in that context are even more complex than the ones we have been examining.

Leites and Wolfenstein, some years ago in a book comparing the movies in different countries, found that in the United States we tend to externalize our conscience. Our Furies, they point out, are not within us but lie in the police car and the siren. Our solution of a problem—say the familiar sex triangle of the older movies—is not internal debate and decision but a car accident in which one of the parties is removed from the scene! The problems to which affirmative action is addressed could of course be reduced to a minimum by external means—by full employment, by universal education and wider opportunities for professional education, by the development of assistance in counselling and in provision of resources for all types of disadvantage. But our society has not worked out such solutions in an institutional way. It has moved slowly toward social security, universal medical care, guaranteed minimum income, and so forth. It needs the greatest imaginative scope to break up questions, to devise a variety of solutions for different types of professions and vocations, different types of labor and learning and teaching. It needs less wielding of general principles that on analysis turn out to be not formulae of justice but bludgeons that will leave things simply as they are. While we mature in all these ways, we need a conscience that will not let the injustices lie no matter how much it hurts us. Affirmative action is such an externalized conscience. That we need it is the mark of our immaturity. Eventually it will give way—we can only hope—to reconstructed institutions and a sensitive humanity that does not even think in the terms that have constituted the groups for discrimination.

VI

Will justice allow us to end on a note that is forward looking, but—oh!—ever so far forward-looking? Conscience, like Rome, cannot be built in a day, and the hope of removing discrimination, together with the conscience that will take care of it, gets postponed in the pressure of continual emergencies. Just as the energy crisis makes inroads on the attempts to end obvious and glaring pollutions, so the economic crisis, with its unemployment, makes inroads on ending obvious and glaring discriminations. This is where justice—the most demanding of moral crises—refuses postponement, and that is the beat to which affirmative action marches. If there have to be sacrifices to meet crises then the theory of equitable sacrifices must include readjustments to diminish discrimination.

Reason and experience add their voice to this demand. If anything is clear in our economic development, it is that the numbers in agriculture and manufacturing and industry generally have gone down almost without end—when I last looked at it the agricultural was down below 5% and the industrial moving below 25%, perhaps by now much lower as automation moves apace. The one area growing and capable of almost indefinite expansion is the service industry. If we look at the picture as a whole, our choice is between supporting a large part of our population on welfare and in unemployment or developing some rational plan for the total use of our population in useful work. This means the acceptance of the goal that was raised in the 1940s of full employment whether or not we export sufficiently to "cover costs." We do not engage in such reckonings when we are at war; we make whatever social arrangements are required to do the job.

So, too, full employment is the only alternative to the bitter struggle over scarce jobs in which not only justice and the voice of justice is lost, but all sense of dignity.

To maintain dignity means participation in meaningful work, not make-work or bread and circuses. It is time to exercise a collective imagination on developing the kinds of jobs that the society needs. Some are obvious: Instead of talking of an over-supply of teachers with present large classes in both the lower and higher schools, we could use an almost endless supply of teachers in the proper pursuit of education. The care of the aged is another domain (in which we could take a few lessons from Sweden). Keeping our streets clean all the time and our beaches and rivers clean could involve endless labors as well as strong civic passions. And the advancement of knowledge and the development of a rich cultural life for the people as a whole could add a wide sector of satisfying labor. And so on and on.

Unless we follow such paths we shall be prey to the irrationalities we find about us. What is more self-defeating than demanding an arsenal be kept on just because people are employed in it, rather than that there be a reconversion of labor and facilities for useful production? The same argument applies to our automobile recession. If there is no demand for cars or large cars—except Cadillacs—and no real need for an over-expanded production of cars in a long-range plan for transportation and for avoiding pollution, what we need is planned reconversion of the industry just as when it was reconverted from war uses. Our present pattern of goals reminds me (putting together two historical cases) of the hoopers' objecting to the introduction of coffee because it was pushing down beer consumption and so diminishing the demand for hoops on beer barrels! And our strategies of solution are little better than—to take a recent example—two states fighting in the courts, one to stop the other from seeding the clouds and so robbing it of the rain that the prevailing winds would normally bring into its territory. An interstate or a national plan for conserving and developing water-supplies is so obviously the rational strategy.

It may very well be that the depth of discrimination in our present life will be the point of pressure at which a sober rationality will be brought home to us in our total national life. Historical causality, as the philosophers are fond of pointing out, follows strange paths. Perhaps it is time to do self-consciously what Hegel appealed to as the cunning of reason—that is, do our own planning rather than let patterns emerge from the blind play of forces. If the situation that has produced and supported affirmative action does have such an historical impetus, justice will have brought more than its own reward.

NOTE

1. For a fuller discussion of such issues, see the forthcoming article by Elizabeth Flower, " 'Affirmative Action and the Principle of Equality' Reconsidered," in *Studies in Philosophy and Education.*

Realizing the Equality Principle

RUTH BADER GINSBURG

ALMOST HALF A CENTURY ago Burnita Shelton Matthews, in the 1920s counsel to the National Woman's Party and since the 1940s United States District Judge, said in answer to a male lawyer's criticism of the Equal Rights Amendment: "It is of course disappointing to women that men of the legal profession are unable to see equality as equity when applied as between men and women. But then it is not surprising when one remembers that this defective vision, this regard of discrimination as 'protection,' is traditional."[1] Earlier, in 1837, Sarah Grimke, noted abolitionist and feminist, spoke with less restraint: "I ask no favor for my sex. . . . All I ask of our brethren is that they take their feet off our necks."[2] Both women were responding to a familiar argument—that women need privileges, not equality, because "[t]he physical handicap which nature places upon [them] cannot be removed."

Women's supposed inherent handicap becomes an increasingly artificial prop for their special protection in a society in which most jobs do not demand extraordinary physical strength. Even for jobs that require above average strength and endurance, classification by sex is a crude measure: It excludes women who could pass a test of actual capacity and fails to screen out men who could not.

Realizing the equality principle, however, will require a persistent effort, after artificial barriers are removed, to prevent perpetuation of the effects of past discrimination long into the future. For example, with respect to one branch of the military, Admiral Elmo Zumwalt commented:

> [Women] are able to do their work in any rating, and there is no question but what women will be able to serve on all ships effectively when the law in contravention thereof is struck down. . . .

... I see no limitations on the managerial or leadership capabilities of women and I see no reason, in principle, why some day a Chief of Naval Operations should not be a woman who has had the opportunity to ... work up through the necessary experiences.[3]

Up to now, most gainfully employed women have been denied opportunity to "work up through the necessary experiences." Hence the need for affirmative action, designed not to confer favors but to assure that women with capacity to do the job are set on a par with men of similar capacity who, through a discriminatory system, have been permitted to monopolize the calling.

Further, indeed above all else, the home-work gap must be confronted. In 1961 Eva Moberg, a young woman in Sweden, wrote an essay she called "The Conditional Emancipation of Woman."[4] In it she deplored the state of affairs existing in her country, as in this one, that women in the work force were nonetheless expected to maintain their traditional function inside the family. Why should the woman have two roles and the man only one was the question she posed. At first, her view shocked some and was ridiculed by many. Today the idea of bridging the home-work gap is less novel, although few practical steps have been taken in that direction.

I

As in the case of discrimination against racial and ethnic minorities, the ultimate goal with respect to sex-based discrimination should be a system of genuine neutrality. Movement in that direction, however, requires remedies necessary and proper to alter deeply entrenched discriminatory patterns. But changing those patterns entails recognition that generators of race and sex discrimination are often different. Neither ghettoized minorities nor women are well served by lumping their problems in the economic sector together for all purposes.

With respect to race the effects of officially sanctioned segregation are still very much with us. Doctrine directed to the continuing impact of race segregation is not necessarily applicable to gender discrimination.[5] The difference is perhaps best illustrated by reference to educational experience. Females have not been impeded to the extent ghettoized minorities have been by lingering effects of officially sanctioned segregation in education, housing, and community life. Females have been significantly disadvantaged by some aspects of educational programs, vocational and athletic training most conspiciously.[6] But on the whole, girls tend to do at least as well as boys in elementary and high school academic programs. For many females the record of achievement continues in higher education. For example, since 1971 women have outscored men on aptitude tests for the study of law.[7] In short, most nonminority females do not encounter a formidable risk of "death at an early age."[8]

The problem of growing up female is that from the nursery on a certain attitude is instilled insidiously. The attitude is described in a nutshell in graffitti etched on a library carrel in a New England women's college in the 1950s.[9] The epigram reads:

Study hard
Get good grades
Get your degree
Get married
Have three horrid kids
Die, and be buried.

From the first three lines the sex of the writer is impossible to determine. From the second three *her* sex is impossible to mistake. To cure the problem felt so acutely by the young woman who wrote those lines (and so many others like her) the overriding objective must be an end to role delineation by gender and, in its place, conduct at every school level, later in the job market, signalling that in all fields of endeavor females are welcomed as enthusiastically as males are.

To achieve that objective "affirmative action" is needed. The meaning of the umbrella term "affirmative action" bears clarification. Equal opportunity policy implies action of two kinds. The first is a stop order, in judicial decrees, an injunction terminating discriminatory practices responsible for systemic preferences to whites over nonwhites, male over females. The second, affirmative action, involves forward motion, positive measures to correct accumulated consequences of the pattern enjoined. Pursued with intelligence and good faith, affirmative action should ultimately yield neither a pattern of "reverse discrimination" nor abandonment of the merit principle. On the contrary, it should operate to assure more rational utilization of human resources.[10]

Affirmative action remedies routinely authorized in employment discrimination cases brought under Title VII of the 1964 Civil Rights Act[11] include: special efforts to seek out and recruit qualified members of groups once excluded or subjected to disadvantageous treatment; elimination of employment tests, standards and qualifications that are not reliable predictors of requisite performance; in-service training programs; back pay and "front pay" (compensation during training at the pay rate for the post to be achieved); and, in settings where other measures will not accomplish the necessary alteration, numerical remedies—goals and timetables or outright quotas for a transition period.

Numerical remedies present a problem of particular sensitivity. As a corrective for an employer's wrong-doing, for his past practice of acting on the basis of a racial or gender characteristic, by hiring only whites or males, or according them preferential treatment,[12] courts have approved initial, short-run numerical relief with virtual unanimity. However, interests other than those of the immediate parties are inevitably affected by hiring and promotion quotas. Absolute preferences have so far been rejected,[13] and courts have turned to alternate solutions where numerical relief would unduly trammel employment opportunities or interfere too harshly with promotion expectations of persons in the once preferred group.[14]

In some settings redressing gender discrimination can be accomplished effectively by altering recruitment patterns and eliminating institutional practices that limit or discourage female participation. This seems to be the case with respect to educational opportunity. Indeed, numerical approaches may operate to the disadvantage of females in academic programs. For example, a federal appellate court recently declared unconstitutional a San Francisco school district's policy, established for a special high school offering advanced, college-preparatory courses designed to produce an equal number of boys and girls.[15] To achieve this 50–50 ratio, it was necessary to set higher admission standards for girls than for boys. The entrance requirement for males was a 3.25 average on a 4-point scale; for females the requirement was a 3.50 average.

Non-numerical affirmative action seems the course appropriate to the challenge of female enrollment in law school for example. Women's intellectual credentials for the study of law are at least equal to their male counterparts'. In the past, however, many law school faculties have been, at best, passively receptive to women applicants.[16] The cure, as a women's law student organization at Berkeley has publicized, is clear posting of the welcome sign.[17]

Professional schools as eager to attract qualified women as they are to attract qualified men might be expected to introduce a number of changes in traditional ways of behavior. For example, in evaluating non-quantitative credentials, deferral of an education to raise a family or to finance the education of a spouse might be regarded with the same favor as accomplishments of college athletes or politicians. Transfer and degree granting policies bear revision to remove inappropriate impediments to completion of graduate education. Extended study programs might be provided for students unable to undertake full-time study because of special family obligations that cannnot be met by customary financial aid (notably, care of pre-school children).[18] Placement policy should reflect firm refusal to assist employers not yet willing to give equal opportunity to women.[19] Comic relief through stereotyped characterizations of women in textbooks and class presentations should be recognized as the elephantine humor it is.

In the labor market abandonment of standards and tests not reliably related to job performance will sometimes prove sufficient remedial action. For example, courts have invalidated arbitrary height/weight specifications that operated to screen out women and members of certain ethnic groups fully capable of quality performance on the job.[20] A dumbbell overhead weight-lifting test for slide projectionists was a recent *cause célèbre* in the New York courts.[21] The test ousted two women from jobs as audio-visual aid assistants at Hunter College. One had held the post for close to seven years when the test was administered; the other had been on the job for nearly two years. Both had eminently satisfactory performance ratings. The overhead lifting posture required by the test is peculiarly difficult for women; their center of gravity counsels a less spectacular, but far safer, method of carrying equipment.

Moreover, throughout history women have demonstrated their skill at carrying the weight involved (25 lbs.) safely and effectively. The dumbbell weight corresponds to the weight of an infant between the first and second year of life.

Catch-up training programs and abbreviated waiting periods before promotion are remedies particularly appropriate when artificial barriers have blocked the way to equal opportunity. Consider this not so hypothetical case in point.[22] Policewomen wish to take the exam for promotion to police sergeant. They are barred for lack of patrol duty experience. Why did they lack this experience? Because patrol jobs were closed to women. The affirmative action called for in this situation is to provide women, on an expedited basis, with the training needed (and up to now denied to them) to qualify for sergeants' jobs. During the catch-up program, they should be awarded "front pay," both as compensation for past denial of equal opportunity, and as an incentive to discourage foot-dragging by the employer.[23]

Finally, there are situations in which numerical relief is "the most feasible mechanism for defining with clarity the obligation to move employment practices in the direction of true neutrality."[24] *Leisner* v. *New York Telephone Co.*[25] is illustrative. The charge was gender discrimination in hiring and promotion of women in management jobs. The general personnel supervisor explained that after assessing objective factors, ultimate decision was based on a "total person concept." In practice, results were that men—white men—were hiring white men. At the hearing, the general personnel supervisor was asked how he knew experience as a military officer was more valuable for the company's operation than experience as a teacher. He replied, "I guess I'm paid to make this type of judgment."[26] No studies or evaluations had been attempted to validate his judgment on this point or any other component of the "total person" concept. The solution, eventually incorporated in a consent decree,[27] was not to order the company to replace subjective individual assessment with totally objective criteria, criteria perhaps impossible to formulate. Nor was it appointment of a court officer to look over the shoulders of persons responsible for hiring or promotion decisions, a course that would have interfered directly and substantially with business operations. Rather, goals and a timetable for increasing hiring and promotion of women were established so that the company, with minimal outside intrusion, would dismantle the discriminatory pattern and change the results which had unjustifiably occurred.[28]

In academia, too, goals and timetables seem an essential part of the initial program necessary to accomplish equal opportunity. Alan Pifer, President of the Carnegie Corporation, offered this appraisal:

> I regret that it has become necessary, because of intransigence, or at least a lack of perceptiveness, on the part of higher education, for government to take coercive action. . . . Measures [included in affirmative action requirements] seem to me to constitute an invasion of campus autonomy and an abridgment of academic freedom. On the other hand, government has a basic obligation to protect the rights of its citizens—yes, even the women—and without the threat of coercion it seems unlikely that higher education would have budged an inch on the issue. Certainly it had every chance to do so and failed.[29]

The Carnegie Commission on Higher Education, after a comprehensive study of the problem, concluded that fears of dilution of academic excellence were not supported by the evidence regarding women's potential:

> We do not share the views of some male academic critics of affirmative action for women whose writings imply that increasing the number of women on faculties will inevitably lower quality. Such views are inconsistent with the evidence we have presented relating to the relative ability of women holding doctor's degrees. We do believe, however, that some of this criticism has arisen because departments or schools have unwisely explained the rejection of particular white male candidates on the ground that their institution's policies force them to hire women or minority groups. We believe such explanations often provide a convenient way out of informing a particular candidate that he is not the most qualified applicant for a position. . . .
>
> Another extremely important point, which tends to be overlooked in much of the discussion of these issues, is that most women who are qualified for academic positions very much

want to be considered on their merits and do not want to
be given preference over a more highly qualified man.[30]

In sum, transition period affirmative action, tailored to the particular setting, far from compromising the equality principle, is
an essential part of a program designed to realize that principle.
The concern engendered by the concept may cover an underlying
fear. The matter was put this way by Susan Brownmiller in a
journal for business executives and graduate business students:

> A mediocre man . . . will suffer the pinch most sharply. No
> longer will he be assured a comfortable berth. . . . He stands
> to be displaced . . . by top-flight women on their way up
> and he will be under assault from equally mediocre women
> who are perhaps a shade more aggressive or sociable or better
> connected. Mediocre women have a right to equal treatment,
> too.[31]

I leave it to you to judge whether there is more than a kernel of
truth in that remark.

II

Customary responsibility for household management remains
the most stubborn obstacle to equal opportunity for women. Care
of young children, particularly, poses formidable psychological
and logistical barriers for women who pursue and seek advancement in gainful employment.[32] Solutions to the home-work problem are as easily stated as they are hard to realize: Man must join
woman at the center of family life, and government must step in
to assist both of them during the years when they have small
children.

Many men and women generally sympathetic to the elimination
of impediments to equal opportunity for women find the notion
of a central home and family role for men disquieting. The idea
evokes a feeling of strangeness and the resistance that often at-
tends the unfamiliar. Constitutionalizing the equality principle
through the equal rights amendment will not effect sudden alteration in long-standing habits of thought. However, it will fa-

cilitate development of new patterns by men and women who are not wedded to old ways.

In 1971 Elizabeth Duncan Koontz, then Director of the Department of Labor's Women's Bureau, called attention to the overbreadth characteristic of responses to "maternity" in the employment sector.[33] She called for sharp distinction between childbearing, something no man can accomplish, and child rearing, which can be the responsibility of a father as well as a mother, can be shared between parents, and can enlist the services of persons and institutions outside the home. Realizing the equality principle will require a concerted effort to distribute responsibility for the nation's future population more widely than we have done up to now.

Childbearing, and the normally brief period of physical disability associated with it, is, as one court has said, "ineluctably sex-linked,"[34] the result of a biological potential that, more than any other characteristic, defines a person as a member of the female sex. This biological function, originated by both a man and a woman, is one of the few matters characterized by the Supreme Court as a "fundamental right."[35] Ironically, for many women, the negative side of the right is better secured than its positive aspect. A labor analyst, referring to the treatment of pregnant women as workforce outcasts, warned:

> [F]ailure to face the issue of the rights of pregnant women
> has created a very real threat of economic blackmail.... [With
> access to abortion], it is not unreasonable to expect both
> public and private employers to resort to this kind of pressure.
> It will be especially effective where the woman's threatened
> income is essential to her family's financial security.[36]

In 1970 the presidentially appointed Citizens' Advisory Council on the Status of Women adopted the following Statement of Principles:

> Childbirth and complications of pregnancy are, *for all job-related purposes*, temporary disabilities and should be treated as such under any health insurance, temporary disability insurance, or sick leave plan of an employer [or] union.... Any policies or practices of an employer or union, written

or unwritten, applied to instances of temporary disability other than pregnancy should be applied to incapacity due to pregnancy or childbirth, including policies or practices relating to leave of absence, restoration or recall to duty, and seniority.

No additional or different benefits or restrictions should be applied to disability because of pregnancy or childbirth, and no pregnant woman employee should be in a better position in relation to job-related practices or benefits than an employee similarly situated suffering from other disability.[37]

In other words, no special pedestal or disadvantageous treatment for pregnancy, simply the same treatment that would be accorded an employee temporarily away from work for other nonoccupational disabilities, among them, a broken leg, a prostate operation, hair transplant, or cosmetic surgery. The Council's chairman explained that this position rests not on analogy to any male-associated disability, but on the attributes pregnancy shares with all physical conditions occasioning a period of temporary disability—(1) loss of income due to temporary inability to perform normal job duties and (2) medical expenses. Equal Employment Opportunity Commission Sex Discrimination Guidelines, issued pursuant to Title VII in 1972, similarly provide: "Disabilities caused or contributed to by pregnancy, miscarriage, abortion, childbirth, and recovery therefrom are, for all job-related purposes, temporary disabilities and should be treated as such under any health or temporary disability insurance or sick leave plan available in connection with employment."[39]

The Supreme Court, which has so far considered job-related treatment of pregnancy only under the Fourteenth Amendment's equal protection clause, not under Title VII, has championed a woman's right to work while pregnant,[40] but not her right to income maintenance when pregnancy in fact disables her.[41] In January 1974, in *Cleveland Board of Education* v. *La Fleur*,[42] the Court held unconstitutional public school board rules mandating maternity leave or termination of employment for a pregnant teacher, well in advance of term, and without regard to her individual fitness. But the Court avoided questions broader than the right to remain on the job while fit: Is disadvantageous treatment of pregnancy gender discrimination? Must disability due to pregnancy be blanketed with other disabilities for job-related purposes? These questions figured in *Geduldig* v. *Aiello*,[43] a case decided some five months after *La Fleur*. No clear answer was supplied to the first question. As to the second, equating disability due to pregnancy with other disabilities, the response was that the Fourteenth Amendment requires no such equation. The Court held in *Aiello* that California did not deny equal protection to pregnant women workers when it singled out for exclusion from its workers' disability insurance system normal pregnancy and delivery.

The *Aiello* problem remains live under Title VII of the 1964 Civil Rights Act and, if it is ratified, the Equal Rights Amendment. Under Title VII any employment practice that places women at a disadvantage in the labor market should attract close scrutiny, not the "deferential" review accorded under a constitutional standard adopted a century ago, when racial equality, but surely not eradication of gender-based discrimination, was made a national commitment.[44]

Under the Equal Rights Amendment, classifications based on physical characteristics unique to one sex would be an exception to the general rule that gender is an impermissible factor in determining the legal rights of people. Indeed, flat prohibition of such gender-linked classifications would lead to absurd results: Laws relating to the nursing of children or donations to sperm banks would be rendered invalid even though noninvidious, narrowly drawn, and serving a legitimate purpose. Presumably, however, classification based on a sex-unique characteristic would be subject to strict scrutiny to insure that the design of the basic principle— to establish full equality of the sexes—is not undermined.[45]

If we are genuinely committed to the eradication of gender-based discrimination, the problem of job and income security for childbearing women workers must be confronted and resolved head-on. Comparative side-glances may be useful in determining our ultimate direction. One model is an International Labor Organization Convention[46] calling for comprehensive income protection and medical benefits for pregnancy and childbirth, financed through compulsory social insurance, taxed to employers and/or employees based on the total number of women and men employed by the enterprise.[47]

With respect to child rearing, perceptible change toward a sex-neutral approach is occurring in employment contexts. Child care as mother's work is still the pattern in social welfare and family law. The priority that should be assigned to public support for child care outside the home remains at the debate stage.

Lawsuits to establish a father's right to child care leave have been initiated,[48] the Equal Employment Opportunity Commission has interpreted Title VII to support the fathers' claims,[49] and parental leaves which may be taken by mother or father are beginning to appear in collective bargaining contracts.[50]

In contrast, social security law provides a mother's benefit for the caretaker of the child of a deceased wage earner but no corresponding father's benefit.[51] Under the Aid to Families with Dependent Children (AFDC) program, assistance for intact families (families with two able-bodied parents) is available only if mother is child tender and father, the temporarily out-of-work breadwinner.[52] Should the family order its life differently, with father assuming management of the household and mother seeking employment, AFDC assistance will not be supplied.

Mother preference remains marked in custody decisions.[53] For example, a father's equal protection objection to a presumption that "the mother is best suited to care for young children" received this assessment in 1974 from the Utah Supreme Court: "The contention might have some merit to it in a proper case if the father was equally gifted in lactation as is the mother."[54] In this particular case, the parents had separated when their child was less than one and a half years old, and the father was given temporary custody due to psychological problems then troubling the mother. Her problems under control, the mother sought custody when the child was over three years old. At that stage mother's milk could not be expected to assist greatly in the child's development. Urging the United States Supreme Court not to review the case, the mother's attorney concluded his presentation on this ringing note: "This Court's God required duty is to strengthen the homes of America. To reduce the lofty role of motherhood . . . is more dangerous a doctrine than any yet devised by man."[55]

President Nixon too was concerned with the strength of American homes when he vetoed the first and only comprehensive child care bill to pass Congress.[56] He complained of "family weakening implications" and refused to commit "the vast moral authority of the National Government to the side of communal approaches to child rearing over against the family centered approach."[57] (More recently, President Ford indicated his ambivalence on the question. He called the "highly motivated, extremely well-disciplined" young people in China a challenge to the American educational system.[58] However, he expressed "serious reservations about the desirability of creating a program of Government-financed child care centers."[59]) President Nixon did consider a communal approach for some children; he approved "day care centers to provide for children of the poor so that their parents can leave the welfare rolls to go to the payrolls."[60]

Apart from the dubious policy of isolating children of the poor in centers where they will not encounter non-welfare children, revolving door, penny-wise-pound-foolish results are achieved by limiting government-aided facilities to the most sorely pressed families. As one mother explained it in August 1974 when she was notified that her child must be withdrawn from a municipal day care center because she and her husband had progressed past the earnings limitation: "Even though my husband and I both work, we just make it. We need the center. Without it, I'd probably have to go on welfare, which I don't want to do—it's crazy. And having to take my son out of here, where's he's been so happy, would really kill me."[61]

The cost of comprehensive care for young children is large.[62] How that cost is allocated reflects national values and priorities. Currently, in contrast to public education for school-age children,[63] the burden of care for the very young is imposed upon a relatively small portion of society. In many cases, for lack of a viable alternative, mother abandons education, training or gainful employment while father attempts to supplement family income alone. But despite the economy effected by "free" mother's labor, one-earner families with children enjoy a lower standard of living.[64] To attain a better living standard and avoid a drop-out period that may have devastating effects on a woman's lifelong earning and self-fulfillment potential, outside child care, however makeshift,[65] is the "solution" increasingly adopted. The unpleasant reality is that numbers of children currently have minimal care, while others receive needed attention at a disproportionate cost to the family in terms of the mother's qualifications for gainful employment and reduction of the family's living standard. In either case, the United States is providing an environment of questionable quality for a significant portion of its youth. The child rearing problem, in short, ultimately concerns all of society. We will continue to shortchange parents, particularly mothers, and children until child rearing burdens are distributed more evenly among parents, their employers and the tax-paying public.

III

The inadequate attention so far paid to pregnancy, childbearing and child rearing as they relate to equal opportunity for women reflects a larger ambivalence. Conditions of contemporary life demand recognition that distinct roles for men and women coerced or steered by law are antithetical to the American ideal of freedom of choice for the individual. But action based on that recognition is deterred by fear—fear of unsettling familiar and, for many men and women, comfortable patterns.[66]

The Supreme Court's most recent decisions in gender discrimination cases display this ambivalence. In 1973 the Court held, in *Frontiero* v. *Richardson*,[67] that married male and female members of the uniformed services are constitutionally entitled to the same fringe benefits. The Court rejected a law providing family housing allowances for male members only, a law based on the assumption that the serviceman's wife, not the servicewoman's husband, is appropriately typed "dependent." And recently in *Taylor* v. *Louisiana*,[68] the Court ruled that a criminal defendant, male or female, is entitled to a jury drawn from a cross-section of the community— a jury drawn from a roll that includes women to the same extent that it includes men.

On the other hand, in a 1974 decision, *Kahn* v. *Shevin*,[69] the Court reverted to an old theme to approve a legislature's benign paternalism in conferring a property tax exemption on the blind, the totally disabled, and widows.[70] In *Geduldig* v. *Aiello*,[71] another 1974 decision, similar deference was paid to a legislative judgment excluding from a workers' disability benefit program institutionalized drug addicts, alcoholics, sexual psychopaths, and women with uncomplicated pregnancies.[72] Plainly, the unifying factor is not whether women are aided or disadvantaged by the classification. Rather, in *Kahn* and *Aiello*, the Court affirmed governmental authority to establish rules based on generalized assumptions concerning needs, abilities and preferences of males and females, dominantly, the assumption that breadwinning is man's proper and preferred work, homemaking and child rearing the primary job of woman.[73] Thus in *Kahn*, all widows were presumed dependent, therefore entitled to a palliative,[74] while in *Aiello*, pregnant women were regarded as a special class, persons not entitled to claim full membership in the labor force.

The analogy of pregnancy to other temporary disabilities pressed in *Aiello* may have foundered for a reason not fully acknowledged in the Supreme Court's opinion: assessment of childbirth not as a short-term episode but as an integral part of a long-term process, a process commencing with pregnancy and ending years later when child rearing work is done.[75] Viewed in this way, pregnancy-related disability has no place in a workers' benefit program. For childbirth marks a new period in the woman's life cycle. She will (or ideally should) relinquish her secondary role as gainfully employed worker in favor of her primary role as mother-wife. And in that role, she should be supported by the family's man, not the state or an employer she is destined to leave. (Significantly, the named individual complainant in *Aiello* did not fit this description. Her attachment to the labor force was dictated by necessity.[76])

The breadwinning male/homemaking female division of functions deserves neither special favor nor condemnation by the law. It is a pattern individuals should be free to adopt or reject, without government coercion. The Supreme Court, in some of its recent decisions, showed signs of recognizing the pernicious character of gross gender classifications that ignore the substantial portion of the population unwilling or unable to conform to stereotype.[77] However, rationales were fitted into familiar and separate compartments.[78] Earlier precedent upholding sex averaging by law— legal lines based on characteristics deemed average for one sex or the other—remained largely undisturbed. Some of the recent expression suggests that the Court does not fully perceive, or is unwilling to confront the particular gender discrimination cases presented to it as part of a pervasive design of government-steered sex-role allocation. Reluctance to move forward to the extent motivated by an historical consideration—the absence of any intention by eighteenth and nineteenth century Constitution-makers to eradicate gender-based differentials—will terminate with adoption of the Equal Rights Amendment. That development should attract the full support of persons committed to individual freedom and equal justice under law.

NOTES AND REFERENCES

1. Burnita Shelton Matthews, "Women Should Have Equal Rights with Men, A Reply," 12 *American Bar Association Journal* 117, 120 (1926).

2. S. Grimke, Letters on the Equality of the Sexes and the Condition of Women; Addressed to Mary Parker, President of the Boston Female Anti-Slavery Society, x (1838).

3. Conversation with Senator Charles H. Percy, recorded June 28, 1974.

4. Cited in Palme, Address at the Women's National Democratic Club, Washington, D.C., June 8, 1970. Reprinted in Davidson, Ginsburg, and Kay, *Text, Cases and Materials on Sex-Based Discrimination*, pp. 938, 940 (1974).

5. Cf. Emerson, "In Support of the Equal Rights Amendment," 6 *Harvard Civil Rights–Civil Liberties Law Review* 225, 229–30 (1971).

6. See Davidson, Ginsburg, and Kay, *op. cit.*, pp. 841, 847–63, 868–69.

7. *Ibid.*, p. 883; Ruud, "That Burgeoning Law School Enrollment Is Portia," 60 *American Bar Association Journal* 182 (1974).

8. J. Kozol, *Death at an Early Age* (1967).

9. In W. Warren Wagar, *Building the City of Man*, p. 100 (1971).

10. See Cooper, "Equal Employment Law Today," 5 *Columbia Human Rights Law Review* 263, 278 (1973).

11. *Ibid.*, pp. 269–74.

12. Under Title VII, the effect of an employment practice, not the employer's intent, is the critical factor. Lack of a design to discrimination is not a defense. *Griggs* v. *Duke Power Co.*, 401 U.S. 424 (1970).

13. See *Carter* v. *Gallagher*, 452 F.2d 315 (8th Cir. 1972), cert. denied, 406 U.S. 950 (1973). But cf. *Morrow* v. *Crisler*, 491 F.2d 1053 (5th Cir. 1974) (where less drastic remedies fail, temporary freeze on white hiring may be directed).

14. See *Bridgeport Guardians, Inc.* v. *Bridgeport Civil Service Commission*, 482 F.2d 1333 (2d Cir. 1973).

15. *Berkelman* v. *San Francisco Unified School District*, 501 F.2d 1264 (9th Cir. 1974).

16. See Davidson, Ginsburg, and Kay, *op. cit.,* pp. 882–83.

17. One of the information and recruitment brochures prepared by the Boalt Hall Women's Association reads, "Wanted by the Law: Women."

18. See Davidson, Ginsburg, and Kay, pp. 884–85.

19. See *Kohn* v. *Royall, Koegel & Wells,* 59 E.R.D. 515 (S.D.N.Y. 1973); Baker, "The Impact of Title VII of the 1964 Civil Rights Act on Employment Discrimination Against Women Lawyers," 59 *American Bar Association Journal* 1029 (1973).

20. See *Meadows* v. *Ford Motor Co.,* 7 EPD 9103 (W.D. Ky. 1973); *Smith* v. *City of East Cleveland,* 363 F. Supp. 1131 (N.D. Ohio 1973).

21. *Sontag* v. *Bronstein,* 351 N.Y.S. 2d 389 (1973).

22. *Matter of Berni,* 40 A.D. 2d 701, 336 N.Y.S. 2d 620 (1972), aff'd, 32 N.Y. 2d 933, 347 N.Y.S. 2d 198, cert. denied, 414 U.S. 1045 (1973) (denying relief). But see *United States* v. *Libbey-Owen-Ford Co.,* 3 EPD 8052 (N.D. Ohio 1971); *Ostapowicz* v. *Johnson Bronze Co.,* 7 EPD 9280 (W.D. Pa. 1974) (ordering affirmative relief, including training programs for women).

23. See Cooper, p. 274.

24. *United States* v. *Lee Way Motor Freight,* 7 EPD 9066 (at 6500) (D. Okla. 1973); cf. *Legal Aid Society* v. *Brennan,* 8 EPD 9483 (N.D. Calif. 1974).

25. 358 F. Supp. 359 (S.D.N.Y. 1973). Accord, *United States* v. *Household Finance,* 4 EPD 7680 (N.D. Ill. 1972); *N.O.W.* v. *Bank of California,* 6 EPD 8867 (N.D. Calif. 1973) (numerical remedies for women in managerial posts).

26. 358 F. Supp. at 369.

27. 6 EPD 8871 (S.D.N.Y. 1973).

28. See Cooper, *op. cit.,* 270; cf. Davidson, Ginsburg, and Kay, *op. cit.,* pp. 778–81.

29. Speech before the Southern Association of Colleges and Schools, November 29, 1971.

30. Carnegie Commission on Higher Education, *Opportunities for Women in Higher Education: Their Current Participation, Prospects for the Future and Recommendations for Action* (1973), pp. 138–39.

31. MBA magazine (March 1971).

32. See Davidson, Ginsburg, and Kay, pp. 470–84.

33. Koontz, "Childbirth and Child Rearing Leave: Job-Related Benefits," 17 *New York Law Forum* 480 (1971).

34. *Gilbert* v. *General Electric Co.,* 375 F. Supp. 367 (E.D. Va. 1974); see *Wetzel* v. *Liberty Mutual Ins. Co.,* 372 F. Supp. 1146 (W.D. Pa. 1974).

35. See *Skinner* v. *Oklahoma,* 316 U.S. 535 (1942); *Roe* v. *Wade* 410 U.S. 113 (1973).

36. Petitioner for rehearing, *Schattman* v. *Texas Employment Commission,* 459 F. 2d 32 (5th Cir. 1972), cert. denied, 409 U.S. 1107, rehearing denied, 410 U.S. 959 (1973). See also, "Comment, Love's Labors Lost: New Conceptions of Maternity Leaves," 7 *Harvard Civil Rights—*

Civil Liberties Law Review 260 (1972); Cary, "Pregnancy Without Penalty," 1 *Civil Liberties Review* 31 (1974); Hayden, "Punishing Pregnancy" (ACLU Report, 1973).

37. Citizens' Advisory Council on the Status of Women, "Job-Related Maternity Benefits," CACSW Item No. 15–N (Nov., 1970).

38. Address of Jacqueline G. Gutwillig, delivered at the Conference of Interstate Associations of Commissions on the Status of Women, St. Louis, 1971, quoted in Koontz, p. 496 n. 88.

39. 29 C.F.R. §1604.10, 37 Fed. Reg. 6837 (1972).

40. *Cleveland Board of Education* v. *La Fleur*, 414 U.S. 632 (1973).

41. *Geduldig* v. *Aiello*, 417 U.S. 484 (1974).

42. *Supra* note 40.

43. *Supra* note 41.

44. Discriminatory impact upon a protected group suffices to render an employment practice vulnerable under Title VII, and to cast a burden of justification on the employer. See *Griggs* v. *Duke Power Co.*, 401 U.S. 424 (1971); Cooper, *op. cit.*, 263. Unlike the Fourteenth Amendment, Title VII does not carry a substantially weaker test for sex-based discrimination than for racial discrimination. See, e.g., *Rosenfeld* v. *Southern Pac. Co.*, 444 F.2d 1219 (9th Cir. 1971); *Sprogis* v. *United Airlines, Inc.*, 444 F.2d 1194 (1971).

45. Cf. Brown, Emerson, Falk, and Freedman, "The Equal Rights Amendment: A Constitutional Basis for Equal Rights for Women," 80 *Yale Law Journal* 871, 894 (1971); Note, 72 *Michigan Law Review* 800, 813 n. 90 (1974).

46. ILO Maternity Protection Convention of 1952 (rev., no. 103).

47. *Ibid.*, art. 4 para. 7.

48. *Danielson* v. *Board of Higher Education*, 358 F. Supp. 22 (S.D.N.Y. 1972); *Ackerman* v. *Board of Education*, 372 F. Supp. 274 (S.D.N.Y. 1974).

49. The determination was made on December 12, 1972 in response to the Title VII charge filed in *Ackerman* v. *Board of Education, supra* note 48.

50. See, e.g., Kitch, "AFT Negotiates Change for College Women," AFT item no. 619 (1974).

51. 402 U.S.C. §402 (g). This differential was declared unconstitutional in *Weinberger* v. *Wiesenfeld*, 420 U.S. 636 (1975).

52. 42 U.S.C. §607; see Griffiths, "Sex Discrimination in Income Security Programs," 49 *Notre Dame Lawyer* 534, 541–43 (1974).

53. See Davidson, Ginsburg, and Kay, pp. 271–74.

54. *Arends* v. *Arends*, 517 P.2d 1019 (1974), cert. denied, 43 U.S.L.W. 3213 (1974).

55. Answer to the Petition for a Writ of Certiorari, *Arends* v. *Arends*, *op. cit.*

56. Economic Opportunity Amendments of 1971 (S. 2007).

57. Weekly Compilation of Presidential Documents (December 9, 1971), p. 1635.

58. *New York Times*, August 31, 1974, p. 1. See R. Sidel, *Women and Child Care in China* (1972).

59. *New York Times*, September 7, 1974, p. 28.

60. *Supra* note 57.

61. *New York Times*, August 31, 1974, p. 23.

62. 1970 estimates placed the cost at $2000–$3000 per child. See Davidson, Ginsburg, and Kay, p. 477.

63. Expansion of publicly supported care for school age children has also been proposed as an appropriate response to the increasing two-earner family pattern. For example, an expert commission in Sweden, headed by the director general of the National Board of Education, has recommended that public schools serve, after instructional hours, as recreational and care centers for children whose parents are at work. The proposal was prompted by the fact that seventy per cent of all mothers with children in the seven-to-ten age group work at jobs outside the home. See Swedish Information Service Release No. 1022 (August 1974).

64. See 1969 *Handbook on Women Workers*, Women's Bureau Bulletin no. 294, U.S. Department of Labor, p. 130.

65. See Low and Spindler, *Child Care Arrangements of Working Mothers in the United States* (Children's Bureau Pub. No. 461–1968, rptd. 1969); M. D. Keyserling, *Windows on Day Care* (1972).

66. See generally E. Janeway, *Man's World, Woman's Place* (1971).

67. 411 U.S. 677 (1973).

68. 43 U.S.L.W. 4167 (January 21, 1975).

69. 416 U.S. 351 (1974); cf. *Schlesinger* v. *Ballard*, 43 U.S.L.W. 4158 (January 15, 1975).

70. See Johnston, "Sex Discrimination and the Supreme Court, 1971–74," 49 *New York University Law Review* 617 (1974).

71. *Supra* note 41.

72. A state court decision had interpreted the statutory pregnancy bar to encompass only normal delivery and recuperation, not disability resulting from medical complications arising during pregnancy. See 417 U.S. at 484.

73. See Johnston, pp. 661–688.

74. In addition to the differential treatment accorded widowed men and women, the Florida statute in Kahn exhibited a further questionable feature. If the purpose was "to reduce the disparity between the economic capabilities of a man and a woman," why was the exemption withheld from the female head of household who never married, or whose marriage terminated by divorce?

75. See Johnston, p. 654.

76. "Except for her husband's educational expenses, her income was the sole support for herself, her husband, and their baby." 359 F. Supp. 792 (1973).

77. See especially *Frontiero* v. *Richardson*, 411 U.S. 677 (1973).

78. See Johnston.

Preferential Treatment: Some Reflections

DEAN RUSK

MY REMARKS will be kaleidoscopic, impressionistic, informal. I do not pretend to be an expert on the subject under discussion, but in order that you might ascertain some of my biases along the way, I might confess some of the peepholes through which I've had a chance to look at this problem over the years. At the end of World War II, I served for a time as Special Assistant to Secretary of War Robert Patterson in the Pentagon, and one of my assignments was to work on the problem of desegregation of the Army. There were many problems and it was rough going, but I think it is interesting to look back to the probability that the Armed Forces were among the first major segments of our society that moved seriously on the problem of integration. Also, I served on the General Education Board in New York, alongside of my work at the Rockefeller Foundation. The General Education Board, which had been established to contribute to education in the United States, had a very strong tilt toward upgrading the education of blacks in the South; and a very heavy portion of its funds over the years, until it spent itself out of existence during the Fifties, went to black education.

Reverse discrimination—illegal, contrary to public policy? Probably not. It was my privilege to participate in the political process through which the various civil rights acts of the 1960s came into being, and I shared some of the negotiations which led to the battery of adjustment and compromise which evolved in that era. Those processes made it possible for the Civil Rights Acts to come into being even with their weaknesses and their unfinished business. I was an equal opportunity employer when I was in charge of the Department of State and saw some of the exhilaration (but also some of the complications and difficulties) which come out of a serious attempt to achieve equal opportunity.

You would not now believe the situation with respect to civil rights in our national capital in 1961. A black ambassador could drive his family down to a beach in Maryland for a weekend and be turned away. An ambassador to the United Nations, of dark color, coming in from a country south of here, landed in the Miami Airport and, while the other passengers were taken into the airport dining room to have lunch, he was put on a folding canvas stool in a corner of a hangar and brought a sandwich in wax paper. It was very difficult for blacks to know where they could have a meal in our national capital. Wives of black ambassadors would ask wives of Foreign Service officers of the Department of State to accompany them to the supermarket because they were afraid of incidents. Housing, apartments, office space for embassies—all were extraordinarily difficult to come by. The Department of State learned very quickly that you cannot deal with these civil rights issues on the basis of diplomatic passports. You can only deal with them if the situation is right in the entire community; so the Department went to work very hard on these issues during that period. Now I am involved with the problems of affirmative action at the University of Georgia, more particularly in the Law School.

I am very wary of the phrase "compensatory justice." For weeks I have been circling it like an old hound dog circling a skunk. I'm not quite sure who pays what compensation to whom for what, and I suspect that there are some ideas that have been tossed around that get in the way. For example, I find it very difficult to deal with the issues of compensatory justice on the basis of personal guilt. I am told that an ancestor of mine was a foreman on John Calhoun's plantation over in South Carolina. Am I responsible for some of the things he probably did while he was serving in that capacity? What is the nature and the range of my personal responsibility for what is going on in the schools of South Boston? I'm very wary of group guilt. As a matter of principle, and as a matter of practice, I think there is rather considerable danger in approaching these problems from that direction because words like "guilt" and "reparations" will raise feelings of anger, resistance, and violence which will stand in the way of the equitable solutions which we all ought to be striving for with all of our might. I'm also a little wary about relying too much upon class designation. There is an infinite variety among real live human beings. Each is unique, and I'm not sure that one says much when one says male, white, woman, black, Chicano, Asian, Indian. It may be that the relevance of those class designations needs to be looked at. We need to be a little more sophisticated in knowing just what it is we're talking about. There is such a thing, I suspect, as abuse by generalization.

I am very pleased that some thinkers do not approach the problem of compensatory justice from the point of view solely of the law, and I would hope that those who discuss the issues would not consider themselves confined by the verbal logic which can be built upon the words of the Fourteenth Amendment as the point of departure for our discourse. The Fourteenth Amendment is a hundred years old. Laws come to reflect the desires of our people in a democratic society. The criminal laws of England were radically reformed when juries simply quit bringing in verdicts of "guilty" in large numbers of criminal charges where the penalty was capital punishment, even as late as the beginning of the nineteenth century. I would hope that the Fourteenth Amendment would not be taken as a barrier because there can be another amendment and the judges just might someday remind themselves of words which the Supreme Court has used: The Constitution is a living instrument, reflecting the total context of the society in which we live.

A lot of this problem rests at what might be called the sub-legal level. There are ways of dealing with it which cannot be really dealt with by the law, both negatively and positively. For example, forty years ago the Foreign Service of the United States was a near monopoly of the Ivy League of the northeastern seaboard. Today some 16,000 young people take the Foreign Service examination each year. Of those, some 3,000 will pass. It's a difficult exam because one of its functions is to reduce 16,000 to 3,000. Those that pass the written examination then go into an oral interview with a board of 3 or 4 officers of the Department of State in an interview that might last an hour or two. Out of that oral discussion has come a steady expansion of the Foreign Service, with some 700 universities and colleges now represented in the Foreign Service and a steady increase in the numbers of blacks and women admitted to the service. I suggest that this procedure cannot be touched effectively by the law because the elements of discretion that are present in the oral interviews are very difficult to challenge. I suspect in one sense that the Law School of the University of Washington was perhaps too formal, maybe too honest, maybe too candid with regard to the matters in the DeFunis case; and I compliment them for it. But there would have been ways in which they could have handled affirmative action without embarrassing the judges by raising issues which the judges would find it very difficult to deal with, sub-legal or non-legal in character.

My own approach to affirmative action is based upon two elementary notions. One is, what does justice require in our constitutional system here and now? Without being chauvinistic, I happen to believe that when one says, "I am an American citizen," that that is a most profound statement. Because it means that we are a part of a society, almost unique in the world, where there is a constitutional system enforced by the courts, establishing certain protections for individual liberty which not all the king's horses and all the king's men, not a Parliament, nor the Congress, can intrude upon, where at the end of the day there is a sovereign citizen entitled to all of the promises made in those glorious first 200 words of the Declaration of Independence and the pledges made in our Constitution.

What is justice? Well, it's very hard to know in complete detail just what justice means. There is a never ceasing search for it and I am glad that the philosophers are continuing that search and are not manacled by the definitions of present law. We are, as I write, in our Bicentennial year. I hope very much that we will not use the occasion simply for the incantations of all the old words, with bands playing and flags flying. I like bands and I revere the flag, but I hope that we would subject those elementary notions of our political system to the most searching examination to try to understand their relevance and meaning in the latter part of the twentieth century. Surely it means something different today to say that all men are created equal—in the first place it means all men and women, doesn't it?—than it did when Thomas Jefferson penned those words in 1776. We have an opportunity here to restoke our furnaces, to get a fresh start, to do the kind of self-examination which does not mean self-flagellation, and to provide an occasion for a rededication to the simple ideas on which our nation was embarked.

I happen to believe, for example, that the simple notion that governments derive their just powers from the consent of the governed was a rather elegant summary of a great deal of discussion for more than 2,000 years about the political consequences of the nature of man. I know that the philosophers can chew it up, and quarrel about it, examine it, and see what it means. But it just happens that it is the most powerful, revolutionary and explosive political idea in the world today. What does it mean in detail when we talk about the status of our women, the opportunities for our minority groups? We require not a one time consent back in 1776 but the continuing consent that is essential to a democratic society. The continuing consent has to be won by those who exercise public power every day, every week, every month, all over again. What does that mean in terms of binding our citizens and those who govern into a common effort to stabilize and nourish the notions of liberty?

My second approach to affirmative action comes from the needs of the next 3 or 4 decades. When one looks ahead, one sees that the human race now has on its plate certain problems which are different *in kind* from any the human race has ever faced before. Some of these will require a relatively definitive solution by around the turn of the century if *homo sapiens* is going to make it: the unfinished business of nuclear weapons and the possibilities of nuclear war; what we do about the human environment, the population explosion, relations among racial, cultural, religious, other groups, right around the world; how we adjust ourselves to the prospect that some of the non-renewable resources are going to disappear. It is a long list that leaves me with the feeling that we are going to need all the talents, all the imagination, that we can possibly find. If there was ever a time when we need to make a lunge in the search for talent, it is right now—schools, colleges, professional schools, everywhere else.

As a boy who came out of modest circumstances in Georgia, I have a certain bias. When I was going through the public schools of Atlanta, my family lived along the old Central of Georgia Railroad on Whitehall Street. The railroad track was a dividing line between the poor white section and the poor black section in that part of the city. What concerns me is that just across the track, there were talents that were never used, talents that were never drawn upon. Talent can come from unpredictable, improbable places. The search for talent drives us to open the doors to women, to minority groups, or whatever source, because we cannot afford to be without it.

I must confess that I feel that affirmative action is most appropriate at the door marked "entrance." I have some concern about how far we can go at the door marked "exit" in our educational system. I don't believe that I would want a surgeon to take out my kidney with boxing gloves because my surgeon was a woman or a Chicano. Now, there are obvious replies, "But there are incompetent white surgeons." Of course, but our continued search must be to find the talents that can do the job where increasing capability is required. Does a law school have a right to victimize future clients by turning out incompetent lawyers, white or black, of whatever sex? That bothers me considerably. But I am not bothered with the idea of trying to find out where the talent is. But, unfortunately, through sheer mass in our educational system, we have made it very difficult. Justice Douglas, in his dissenting opinion in the *DeFunis* case, said some things about the Law School Admissions Tests and grade point averages that struck quite a responsive chord in me. We found in making some serious studies of the written examinations for the Foreign Service that there was a considerable premium earned by those who had had a lot of experience in their own colleges in taking that type of examination, that the technique of taking exams counted a good deal over against what might be called the basic talents and capabilities of the persons involved. But when you talk about, say, 2,000 applications to a law school, it isn't easy to have a serious, personal, individual, consideration of each case, simply from an administrative point of view. If we try to find ways to take into account factors other than numbers in our search for the kinds of talents we need from all elements in our population, and in the short run can do so without bringing the courts down upon us, I for one would be in favor of it.

In conclusion, let me remind you of an hour's television program which consisted of a conversation with Justice Hugo Black. Some of you may have seen that extraordinary hour which he spent in reflecting upon his experience on the Supreme Court. These are not his exact words, but I remember that when the question of the

Brown case came up, he said, in effect, "I didn't have to have distinguished lawyers tell me that separate was not equal. I knew it. They didn't have to argue that with me." I put it to you, without pointing the finger of guilt. We know that we have not opened wide the doors of opportunity to women, racial, religious, ethnic groups, in our society. We've done a lot of things, but there is a lot of unfinished business, and my guess is that if we look ahead, we'd better get at that unfinished business, both at the level of law and at the level of societal actions which cannot really be penetrated by the law.

Discrimination Against Blacks in Education: An Historical Perspective

PRINCE E. WILSON

INTRODUCTION

THE PURPOSE of this paper is to analyze the major trends in the history of the United States relating to both the provision and the denial of education to black Americans. Although this conference is concerned with what is called "compensatory justice," this study reveals the basis on which some Americans claim the need for compensation in justice for blacks. It is also designed to discover, if possible, the major influences which determined in the past whether Americans as a group would be permissive or restrictive regarding the education of blacks. A major presumption in this paper is that problems regarding "compensatory justice" or "reverse discrimination" or "quotas in education" or whatever other slogans are used assume a more significant and clearly understood role when viewed in the light of historical perspective. The great French observer of the American scene in the 19th century, de Tocqueville, prophetically described the tenacity of the problem when he wrote: "If ever America undergoes great revolutions, they will be brought about by the presence of the black race on the soil of the United States; that is to say, they will owe their origin, not to the equality but to *inequality of condition*."[1] [Italics mine.] Likewise the great black intellectual, William E. B. DuBois, observed in 1907 that the color problem is the major problem of the 20th century.

This historical overview describes three cycles of alternating, contracting, and expanding opportunities for black Americans in education. The first cycle includes the Colonial and American Revolutionary Periods; the second embraces the so-called National and Civil War–Reconstruction Periods; and the third what I refer to as Pre– and Post–World War II Periods. Let us repeat that these three cycles embraced alternating periods of positive, inclusive, expanding opportunities tied with yet another period of negative, exclusive, highly discriminatory and contracting educational opportunities. It is my view that each of these three cycles or six periods carries meaningful information for our understanding of the dilemma we face today in meshing our highest moral ideals with our racism and competing survival techniques.

THE FIRST CYCLE: COLONIAL AMERICA AND REVOLUTIONARY AMERICA: 1619–1770 AND 1770–1800

Colonial America bequeathed 150 years of steadily contracting, discriminatory, or negative, history in black education. English America in the 17th century dedicated its energies to removing as much African culture as possible from the blacks and then, after considerable debate, decided to provide only the most limited educational resources for them. Totally rejecting the Spanish and French examples of legally requiring the slave owners to teach the blacks to read and write, the English engaged in polemics with each other over whether slaveowners would be forced to free the slaves if they taught them to read and write. The dilemma came from the belief that the only real reason for learning to read was to read the Holy Bible and the catechisms for the purpose of becoming a Christian. And, after all, it was for the purpose of spreading God's Kingdom that many of the colonies were founded. It was unthinkable to many for one Christian to hold another Christian in bondage.

In 1665 the Bishop of London cleared the path in a sermon indicating that the Christianizing of blacks did not force their freedom as a result. Several other Bishops of the Church of England followed suit and within 19 years (1695) the first school for blacks in British Colonial America was established by the Reverend Samuel Thomas in Goose Creek Parish, South Carolina. On leaving the colony he reported that he had taught many of them to "read the Bible distinctly, and great numbers of them were learning when I left the province."[2] It may be suggested, therefore, that in a sense the religious promises of heaven were denied to blacks until the rewards of the world were guaranteed for whites.

Yet it is also to be observed that, once the obstacle was removed, many whites sought to offer the rudiments of education to blacks. The famous British missionary group, the Society for the Propagation of the Gospel, established several schools for Negroes; taught them to read the Scriptures, poems, and other useful books, while grounding them in the catechism of the Anglican Church. The Society of Friends, or Quakers, took a very active role and by so doing ran counter to British imposed customs. The Governor of North Carolina in the 1670s prohibited Quakers from teaching blacks unless they had secured a license from the Bishop of London—an Anglican! In anger, the Quakers queried: "Who made you ministers of the Gospel to white people only, and not to the tawny [Indians] and blacks also?"[3] When the famous 18th century Methodist evangelist, the Reverend George Whitefield, joined contemporary Georgians in their efforts to have slavery legalized in the colony, he urged the slave owners to educate the young slaves and give the old ones religious instruction. Perhaps this is one reason that so many blacks joined the Methodist Church in Georgia.

Although the religious-minded sought to teach blacks, there were many who vehemently opposed the effort. Among the most compelling reasons were: (1) the idea that literacy would make it easy for blacks to plan violence and revolution as well as their escape; (2) the fact that Negroes were conceived to be such stubborn creatures that one could not teach them; (3) the belief that Negroes were so far gone in wickedness and evil ways, education would not help them; and (4) the feeling that Negroes did not have time enough away from work to make it worthwhile to try to teach them.

Despite the efforts of certain religious groups, therefore, and even when comparing the very low level of literacy among whites of the period, the Colonial Period was one of very limited education for blacks accompanied with strong practical objections growing out of the needs of whites without regard for the needs of blacks.

The second phase of the first cycle, the American Revolutionary Period, saw about 25 years of slowly expanding opportunities for the education of blacks. Caught up in their own slogans and in the rhetoric of the period, the Founding Fathers supported the education, even the freedom, of the black man. Benjamin Franklin proclaimed that they should be educated not only to make them into Christians or increase their economic efficiency, but also "because they are men." As president of the Philadelphia Abolitionist Society he established a school for blacks which lasted almost a century. Thomas Jefferson spoke of the "natural right" which slaves had to an education although he vacillated on the question of the potential intellectual equality of blacks with whites.

Abolitionist societies took the most dramatic steps and were joined by religious groups. Abolitionist committees of education were established in several colonies and emphasized the development of schools for blacks. Presbyterians and Methodists defended their education. John Wesley proclaimed: "Allowing them to be as stupid as you say, to whom is that stupidity owing? Without doubt it lies altogether at the door of the inhuman masters who give them no opportunity for improving their understanding and indeed leave them no motive either from hope or fear to attempt any such thing [as learning]."[4]

Gripped in the rhetoric of the day, many took what might be today called "affirmative action" regarding black education. Colonial rules against teaching slaves were not enforced; the New York African Free School was established in 1787 and taught as many as 500 black pupils in any given year. The French general Lafayette spoke of that school as having "the best disciplined and most interesting school of children" he had ever seen. Poor whites and blacks in New Jersey and Louisiana saw improved educational efforts. The City of Philadelphia had seven schools for black children in 1797. Quakers in Western North Carolina, where I was reared, reported that most of the Negro children there had had some schooling.

What were the visible results of this expansion? The famous black historian, Carter G. Woodson, estimated that about 20% of the black adults in that period could read. Famous black preachers abounded—Richard Allen established the AME church in Philadelphia; George Liele established the first black Baptist church in Savannah, Georgia. Josiah Bishop was a black pastor of a white Baptist church in Portsmouth, Virginia. A Philadelphia-born black man, James Durham, spoke English, French, and Spanish fluently, and he practiced medicine in New Orleans with his earned M.D. degree. Benjamin Banneker published an almanac, invented a clock, read astronomy, learned surveying, became a scientist, conversed with Jefferson, and helped to plan the city of Washington, D.C. Positive results were therefore clearly visible in this period.[5]

One must hasten to add, however, that there were forces still opposed to the education of blacks. In South Carolina, the state law which prohibited the education of slaves in 1740 was extended to include all blacks, free or slave, in 1800. Boston, Massachusetts, in the 1790s wrestled with the problem of segregated education as they did in 1975—175 years later. One major difference in the 1790s was that blacks propagated the idea of separate schools, hoping to prepare themselves to enter the mainstream of American life after such preparation. They were not advocating segregation as a way of life, only as a temporary tactic.

One should observe at the close of the first cycle that the overall results of its 180 odd years were the complete removal of traces of African culture while haltingly and slowly, and against continuing opposition, providing rudiments of an education for about 20% of the American black population. Religion, variously interpreted, and the rhetoric of the American Revolution were the main supporters of 17th and 18th century "affirmative action" efforts while self-interest (narrowly interpreted), basic prejudice, and racial fears remained the major barriers.

THE SECOND CYCLE: THE NATIONAL AND CIVIL WAR–RECONSTRUCTION PERIODS: 1800–1875

Compared to the other two cycles, the second cycle witnessed intense, passionate, violent, and inflammatory feelings and actions. Education of blacks in America suffered considerable reduction and restraint in the first part of the cycle and equally expansive and optimistic growth in the second part of the cycle.

In the first part, the National Period (1800–1860), white Americans found themselves facing two major developments related to the issue of educating blacks. The first movement was the establishment of what we might call an "agribusiness" base in the "Cotton Kingdom" of the South which demanded millions of slaves working millions of acres of cotton-producing land from Virginia to Texas. The industrial revolution newly developing in England produced textile factories which consumed American cotton as fast as blacks could produce it. The second movement was a growing tendency of slaves to organize escape mechanisms, re-volts, and rebellions. The two movements together combined to practically eliminate any vestige of education for blacks, especially in the South.

Toussaint L'Ouverture's successful black revolt against the hith-erto undefeatable armies of Napoleon Bonaparte in Haiti ap-parently inspired American slaves to action on their dreams for freedom. Gabriel Prosser revolted in Richmond in 1800. Judge Tucker wrote: "Every year adds to the number of those who can read and write; and the increase in knowledge is the principal agent in evolving the spirit we have to fear."[6] Camden, South Carolina blacks revolted in 1816. Denmark Vesey staged a formi-dable revolt in 1822. He had learned to read and had read the accounts of L'Ouverture's revolt. Nat Turner's famous revolt in 1831 was but one of many efforts of black slaves to gain freedom. Like Nat Turner, most of them could read.

Black education thus became the whipping boy of the white "backlash." Virginia prohibited free Negroes from teaching slaves to read and write in 1819; Mississippi in 1823 made it unlawful for five Negroes to meet for educational purposes. Louisiana in 1830 provided life imprisonment for those who published or wrote for the purpose of stirring slave discontent. In 1831 Georgia law prohibited the teaching of Negroes to read or write under penalty of a $500 fine or jail. In 1835 North Carolina even prohibited in-struction of Negroes to the fourth generation removed! Prudence Crandall, the white teacher in Connecticut, found her school for black pupils burned and herself in jail. Cincinnati whites turned cannon on black neighborhoods in 1829 and bombarded the Negroes out of the city. The Episcopal Church South stopped all education of blacks. Methodists and Baptists followed suit. Only Quakers, Catholics, and a few mountaineers in Kentucky, North

Carolina, and Tennessee continued the effort—most often in a clandestine manner.

What results came from this negative action, this systematic suppression of black education? The best estimates indicate that black literacy dropped from about 25% in the late 1820s to about 2% in 1860! Black churchgoers could no longer read even the hymn books and the practice of "lining out" the hymns became almost universal. Sabbath schools which had formerly taught blacks were monitored by "discreet whites" to prevent any more such instruction. One historian described the results in terms of the effects on Negro personality. Deprived of real Christianity, he wrote, they developed habits of stealing, lying, insensibility, and lasciviousness. They became brutish to both animals and people. They saw and adopted the adultery practiced by the white owners.[7]

One must hasten to add that not *all* education disappeared among blacks, although most suffered a mortal blow. Some white parents of mixed parentage blacks taught them despite the law, as did some white friends. One black president of Wilberforce University in Ohio went to school in Bibb County, Georgia, at the age of six and was taught by an old South Carolina white man at the age of 10. The famous black bishop Henry McNeal Turner, whose portrait today hangs in the Georgia capitol building, was taught by an old white woman and a young white boy before his mother hired a white lady to teach him at age 13 on Sundays. The famous black abolitionist Frederick Douglass got his first instruction from his white mistress. When the Union army marched through Georgia in the 1860s, they found a black woman named Deveaux who had operated a school for 30 years in Savannah without the knowledge of whites.

Notwithstanding these developments, it must be concluded that the so-called National Period in American history witnessed an intense deprivation of black Americans in the field of education. It may be stated that this deprivation was of an extremely crippling nature.

The ten to fifteen years constituting the Civil War–Reconstruction Period (1860–1876) was indeed one of intense hatred, hostility, and bloodshed; yet it was accompanied by positive efforts in the education of black Americans. Its duration was too short and its accomplishments too limited to erase the damage done during the National Period.

During and following the Civil War, white and black, military and politician, carpetbagger and scalawag periodically joined hands to create the first public school system supported by state taxes in the history of the South. The Union Army established the first system of free public schools for Negro children supported by taxes levied on the property of citizens. The Congress of the United States established the famous Freedman's Bureau which joined hands with the Congregationalist American Missionary Association to establish thousands of schools and "colleges" for blacks in the South. In five years the Bureau established 4,239 separate schools, hired 9,307 teachers, and provided instruction for 247,333 pupils at a cost of $3.5 million. The best known black institutions of higher learning were formed during this period. Atlanta University, Fisk University, Howard University, Morehouse College, etc., developed from crude beginnings in such out of the way places as abandoned freight cars. For the first and only time in our history there was a black State Superintendent of Education—indeed five states had one. Again, black Americans had their hopes raised that white America would really admit them to the mainstream.[8]

THE THIRD CYCLE: PRE– AND POST– WORLD WAR II ERAS: 1880–1935 AND 1945–1975

Similar to the first two cycles, our third and final cycle featured both educational deprivation and educational promise or affirmation. Compromise between the Bourbons and northern industrialists procured vocational education on a very low level for both whites and blacks in the South. But even that education for blacks was broken on the rock of racial supremacy deliberately fomented by those who would prevent a political coalition between the two groups. Let us examine the dynamics of the Pre–World War Period of about 55 years which followed the departure of the Union troops and the establishment of Bourbon rule in the South.

Affirmative type action receded in the face of the violent negative reaction during and following the withdrawal of the Union troops from the South. The Ku Klux Klan, born in Tennessee, spread its pillaging and burning to Negro schools and homes throughout the South. Two bills in Congress designed to provide federal aid to black education were broken on the rock of prejudice against racial mixing during the 1870s. In New Orleans the son of the black Lieutenant-Governor, P. B. S. Pinchback, was driven out of the high school by white students who insisted that, "They were good enough Niggers. But still they were Niggers." Some whites offered equal public education to blacks if the latter would abandon the struggle for racially mixed schools. Blacks in Bamberg, South Carolina, agreed in 1875 and found that by 1932 the per capita expenditure was $178 per white child and only $8 per black child.

When peace came in the form of rule by the old Southern political leaders who cooperated with dominant northern industry, blacks continued on the toboggan downwards in the area of education as in other areas. Their leaders, called Bourbons, and the poor whites agreed to systematic denial of money in black education and diverted it to whites. A few statistics will illustrate the fact. From 1880 to 1895 white school enrollments doubled while Negro enrollments grew one-half as fast. In 1890 expenditures for white children exceeded those for black children by 22.4%, and by 1911, by 459%! Horace Mann Bond, the father of Georgia State Senator Julian Bond, found that by 1930 black children were getting about one-third of the expenditures that were received by white children. In Alabama, 36%; Arkansas, 40%; Florida, 31%; Georgia, 28%; Mississippi, 21%; South Carolina, 22%; North Carolina, 48%.[9]

Student-teacher ratios for black schools were staggering. In 1912–13, it was 1 to 67. During 1921–22, it was 1 to 50. The national average in 1924–25 was 1 to 31.9. Black teachers were paid about 60% of the salaries paid white teachers. The average daily attendance for black pupils, who were forcibly taken out to pick the cotton fields, was about four-fifths of that of the white students. By almost any index the education of black Americans was again decimated and almost eliminated.

White racists and pseudo-scientists now found that they could prove the inherent ineducability and intellectual inferiority of the black American. Against such a backdrop of extreme educational deprivation many studies were released. Alice Strong measured black and white children in South Carolina in 1913 and concluded that blacks were 20% below whites. William H. Pyle in 1915 administered his "intelligence tests" and again proved Negro children to be inferior to whites. The famous "Alpha" tests used with World War I soldiers concluded that the average mental age of the white recruit was 13 years and that of the black was only 10. While the purpose of this paper is not to examine the validity of intelligence tests, it seems evident that the systematic and extended, even violent, exclusion of black children from equitable access to the resources of American education must necessarily result in some major differences in their educational achievement levels. Nevertheless, whites often concluded that blacks are inherently and biologically inferior to whites. This kind of argument extends to the Riesmans and Jenckses and Shockleys of today. Perhaps if they really knew more about the history of blacks in America they might revise their conclusions—an important role for Black Studies in the curricula of our institutions.

With regard to this Pre–World War II Period, it is quite obvious that these fifty-five years of educational deprivation, heaped upon the 180 during the Colonial Period and the 60 during the National Period, make a total of about 275 years of systematic, negative, deprivation of education for blacks, compared to about 90-odd years of either the absence of negative deprivation or some significant and recognizable gains. These are not odds which modern chance takers would consider good.

Yet, despite these odds, somehow in their subconscious, American blacks moved into the period of World War II and afterwards with increasing vigor and even increasing hope for working out their solutions within the American system, despite the Communist efforts to court blacks during the 1930s. Black Americans increasingly began to take their destinies into their own hands and abandoned much of their hope that individual liberal white Americans would truly help them in the crisis periods. They began to work on making the "system" work for blacks.

Turning first to law they began to make direct, although gradual, assaults on the legal bastions of segregation. The famous Supreme Court decision of *Plessy* v. *Ferguson* in 1896 had established segregation as the law of the land. As revealed in the 1927 case of *Gong Lum* v. *Rice* even Chinese could be classified as colored and made to attend Negro schools. But the legal attack began. In 1935 in the Donald Murray case, the courts agreed that paying out-of-state tuition to Negroes was not "separate but equal" as demanded by law. Lloyd Gaines won the right to go to school in Missouri through court action. One scholar commented: "The decade following the Murray and Gaines cases witnessed the most revolutionary change to take place in the whole history of education in the South; the entire South began to spend an unprecedented proportion of its income for the education of Negro children in public schools." [10] But it was a case of "too little, too late." Legal action continued apace: *McLaurin* v. *University of Oklahoma*, *Sweatt* v. *University of Texas*, *Sipuel* v. *University of Oklahoma*, etc. In 1954 five pieces of litigation were coalesced into one major class action assault on the very concept of segregation as being inherently unequal. After much research the Supreme Court in 1954 did rule, in the famous Brown decision, that segregation was inherently unequal. School systems were requested, in what has come to be called BROWN II, to desegregate "with all deliberate speed."

Again, the hopes of black Americans were to fade under harsh white reaction. "All deliberate speed" came to be interpreted as gradualism, as circumvention, as massive resistance, as state tax support of private schools, as even threats of a 20th century type of secession. Six years after the law was established, only six percent of the Negroes in the elementary and secondary schools in the South were in schools with whites. Extrapolating from that "deliberate speed" of an average of one percent per year, it would take 100 years before desegregation would take place fully.

It must be hastily added that some progress for black education came about as the Americans began to believe that courts would indeed outlaw segregated schools. The expenditures of money in black schools noticeably increased, but they never got above 60% of that spent for whites during the 1950s. In Mississippi, for example, only 77% of the black children were in school compared with 89% of the whites in 1956. Much of white America seemed ready to join Governor George Wallace in 1957 as he opposed the desegregation of Alabama schools, proclaiming: "I draw the line in the dust and toss the gauntlet before the feet of tyranny; and I say segregation now, segregation tomorrow, segregation forever."

In the 1960s black education became intertwined with the general civil rights movements initiated by the students at A & T College in Greensboro, North Carolina. Students at the Atlanta University Center institutions, again including Julian Bond, joined to forge well organized systematic civil rights efforts, founded the Student Non-Violent Coordinating Committee (SNCC), and joined Martin Luther King's Southern Christian Leadership Conference (SCLC). America had never witnessed before such a movement of young black and white students making massive assaults on "the system." Boycotts, sit-ins, wait-ins, ride-ins, pray-ins, etc., became a familiar story. The Supreme Court found a new ally in its attack on desegregation in Presidents Eisenhower (however reluctant), Kennedy, and Lyndon Johnson. Whites and blacks were murdered in the South as civil rights laws were enacted and federal troops again entered the South to support an open system of education for blacks. Hallmark legislation was passed in 1965 when Congress enacted the Elementary and Secondary School Act (ESSA) designed to provide massive federal aid to those schools. The Higher Education Act of 1965 also passed with a special section, Title III, for developing of minority colleges and universities. In October 1969 the Supreme Court ordered an immediate end to all school segregation and thus replaced the 15-year-old doctrine of "all deliberate speed" of 1954. Although not directly related to education, the Supreme Court's support of the so-called "Philadelphia Plan" in January, 1970, was to lead to other kinds of affirmative action demands in the schools in the middle '70s. The Philadelphia Plan required state contractors to give assurances that they would employ a specified number of black workers in projects constructed with federal funds—a kind of "quota system" thus gained federal court approval. President Richard Nixon's adoption of a policy of "benign neglect" coupled with his decision to be concerned only with *de jure* segregation and not with *de facto* desegregation was insufficient to stop completely the effort for legal affirmative action. The Labor Department and the Department of Health, Education and Welfare found themselves along with the U.S. Civil Rights Commission committed to some degree to affirmative action and desegregation of the schools, both north and south, in the United States.

Despite the strong opposition, it seems clear that opportunities for blacks to get an education in the 1970s were significantly better than they had been in 1930. But let us examine closely some of the statistics to discover more hard data on the conditions in the 1970s. In 1972 the median number of years of schooling completed by blacks was 10.3 years compared with 12.2 for all races. The percentage of black families earning over $15,000 annually in 1971 was 12.2 while 26.4 percent of white families so earned. Rates of unemployment for whites in 1974 were estimated at around 6% while that for blacks approximated 14%. The U.S. Bureau of Labor Statistics listed blacks holding white collar jobs at 29.8% in 1972 compared with 50% of whites, while Negroes were listed at 27.2% for service industries compared with whites at 11.8%. *Ebony* magazine in 1969 reported that blacks were half the population of Newark, New Jersey, but owned only 10% of the licensed businesses. Washington, D.C.'s population was 63% black but they owned less than 13% of the businesses. Not one black firm ranked among the 500 largest U.S. corporations. All 46 black insurance companies control 0.2% of the industry's total assets. Only 1.47% of the nation's state troopers are black. Less than 1% of the Ph.D. degrees in the nation are held by blacks. The effort to make a big public relations stunt out of the growth of the black middle class (a short time ago) is again a failure to read the basic general statistics of the blacks in the nation's mainstream.

CONCLUSIONS

This paper, I believe, has demonstrated that America has systematically and over a very, very long period of time, legally, illegally, peacefully, violently, religiously, openly and subtly seriously deprived its black citizens of equal access to the educational and other resources. The efforts to establish affirmative action and so-called "compensatory justice" in the 1970s is, in the light of these 350 years of history, apparently necessary, although insufficient.

It is perhaps significant, as recently pointed out by the Office of Civil Rights, that college and university officials are making the loudest noises against what they wrongly call the "quota system," now officially disclaimed by HEW and the Office of Civil Rights. It would appear that colleges would look over their shoulders at big foundations and big business which are currently approaching the problem of black deprivation with major efforts to increase the resources and facilities open to blacks and to train more of them to enter managerial and executive positions. Instead of protesting the unfounded rhetoric of "reverse discrimination" America's big business has adopted affirmative action and is moving to pour millions into degree programs for the training of black engineers and managers. The Sloan Foundation is only one of those currently doing so.

Finally, it must be observed that the bulk of historical evidence suggests that (1) there is a part of the American mystique or dream which wants all Americans, including blacks, to be well educated; and (2) there is a part of the American (white) psyche which demands the exclusion, or at least the limitation, of blacks in access to true equal educational opportunities. When measured against the time line of history, the evidence suggests that white Americans tend to be more permissive toward black education in times of serious national crises (mainly military) and that almost a one-to-one correlation exists between our concern for our national existence and our permissiveness toward black Americans. Witness the American Revolution, the Civil War, and World War II—the only three points in our history when we made significant turn arounds in our equal opportunity affirmative action efforts for blacks.

NOTES AND REFERENCES

1. Quoted in *Ebony*, Aug. 1969.
2. Carter G. Woodson, *The Education of the Negro Prior to 1861* (Washington, D.C.: Associated Publishers, 1919), p. 27.
3. *Ibid.*, p. 45.

4. *Ibid.*, p. 68.
5. *Ibid.*, pp. 70ff.
6. *Ibid.*, p. 157.
7. *Ibid.*, p. 199.
8. See Horace Mann Bond, *The Education of the Negro in the American Social Order* (New York: Octagon Books, 1966), pp. 13ff. Also see John Hope Franklin, *From Slavery to Freedom* (New York: Alfred Knopf, 1969), for general discussion of the period.
9. Bond, pp. 88ff. See also John P. Davis, *American Negro Reference Book* (New York: Prentice-Hall, 1966), for discussion of the period and the court cases on the matter.
10. Virgil A. Clift, Archibald W. Anderson, and H. Gordon Hullfish, *Negro Education in America* (New York: Harper and Brothers, 1962), pp. 371–72. See also Henry A. Bullock, *A History of Negro Education in the South from 1619 to the Present* (Cambridge, Mass.: Harvard University Press, 1967).

Equality and Inviolability:
An Approach to Compensatory Justice

MAXINE GREENE

AMERICAN SOCIETY is pluralist; American citizens are ineluctably diverse. We vary in temperament, talent, and capacity within all groups and categories, including those of sex and race. We locate ourselves in the world in the light of our own particular biographical situations, in the light of experiences we build up over time. We interpret the realities we confront through perspectives made up of particular ranges of interests, occupations, commitments, and desires. Each of us belongs to many social groups and plays a great variety of social roles; and our involvements affect the ways we use "the stock of knowledge at hand"[1] to make sense of the social scene. The stock of knowledge, the disciplines, the schemata made available to us not only give our culture its identity, they also enable us to participate in a common meaning structure, to inhabit a common world. Even as we do so, however, we maintain our individual perspectives; we make personal interpretations of what is shared. Each of our undertakings, therefore, each of our projects remains distinctive; each vantage point is unique for all the association and communication essential to communal life.

I begin this way because my concern is as much with persons and their life-worlds as it is with equity in the social system. I am as interested in personal emancipation as I am in equality and justice. At once, I am entirely aware that the traditional liberal reliance on a morality based upon individual rights has not resulted in equal opportunity for many, many individuals—females and members of minority groups who continue to suffer from disadvantages that are undeserved. I want to try to develop an approach to equality and justice that rests upon a conception of individual inviolability and critical self-consciousness, one that takes into account the way inequity and exclusion actually afflict individuals struggling to define themselves in the world. I want to try to develop an approach that allows me to move back and forth between the objective arrangements made by the social system and the experiences people have with opportunities, provided *and* withheld. It is important, for instance, to hold in mind the idea that "an individual experiences what we have defined in the objective sense as an opportunity for a possibility for self-realization that stands to his choice, as a chance given to him, as a likelihood of attaining his goals in terms of his private definition of his situation within the group."[2] It is important to hold in mind the differences between what equality means to the one who feels discriminated against and what it means to those whose status the outsider wants to attain. It is important, also, to hold in mind the split created in consciousness when an individual is identified in terms of group membership, even when he or she is convinced that only through alliance with groups can individuals overcome inequities.

One of the crucial issues that confronts us, of course, is the matter of group rights and the break with pluralistic liberalism an emphasis on group rights entails. Another has to do with preferential treatment and the relationship of such treatment to social justice. Still another has to do with the problem of collective compensation to groups and the ways in which such compensation is distributed to individual members of such groups. Does "affirmative action" mean, as one critic believes, an "erosion of legal principle"?[3] Can reverse discrimination be carried on in accord with principles that are relevant from the point of view of justice? What does justice, what does fairness entail?

None of these issues can be addressed without a clarification of concepts like "rights," "equality," "justice," and "compensation"; and it seems to me that no one of them can be clarified except within specific contexts, in reference to what Alfred Schutz calls prevailing "systems of relevance." The system of relevance that has won most social approval over the years in our culture is the one associated with meritocracy. We are so familiar with it, we take it so much for granted that we are likely to forget that the meritocratic reality is a constructed one like every other example of social reality.[4] The explanations and legitimations connected with meritocratic thinking represent one mode of interpreting economic and social relationships, a mode so hallowed by tradition that we tend to confuse it with objective reality. Fundamental to the construct is the idea that human beings are to be judged and rewarded on the basis of individual merit. Achievement rather than ascription is to determine success. The assumed purpose of social and political arrangements is to enable diverse individuals to compete for places open to persons of comparable talent and ambition. From the point of view of the meritocratic system this satisfies the requirements of efficiency. Equality of opportunity can be taken for granted because barriers of birth and wealth are not permitted to bar the way. In the last decade, as we know, efforts were made to help certain persons overcome specific deficiencies and thus compensate for previously unregarded disadvantages. Once this was done, it was believed, each individual would have a fair chance to realize his or her potentialities, to satisfy his or her desires. Natural rights (to life, liberty, and the pursuit of happiness) were assumed to be secured. Because everyone would be offered the same chance, the system was described as just.

Recent historic events and disclosures have made clear to many people that, even with compensatory arrangements, the meritocracy does not provide equal chances for all individuals, nor does it protect everyone's natural rights. Many have come to realize that true equality of opportunity is in any case impossible. R. S. Peters says flatly:

> The obvious fact is that, descriptively speaking, there is no equality of opportunity and never can be unless equalitarians are prepared to control early upbringing, size of families, and breeding. Without taking such steps there will always be ineradicable differences between people which will affect how any system works in practice. Were there not such differences the principle of equality would have little point.[5]

To speak of a principle of equality is to speak of equality of consideration, of equity in the treatment of persons whose skills, strengths, and talents are necessarily diverse. Peters is concerned with justice in the making of distinctions, when it is important that distinctions be made. "The notion basic to justice," he writes, "is that distinctions should be made if there are relevant differences and that they should not be made if there are no relevant differences or on the basis of irrelevant differences."[6] The interesting question has to do with the criteria of relevance. Are considerations of efficiency, for example, more important than considerations of self-development? Is a concern for interests as important as respect for persons? Is achievement more significant than self-respect? It is easy enough to say that sex and race are not relevant when choices are made in hiring. What does determine relevance? What warrants distinctions being made?

John Rawls, in *A Theory of Justice*, has devised a formal system that takes into account what he considers to be the most profoundly relevant differences: between the most and the least favored in a society. His approach explicitly challenges the meritocratic view; his prime considerations are equality and self-esteem. He believes that meritocracy is unfair; because, under meritocratic arrangements, equality of opportunity signifies an equal chance for the more fortunate to leave the less fortunate behind. To be less fortunate, he says, is a matter of contingency. Disadvantages, deficits, inequalities due to birth and endowment are undeserved and call for redress. Clearly, this breaks fundamentally with what is taken for granted in our culture. People all too often confuse success in the meritocratic hierarchy with individual worth; and there is no question but that self-esteem in this culture is a function of the ability to achieve. Individuals are held responsible for their failures as well as their successes. Offered an equal chance, a person who does not "make it" is considered to be less valuable as a person—and has little chance to develop self-esteem. He or she may be undisciplined and aggressive, uninterested in learning to read. He or she may be poorly fed or unclean; his or her test scores may be appallingly low. All these, suggests Rawls, are deficits and undeserved.

The social ideal he develops is one in which equality, for reasons of justice, is given priority. Justice, he writes, is the primary virtue of social institutions. It provides a standard for determining whether the distribution of goods in a given society is fair or unfair. The conception most rational men would accept, he says, is one that requires social and economic inequalities to be so arranged that they benefit the least advantaged in the society.[7] Not only is there to be redress for deprivation; there is to be a "difference principle" requiring that resources be allocated in such a way as to improve the long-term expectations of the least favored.[8] In connection with all this, "positions of authority and offices of command must be accessible to all"; inequalities in general must be attached to offices open to all in such a fashion that everyone benefits. Prior, however, to the principles regulating inequalities is a principle of liberty. Rawls asserts that every member of society has an inviolability founded on justice "which even the welfare of everyone else cannot override." He believes that no proper conception of justice or fairness can affirm that "the loss of freedom for some is made right by a greater good shared by others."[9] He is not a leveler; he is not asking that handicaps be evened out, nor that individuals be denied the freedom to achieve. He is saying that higher achievement and greater advantage are to be justified not by the individual satisfaction they produce (nor by the net balance of satisfactions) but by the contribution they make to the welfare of the least advantaged.

How, guaranteed inviolability and freedom, can human beings be expected to attend to those born into less favorable social positions or into less advantaged groups? Why would anyone who is better endowed and more advantaged concern himself with the life prospects and expectations of the least favored? Rawls, positing a rational and rule-governed society, speaks of mutual benefits and the capacity of human beings to treat others with respect. The principles that support self-respect and make social cooperation more effective are that "each person is to have an equal right to the most extensive total system of equal basic liberties compatible with a similar system of liberty for all" and the principle that the arrangement of inequalities should be to the benefit of those least favored. No longer is equal opportunity to be used mainly to unleash energies for the pursuit of wealth and power. The higher expectations of the gifted and better situated citizens are to be considered just "if and only if they work as part of a scheme which improves the expectations of the least advantaged members of society."[10] Self-respect is the primary good in this system; indeed, it is the primary motivation. Self-respect, for Rawls, refers to a rational individual's sense of his or her own worth and to his or her conviction that the life plan he or she has developed is worth carrying out. In addition, there is a confidence in the ability to fulfill whatever his or her intentions are. Justice supports such self-esteem, Rawls says; life itself has more value if we are appreciated by others whom we ourselves esteem. So a sense of their own worth must be sought for the least favored as well. The point of education, in fact, is to enrich personal and social life even more than to train productive abilities.

Daniel Bell finds all this extremely radical; he sees Rawls's theory, in fact, to be a "socialist ethic." It should be pointed out, however, that Marxists would disagree in almost every particular with Rawls. For one thing, most of them believe that class struggle is necessary if inequalities are to be effectively reduced, especially since the most favored class in society is a ruling class with a need for wealth and power and little desire for social cooperation based on a difference principle.[11] Marxists would object vehemently to Rawls's neglect of the problem of class interest; they would find meaningless the concern for self-esteem within the free competitive society that is assumed. Bell's charge of radicalism is primarily based on the belief that Rawls makes the disadvantaged identifiable in group terms. Therefore, says Bell, he is making a claim for group rights that "stands in formal contradiction to the principle of individualism, with its emphasis on achievement and universalism."[12] Why not, he asks, provide for greater incentives "for those who can expand the total social output and use this larger 'social pie' for the mutual (yet differential) advantage of us all?"[13] Granting the fact that few people yet conceive society "as a cooperative venture for mutual advantage," granting the fact that Rawls's social ideal may be unrealizable, I find it difficult to see how Bell's "just meritocracy" deals with the inequities confronting us today. He says that all we have to do is to realize the traditional ideal of equality of opportunity fairly; and he is convinced that questions of inequality have little to do with meritocracy, which is made up of those "who have earned their authority."[14] Is it the fact that women and blacks remain relatively disadvantaged because they have *not* earned the right to success and authority? When I consider the empirical realities of the hiring situation as it pertains to women and blacks, I find it less than satisfactory to be told to wait for the advent of a "just meritocracy." I find it frustrating to read over again that "we must insist on a basic social equality in that each person is to be given

respect and not humiliated on the basis of color, or sexual pro-
clivities, or other personal attributes." The social equality Bell
has in mind is not the kind that leads to democratization in every
sphere of life. It is qualified by his conviction that, in the techno-
cratic society, there must be a regard for intellectual authority,
significant achievement, earned status confirmed by a person's
peers. The question is whether these considerations exclude a concern for the plight of those discriminated against or kept (by accident, prejudice, thoughtlessness, or neglect) from developing
themselves and attaining a sense of worth.

The Educational Testing Service recently conducted a study on
persons awarded Ph.D.s and Ed.D.s in 1950, 1960, and 1968. The
study concluded that "women, having often subordinated their careers to family responsibilities, have consistently received lower
pay, less prestigious jobs and fewer employment opportunities"
and that this has changed little over the years. The report goes on
to state that disparities in income between men and women with
doctorates increase with years of experience. Because of marriage
and motherhood, many women have had to work part-time. "Men
with full-time positions received the grants, published the research, and got the promotions."[15] Is this required by a just meritocracy? Is it, from any point of view, fair?

Unnecessary though it may be to review the details, I must emphasize that, in 1970, only 18 percent of the professional staffs of
institutions of higher education were women.[16] The proportion
of women professors has decreased since 1920, despite the increased number of women in the labor force. It is well known
that, after the change in the character of that labor force during
World War II, 51 percent of all mothers with children aged 6–17
were employed; and a middle-class woman was as likely to be
working as one from the working class. This fact is one of many
that accounts for the growing ambivalence of women in all classes
towards traditional family roles. Their ambivalence, yes, and rest-
lessness, along with rapidly increasing access to higher education,
have led to an expanding pool of potential female participants in
the work life and the professional life of this country. These factors are countered, to a significant although decreasing degree, by
women's culturally conditioned fears of success.[17] They are countered as well by an educational system that reflects society's values

and therefore imposes expectations on women that differ from those imposed upon men; from the beginning of school, little girls learn from textbooks, toys, and teachers that they are inferior in important respects to little boys.[18] Efforts are being made to alter the toys and textbooks made available to girls to the end of releasing expectations and promoting self-respect in what is still regarded as a man's world; but the injustices, whether intended or not, remain. It ought to go without saying that black women, most particularly black women professionals, suffer even more when it comes to status and salary differentials. The sprinkling of black women assistant deans and heads of recruitment programs should not obscure the fact that, in 1973, only 1,073 black females were employed as teaching and administrative personnel in 1,764 two- and four-year colleges and universities—less than one per institution. And the statistics show as well that black women professionals cluster in the low-status schools.[19]

Where blacks in general are concerned, there can be no argument with the claim that too many have been casualties. The long years of exclusion, humiliation, poverty, persecution, and inadequate training have left a fearsome mark. Job discrimination, despite the improvements of the last decade, still abounds. (After all, unemployment in the male black population is twice what it is in the white.) Feelings of "nobodyness" and "invisibility" still afflict many members of minority groups, for all the increase in self-esteem derived from new-found pride in identity. The disadvantages with which they are burdened are of a different order from those holding women back from self-realization and feelings of worth. The color-blindness that was supposed to result from anti-discrimination legislation has not helped as much as the reformers hoped.[20] The matter of poor qualification still has to be confronted, along with the problem of rising expectations and the bitter sense of unmet needs. Using an old Aristotelian idea, some critics say that, since white society has enslaved and exploited blacks for so long (and been enriched by doing so), justice demands that the victims be compensated. This, they assert, is commutative justice and only right. We have, we are told, a long way to go in achieving a society where race is as irrelevant as eye-color and where minority groups are judged on individual worth alone. When we reach that point, "their history will have left them so educationally, economically, and psychologically disadvantaged that, unless they receive special preference, they and the vast majority of their children will be condemned by our now color-blind society to perpetual deprivation in the midst of surrounding affluence."[21]

More arguments could be amassed to indicate the extraordinary problems involved in the effort to achieve fair employment policies in a basically inequitable society. Affirmative action programs, developed largely in response to pressures by women's organizations, are understood to be the consequence of a lack of enforcement of executive orders preventing discrimination. Once the Civil Rights Office of the Department of Health, Education and Welfare took over the responsibility for holding colleges and universities accountable, the controversy over group rights and preferential hiring began. J. Stanley Pottinger, then Director of the Office for Civil Rights, said, at the time the regulations were devised, that the Executive Order had never been intended to set aside professional qualifications as the primary standard for hiring. He "never understood academic freedom to deny a qualified person an opportunity for appointment or advancement because of race or sex, or the right to pay one person less than a person of another race or sex performing the same job,"[22] and it is difficult to argue with that belief. The problem has been the vagueness of the language used in the directives. Many persons have understood them to call not only for quotas but for preferential hiring. One reason for this is that universities have been asked, not simply to declare themselves against discrimination, but to take positive action to remedy inequities according to timetables worked out in advance. They have also been asked to appraise what their schedules are likely to yield in the future. According to regulations, those predictions must be expressed as statements of goals, which are to be used in measuring the efforts made. One writer says that it may be useful "to look upon the use of goals—and their attendant timetables—as a management information device to allow both . . . the colleges and the regulatory agency (HEW) to monitor more effectively and evaluate the progress being made towards the achievement of actual equal employment opportunity."[23] Others, however, have said that the effort to prove "good faith" has led many universities to spell out their goals numerically. Virginia Black, who finds it logically impossible to show the effectiveness of special treatment mandates, is convinced that affirmative action programs must be discriminatory. Enumeration is necessary, she says, to demonstrate that an organization is in compliance; and this inevitably implies a quota system.[24] The point has also been made that, even though the goals demanded are to operate in favor of minorities and not as ceilings, a numerical requirement in favor of any group must become a restrictive ceiling for others. Although no one defends quotas in the restrictive sense, many of the arguments against affirmative action are based on the assumption that the requirements of the Executive Order make quotas inescapable. Vernon Jordan writes in rejoinder that quotas are "a phony issue, a red flag to divert attention from the real issue of discrimination by falsely categorizing reasonable numerical *goals* and generalized intentions as rigid mathematical formulae. Nevertheless, if numerical goals and timetables are not formulated, as one commentator has stated, 'the future will resemble the past.' "[25] Shifting the ground somewhat, Sidney Hook and others have responded by insisting that the effect of affirmative action is to force institutions to hire unqualified members of preferred groups and discriminate against qualified members of majority groups.[26] Daniel Bell, viewing the setting of "target" figures as equivalent to quotas, says this means that "standards are bent or broken."[27] Most recently (although probably not conclusively) the present director of the Office of Civil Rights has issued a memorandum on college hiring policies that explicitly orders colleges to hire the best qualified and asserts that sex and race must play no part. "The affirmative action process must not operate to restrict consideration to minorities and women only. . . . Job requirements must be applied uniformly to all candidates without regard to race, color, sex, ethnicity."[28]

The aim of those who called for affirmative action in the first place was to take steps to overcome preferential treatment of the white male and to allow groups to compete with all others on the basis of individual merit. As we can see, the issue is in no sense resolved—because of the danger of new inequities, once special treatment for particular groups is required. The prevailing belief seems to be that unqualified people should not, under any circumstances, be hired; and preferential treatment of any sort is taken to mean that something other than individual merit will determine who is chosen. Underlying this is a view of a "natural" distribution of talents that free, unhampered competition makes possible. There must be, according to this view, no arbitrary interference with what is thought to be the "bell-shaped curve" according to which talents are distributed in any society. The presumption that such a curve has some objective existence is profoundly questionable. It is a presumption integral to the knowledge structure that sustains and legitimates what Bell calls the "post-industrial society"; but we need to understand that it is a construct developed over time to serve particular human interests,[29] certainly not all. The very idea of an unequal distribution of talents almost always assumes a conception of single talents, those of most utility to the social system. It becomes all too easy to overlook "the range and variety of human capacities: intelligence, physical strength, agility and grace, artistic creativity, mechanical skill, leadership, endurance, memory, psychological insight, the capacity for hard work—even, moral strength, sensitivity, the ability to express compassion."[30] Granting the fact that college or university hiring policies must now be geared to a selected range of capacities, I still would emphasize the ways in which the notion of merit is linked to a conception of the "given," of the conventional and unquestionable. The requirements universities have in mind when they hire are frequently defined to correspond with what is taken to be the distribution of talents. Yet they are granted an objective status which makes us overlook the fact that they too were created by human beings in the light of interests interpreted over time.

My interest, as I have said, is to develop an approach to equality founded in a commitment to inviolability and critical consciousness. Such an approach requires that we break with either/ors as we break with what we blandly take for granted where fairness, merit, and efficiency are concerned. It also requires that we pay heed to the self-respect and the life plans of many different members of our society, with the idea that each one is entitled to act upon what he chooses, to question, to become what he or she has the capacity to be. If each one is entitled to equality of consideration, as I believe to be the case, the claims of injured groups for compensation cannot override the rights of the white male to act upon his life plan. I am unable to discover principles relevant from the point of view of justice that sanction arbitrary discrimination in favor of certain victims of discrimination; nor am I able to justify preferential hiring if it restricts opportunity for members of the majority group. I am concerned, among other things, about the individual in the nonpreferred group who may have been maltreated for reasons other than sex or race. I am concerned as well with the unfairness of holding the group of young white males responsible for the injuries done blacks and women, even though the individuals in the group may neither have done injury nor profited from exploitation.[31] Like John Rawls, I do not believe that the better situated white male ought to be held back in the name of justice. It seems at least possible that his advantages may be acted upon in such a fashion that they benefit those who are not as well situated as he. In any case, as I shall try to make clear, it seems to me that that should be the focus of our discussions of compensatory justice. My interest is primarily in what individuals, freed from discrimination and domination, can do together to create a more equitable world.

The terrible fact is that social injustice still characterizes this society. In addition, equal attention is not being paid to the individuality of every man and woman. Even when plans are devised for compensating injured groups as groups, there is little concern for the dignity and self-esteem of the persons involved. There is, admittedly, some recognition that amends should somehow be made for unjust discrimination over time, that some compensation is due the victims of inequity. It may be useful to think in terms of what Edmond Cahn calls "the sense of injustice," meaning a response to real or imagined instances of injustice. He writes that all human beings possess the capacity to see injustice to others as personal aggression against themselves. Much depends, however, on whether there can be imaginative identification with the persons who are oppressed. If not, if individuals are "tethered" and remain at a distance from those being victimized, their awareness is dulled. The sense of injustice, then, is a compound of reason and empathy.[32] I believe that it is only as we keep this in mind that something can be done to increase equality while protecting inviolability, taking personal vantage points into account, extending self-esteem.

Cahn seems to me to be quite right when he says that people do not become outraged when a decision violates some dialectical pattern or an analytic conception of justice. They become out- raged when they feel themselves—or someone they can identify with—being treated unfairly. Indeed, ever since the philosopher Hegel pointed it out,[33] there has been a recognition in western philosophy of the human need to criticize constraints upon ex- perience and to struggle against what is felt as unnecessary domi- nation. At the height of the civil rights campaigns, many white citizens were able to empathize with black people because of the way such great leaders as the Reverend Martin Luther King, Jr., where able to present the struggles to them. They could identify with other human beings who were being brutalized, imprisoned, demeaned, oppressed. They became capable of reading black lit- erature as well; and the novels, the poems made it more and more difficult to remain "tethered," to be indifferent to what was hap- pening to other human beings. Somewhat the same thing has hap- pened, although far more slowly and ambivalently, where women are concerned. Some men have read such poetry as Dilys Laing's ("Women receive / the insults of men / with tolerance")[34] or Muriel Rukeyser's ("Praise breakers, / praise the unpraised who cannot speak their name").[35] They can identify with the potential editor condemned to being a typist, with the woman who cannot get a bank loan, with the woman refused a job because she might some day have a child. Certain men can even recognize the domi- nation by household tasks, convention, and routines. There de- veloped, therefore, a sense of injustice through imaginative connection with persons being recognizably oppressed. And out of this came a certain willingness to make amends.

Recent preoccupation with the possibility of preferential hiring has changed the focus of the sense of injustice for many people. Tales are told of young male graduate students unable to secure jobs or even interviews for jobs in colleges and universities. They are being passed over, we are told, by women and blacks, often (we are told) far less qualified. In order to retain their Federal contracts, institutions of higher education try to prove their "good faith efforts" by writing fixed numerical goals and then hiring with those goals primarily in mind. The public consequence has been an outraged response to a new kind of victimization. The sense of injustice is now aroused, not by the plight of blacks and women, but by the plight of the young white male—who (more than all others, it is still assumed) *deserves* the fair treatment superiority demands. Yet the fact is, as more and more observers are discovering, that white males are neither being effectively excluded nor removed from faculties. Nor have the percentages of blacks and women risen sufficiently to suggest that the effects of discrimination have been overcome.

Certainly the facts should be made clear. At once, it should be recognized that the assumptions and the constructs of our culture are such that injustices cannot be overcome through numerical balancing; nor can they be overcome by means of limited compensations to groups. Whatever costs are involved in attaining equity in hiring should be borne by a population larger than the group abruptly nonpreferred. Some have suggested that senior professors, tenured professors, should contribute to the cost by agreeing to early retirement or, perhaps, to reductions in salary. This would not only take the onus off the "innocent bystander" who is the white male;[36] it would, to an extent, enlarge the pie. It would, in other words, provide more opportunities and more financial resources; and a few more members (although not all) of the preferred groups might benefit. The question of how this helps the members not hired, or how it helps the entire group, remains open. The question of what this does to the consciousness and self-esteem of the one hired as a member of a group remains open and troubling as well, even if the one hired is perfectly qualified. And finally there is the life plan of the senior professor; there is the matter of the contribution he or she is capable of making at the moment of full maturity; there is the crucial issue of his or her dignity and self-esteem.

None of the compensatory mechanisms appear to be fair, since each one violates some person's freedom or interferes with a choice of a life. I do not, however, believe that we can return to the kind of color-blindness and apparent disregard for gender that perpetuated inequities for so long. Colleges and universities do have to be held accountable in some way. Those responsible for hiring do have to make deliberate efforts to select candidates from every group in the community for interviewing and assessment, even as they maintain what they conceive to be their standards. Personnel and hiring committees, like search committees, must be organized with care, so that what has so long been taken for granted does not prevent them from recognizing promise and distinctive quality. Interview questions must be sensitively evaluated, so that individuals who have not been members of the "network," not even members of the dominant class, are provided a fair chance to say who they are and what they can do. If at all possible, candidates must be permitted to perform in classrooms, so as not to be judged on credentials or appearance alone. All this suggests an increase in self-consciousness on the part of all the persons involved, a capacity to think about what they are doing, to offer good reasons for the decisions they make, to work in accord with principles. I am not convinced that indirect coercion by federal agencies nurtures this kind of consciousness. Nor am I convinced that intervention by federal agencies is appropriate in academic life. Virginia Black, arguing strongly against reverse discrimination, warns against "short-term policy implants whose function is to coerce the correction of an observed economic imbalance. Social change comes about gradually," she says, "and the only laws that are economically feasible or morally tolerable are those laws that people are ready spontaneously to obey."[37] Not as troubled as Professor Black by the prospect of a rigid class structure emerging from preferential treatment, I am impressed with the notion of people being *ready* to obey, because this suggests the change in consciousness and attitude I believe is required if justice is to be attained. People are "spontaneously ready" when the sense of injustice is aroused. They do not need coercion from without when they can freely identify with individuals endowed in diverse ways and grant them the respect each one requires. Granting such respect, acknowledging the worth of the other, people may be expected to criticize and to refuse unwarranted domination. Seeking their own realization and self-esteem, some may be expected to choose equity and social justice.

But, first, perspectives must change; and people must break with what they take for granted. I do not only have in mind traditional notions of merit, hierarchy, and bell-shaped curves. It also seems to me that we must rethink our attitudes towards differential economic rewards. Thomas Nagel, writing on "Equal Treatment and Compensatory Discrimination," says that it may be unjust for larger rewards to be provided for tasks that require superior intelligence. "This is simply the way things work out in a technologically advanced society with a market economy. It does not reflect a social judgment that smart people *deserve* the opportunity to make more money than dumb people." And later:

> Justice may require that we try to reduce the automatic connections between material advantages, cultural opportunity, and institutional authority. But such changes can be brought about, if at all, only by large alterations in the social system, the system of taxation, and the salary structure. They will not be achieved by modifying the admissions or hiring policies of colleges and universities.[38]

I am as aware as Dr. Nagel is of the unlikelihood of this degree of change in a competitive society like ours. Nevertheless, it is important for people to examine their assumptions about the relation between money and merit. Do individuals actually deserve the financial rewards they receive for what they do? Does the exchange value given a job of work always match its intrinsic value? Are there not other values for which work can be exchanged—respect, for example, the sense of having contributed to others' welfare?

It seems to me that the question of economic justice ought to be separated from the question of equity in the distribution of employment. If this could be accomplished in fact, it would be possible to think in terms of multiple criteria of relevance where equality of consideration is concerned. There are multiple contributions noncredentialed, *relatively* unqualified persons might make to the lives of universities. Not only is there skill-teaching; there are experiences in the several arts that might be opened up in distinctive ways by persons whose unique perspectives have been too long ignored. There are sociological insights to be shared; there are coping capacities to be taught. I am suggesting that, were it not for the linking of money to level of traditional achievement, a great range of occupations might become significant possibilities. If there were greater uniformity of reward, many of these would appear more worthy than they presently do; and new opportunities for self-definition and self-esteem might be created. I am not talking about a kind of second-class citizenship within the system. Nor am I suggesting that qualified members of minority groups not compete with other qualified individuals for traditional university posts. I am suggesting that the opportunities made available be diversified in the light of an expanded vision of merit and competency, an altered approach to rewards. There is, theoretically, no limit to the kinds of services that might be offered in this society, no limit to the need for services. Whether the capacities tapped are those of an elderly woman able to care for disturbed juveniles, a neighborhood block leader, a blues singer who can tell tales about the past, a ham radio operator, or a motorcycle repair man, they all might be conceived as valuable, just so long as they were valued by persons interested in what they had to give. If, in this society, we can create such openings for those who are now among the least favored, if we can make it possible for them to gain self-esteem, we might come far closer to attaining justice. I realize that there would still be the appeal of status, even if rewards were equalized; and I am quite aware that the colleges and universities would still have to make unprecedented efforts to overcome the biases for which they are now made to pay. I believe, however, that legitimate compensation can only be made if living individuals of all kinds are enabled to contribute to the society's store of talents in the manner most appropriate for each one. But this can only happen, as I have said, if we can break with meritocratic conventions and make self-development a criterion of relevance. It can only happen if, through education and work experiences, consciousness can be altered in this culture—and people can begin opting for diversification, for the end of domination and constraint.

Given the need for attentiveness on the part of colleges and universities where the hiring of qualified women is concerned, I believe that here, too, preferential hiring and reverse discrimination will do harm. I think that institutions should indeed define their goals in this domain, and it may be necessary that these be sometimes numerical goals. But this will not solve the larger problems confronting qualified women whose lives encompass more than their careers. Jill Conway, writing in *Daedalus*, talks about increasing differentials between rewards for male and female work and about the fact that access to higher education has not had real impact on the pattern of female employment. The major problem is, she says, for women to find places at the center of academic institutions which create and transmit the culture of the West.

> On the one hand, to be in command of that culture women
> must master skills in mathematics and the hard sciences which
> have traditionally been defined as unfeminine and neglected
> in the education of females. On the other hand, if these skills
> in abstract reasoning are to be applied in a manner which
> draws upon the inner springs of creativity, they must be
> acquired in a way which is no threat to the female identity.
> This can be achieved by an educational experience which is
> critical of many of the assumptions of a male-controlled culture
> and which takes the female as the norm rather than the
> deviant except to the life of the mind. One pre-condition
> for such a view of intellectual life is a sense of solidarity with
> female colleagues.[39]

Women's studies will be necessary, she suggests, and cooperative efforts made to transform male definitions of scholarly roles. Only, in fact, as male faculty members come to see women as potential leaders who can play a part in reshaping institutions will women begin participating consequentially in decision-making bodies. Dr. Conway sees a danger in government efforts to force affirmative action programs on universities. Forced compliance can lead to purely formal action, like the setting up of low-status programs staffed by women. More seriously, coercion cannot change attitudes towards women any more than towards members of minority groups. "It is difficult," writes Dr. Conway, "to build a more comprehensive curriculum or a livelier intellectual experience for either sex in . . . a climate of politicization and confrontation."[40]

Again the matter of consciousness is involved. Again stress is placed on the need to break with the customary, the taken-for-granted. It appears evident that thoroughgoing compensatory justice for women scholars demands fundamental changes, not simply in attitudes, institutions, and curricula, but in patterns of social life. As has been said, women have been held back by family obligations; they have suffered from the inevitable delays in the development of their careers. It is neither sufficient nor wholly fair to place a kind of compensatory responsibility on the shoulders of the husbands, for all the importance of overcoming sexism and oppression in the home. If women scholars become disadvantaged in the society of scholars because they have chosen to rear children, justice would seem to require that the society of scholars justify the undeserved advantages entailed in being free, white, and male by applying their expertise to the creation of new socialization patterns for the young. Not only ought there to be excellent day-care centers on college campuses; there ought to be imaginative alternatives to the home-bound family life now demanded of the informed intellectual woman, who chooses to raise a number of children when she is young. The burden should not be placed solely on the woman, who knows so well that her male classmates are moving up the academic ladder while she is hard put to find the spare moments needed for keeping in touch with her field. The fact that the woman is normally left to make her own arrangements is testimony to how much is taken for granted where opportunity is concerned. It is *because* disadvantages like these are so seldom questioned that numerical quotas have appeared to be necessary. The discouraging reality is that, where there have been quota systems, women have been hired by committees that would never have considered them before.

Preferential hiring, it appears, can be justified on only the most restricted pragmatic grounds: It *has* worked to benefit certain members of disadvantaged groups who otherwise would have been asked to wait for the day of the just meritocracy. Even if, in particular cases, white males cannot claim to have been deprived of employment in consequence, I cannot—on any reasonable philosophical ground—say that the practice is right. From the vantage point of a principle of justice and from the vantage point of a concern for individuality, I find quotas to be indefensible. Yet I know, as Michael Walzer has pointed out, that "they are likely to be resolutely opposed, opposed without guilt and worry, only by people who are entirely content with the class structure as it is and with the present distribution of goods and services." He went on:

> For those of us who are not content, anxiety can't be avoided. We know that quotas are wrong, but we also know that the present distribution of wealth makes no moral sense, that the

dominance of the income curve plays havoc with legitimate distributive principles, and that quotas are a form of redress no more irrational than the world within which and because of which they are demanded. In an equalitarian society, however, quotas would be unnecessary and inexcusable.[41]

This suggests the dilemma of the philosopher concerned about what happens to individuals when they are submerged in groups, concerned about the maintenance of standards in universities, concerned about equity and decency. It suggests the dilemma of the philosopher uneasy with prevailing meritocratic values and aware, as Crane Brinton put it almost forty years ago, that the logical conclusion to be drawn from the principle of equality is something other than meritocracy and *laissez faire.* To bring about the kind of social arrangements in which equality would be meaningful requires collective action, as Brinton said. But, as he also said, the believers in this form of equality are "however, rarely logicians."[42]

All we can hope to do, I think, is to work for increased reflection on the unfairness taken for granted for so long. Of course there have to be short-range efforts: more involvement of women and blacks in hiring committees; workable accountability schemes; expansion of curricula; attention to differential rewards. At the same time, however, work must be done to challenge and to criticize the existing consensus where criteria of relevance are concerned. If we take seriously the idea (as we claim to do) that each person should be treated as an end and never as a means, we have also to think about a plurality of values and a diversity of capacities. Contemplating the emergence of a "service society," we have to consider the range of services human beings can provide—and ascribe value to those not yet included in our hierarchies.

Perhaps, above all, we need to think together about what John Dewey called "the Great Community." Dewey knew well the strength of the forces that work against effective inquiry into the taken-for-granted.[43] He knew the importance of communication and participation by persons moved by their associations with others, but not obliterated in those associations. Perhaps we have to think again what unites individuals in a community, in any great community. What is common to them all is their equal inviolability, their integrity as human beings. If we are to be fair, to take affirmative actions that are just, individuality must be cherished, as justice is pursued. Dewey wrote that Walt Whitman was the seer of the democracy that this implies. And Whitman wrote:

> I swear I begin to see the meaning of these things,
> It is not the earth, it is not America who is so great,
> It is I who am great or to be great, it is You up there, or any one,
> It is to walk rapidly through civilizations, governments, theories,
> Through poems, pageants, shows, to form individuals.
>
> Underneath all, individuals,
> I swear nothing is good to me now that ignores individuals.[44]

No. Nothing is good that ignores individual perspective and opportunity perceived "as a possibility for self-realization" by a particular individual—black, woman, or young white male—entitled to choose, to pursue his or her fulfillment, to strive towards meaningful goals. Nothing is good that ignores the need for critical reflection on the part of each person affected by social policy, reflection on what he or she understands to be his or her situation, not only in the group but in the social system at large. Affirmative action must become emancipatory action, freely undertaken by women and men, working together to reject irrational and unfair limitations, to remake the inequitable world.

NOTES AND REFERENCES

1. Alfred Schutz, "Phenomenology and the Social Sciences," in *Collected Papers I: The Problem of Social Reality*, ed. Maurice Natanson (The Hague: Martinus Nijhoff, 1967), p. 136.

2. Alfred Schutz, "Equality and the Social Meaning Structure," in *Collected Papers II: Studies in Social Theory*, ed. Arvid Brodersen (The Hague: Martinus Nijhoff, 1964), pp. 271–72.

3. Virginia Black, "The Erosion of Legal Principles in the Creation of Legal Policies," *Ethics,* 84 (1974), 93–115.

4. See Peter L. Berger and Thomas Luckmann, *The Social Construction of Reality* (Garden City, N.Y.: Anchor Books, 1967).

5. R. S. Peters, *Ethics and Education* (Glenview, Ill.: Scott, Foresman, 1967), pp. 87–88.

6. *Ibid.*, p. 51.

7. John Rawls, *A Theory of Justice* (Cambridge, Mass.: Harvard University Press, 1972), p. 83.

8. *Ibid.*, pp. 75–78, 101.

9. *Ibid.*, p. 28.

10. *Ibid.*, p. 95.

11. Richard Miller, "Rawls and Marxism," *Philosophy and Public Affairs*, 3 (1974), 188–89.

12. Daniel Bell, *The Coming of Post-Industrial Society* (New York: Basic Books, 1973), p. 445.

13. *Ibid.*, p. 450.

14. *Ibid.*, p. 453.

15. *The New York Times*, January 6, 1975, p. 16.

16. Patricia A. Graham, "Women in Academe," *Science*, September 25, 1970, p. 1284.

17. See Alice Rossi, "Barriers to the Career Choice of Engineering, Medicine, or Science Among American Women," in *Women and the Scientific Professions: The M.I.T. Symposium on Women and the Scientific Professions* (Cambridge, Mass.: M.I.T. Press, 1965); Rossi, "Women in Science: Why So Few?", *Science*, May 28, 1965, p. 1196; Matina Horner, "The Motive to Avoid Success and Changing Aspirations of College Women," in *Readings on the Psychology of Women*, ed. Judith Bardwick (New Work: Harper and Row, 1972).

18. See Judith Stacey, Susan Bereaud, and Joan Daniels, eds., *And Jill Came Tumbling After: Sexism in American Education* (New York: Dell, 1974).

19. William Moore, Jr., and Lonnie H. Wagstaff, *Black Educators in White Colleges* (San Francisco: Jossey-Bass, 1974), pp. 162–65.

20. Kaplan, "Equal Justice in an Unequal World: Equality for the Negro—the Problem of Special Treatment," in Paul M. Dodyk, General Editor, *Cases and Materials on Law and Poverty* (St. Paul, Minn.: West, 1969), p. 482ff.

21. *Ibid.*

22. Quoted in John H. Bunzel, "The Politics of Quotas," *Change* (October 1972), p. 25.

23. Jinny M. Goldstein, "Affirmative Action: Equal Employment Rights for Women in Academia," *Teachers College Record*, 74 (1973), 415.

24. Virginia Black, p. 96.

25. Vernon E. Jordan, Jr., "Blacks and Higher Education—Some Reflections," *Daedalus*, 104 (Winter 1975), 161.

26. Sidney Hook, *New York Times*, November 5, 1971, p. 43.

27. Daniel Bell, p. 418.

28. Peter E. Holmes, quoted by Albert Shanker in "Strong Voices Against Ethnic Hiring," *The New York Times*, January 12, 1975, p. 9.

29. See Jurgen Habermas, *Knowledge and Human Interests* (Boston, Mass.: Beacon Press, 1971).

30. Michael Walzer, "In Defense of Equality," *Dissent* (Autumn 1973), p. 400.

31. Robert Simon, "Preferential Hiring: A Reply to Judith Jarvis Thompson," *Philosophy and Public Affairs*, 3 (Spring 1974), 317–18.

32. Edmond N. Cahn, *The Sense of Injustice* (New York: New York University Press, 1949), pp. 24–27.

33. See G.W.F. Hegel, "Independence and Dependence of Self-consciousness: Lordship and Bondage," in *The Phenomenology of Mind*, tr. J. B. Baillie (New York: Harper and Row, 1967), pp. 228–40.

34. Dilys Laing, "Veterans," in *By a Woman Writt*, ed. Joan Goulianos (Indianapolis: Bobbs-Merrill, 1973), p. 328.

35. Muriel Rukeyser, "Ann Burlak," in *By a Woman Writt*, p. 366.

36. Robert Simon, p. 318.

37. Virginia Black, p. 105.

38. Thomas Nagel, "Equal Treatment and Compensatory Discrimination," *Philosophy and Public Affairs*, 2 (1973), 348.

39. Jill K. Conway, "Coeducation and Woman's Studies: Two Approaches to the Question of Woman's Place in the Contemporary University," *Daedalus*, 103 (Fall 1974), 241.

40. Conway, p. 245.

41. Walzer, p. 408.

42. Crane Brinton, "Equality," *Encyclopedia of the Social Sciences*, 3 (1937), 579–80.

43. John Dewey, *The Public and Its Problems* (Chicago: Swallow, 1954), p. 170.

44. Walt Whitman, "By Blue Ontario's Shore," in *Leaves of Grass* (New York: Aventine Press, 1931), p. 360.

Compensatory Justice and the Meaning of Equity

WILLIAM A. BANNER

IN THE OPENING SECTION of the *Institutes* of Justinian, justice is defined as "the constant and lasting will to give to each man his due."[1] In Book V of the *Nicomachean Ethics*, written centuries before the *Institutes*, Aristotle characterizes justice, i.e., general justice, as more perfect than private virtue, inasmuch as justice is the whole of virtue practiced with respect to others. Man is a social being and the individual is called upon to do what is *fitting* in the many relationships of communal life; indeed, apart from these relationships, the life of the individual is incomplete if not impossible. What is beneficial to the individual is supported through what is fitting in social relationships. And what is fitting in social relationships has its expression in good laws, the lawful being simply the compelling of individuals to do what is virtuous and mutually beneficial. In Aristotle's words:

> For the actions that spring from virtue in general are in the main identical with the actions that are according to law, since the law enjoins conduct displaying the various particular virtues ... and the regulations laid down for the education that fits a man for social life are the rules productive of virtue in general. ... but law ... is a rule, emanating from a certain wisdom and intelligence, that has compulsory force. ... law can enjoin virtuous conduct without being invidious.[2]

With a view to the precise demands of justice in society, Aristotle distinguishes three kinds of *fairness*: namely, fairness in the distribution of honor and wealth, in the compensation for injuries, and in the regulation of commercial affairs. The kinds of fairness, although distinct, are not entirely separate; they are joined together through relation to a mean between having too much and having too little in any division of goods between two persons.[3]

Our interest here is directed to what Aristotle says about compensatory or corrective justice. As distinct from distributive justice, compensatory justice is not proportional, i.e., it is not a giving to each what he deserves according to his *share* as determined by free birth, wealth, or virtue.[4] Compensatory justice concerns private transactions, voluntary and involuntary, and under this mode of justice all parties are *equals*. Compensatory or corrective justice seeks to restore to the individual what he has lost, to compensate the individual for what he has suffered.[5] This justice is a mean between loss and gain; it is a restoration of equality, i.e., a restoration of what the injured party had before becoming a victim of theft, assault, or breach of contract. While the character of the injury or damage to be remedied is indicated in the precise formulation of law, the restitution itself is effected through the office of the judge, who is the medium between litigants and is, so to speak, the embodiment of justice.[6]

It is significant that Aristotle, who recognizes the judge as the ultimate referee in the rectification of grievances under the law, also recognizes the judge as the agent of *equity*.[7] Equity is the rectification of the law itself where the law is defective because of its generality[8] or some other limitation.[9] In the exercise of his best judgment, the judge decides what the wise legislator *would have decided* in a particular case. Although both functions of legislator and judge are required in the state, it is the judge who is responsible for the administration of justice which is "real and expedient."[10] Thus it is that the dispensing of justice would involve not only conduct which is contrary to law and custom but also conduct which is, in the absence of adequate legislation, simply contrary to reason. The appeal to reason and equity is necessary, then, where there is no law, where the law is equivocal or contradictory, or where the conditions of enactment of law are obsolete.[11]

II

Following the general direction of Aristotle's treatment of justice, I wish to hold in this paper that compensatory justice in its concern with loss and gain has two dimensions at least: namely, the correction of abuses committed against the existing law and the correction of abuses permitted by the limitations of the existing law. And, in consideration of what are to be respected as the *rights* of the individual, I wish to hold that compensatory justice is part of the *justice of right reason* in the protection of the individual in the having and enjoying of what is rightfully his as a person. Judgments about loss and gain are judgments which require a review not only of what the law requires but also of what the law should require.[12] In this respect every litigation concerned with loss and gain becomes a matter of equity.

This may not be apparent in many cases where a court is asked to decide in what way a contract has been violated or in what way one individual has been injured through the negligence of others. In observing that the law *is very clear* on a given matter (physical injury, theft, trespass, libel, fraud), there would be needed only the recognition of the fact (and extent) of injury and the arrangement for the compensation of the injured party.

There may, however, be matters with respect to which the law is not clear, in not providing adequately for the handling of all problems of injury and compensation brought before a court of law. This is a defect arising from the generality of law, a defect which is really irremediable, given the complexity of human life and the diversity of situations to which the written law is to be applicable. A law which sought to cover all possible cases would be cumbersome in its detail and would still fall short of coping with the variety and contingency of human affairs. There must be an appeal to the wisdom and judgment of the judge in bridging the gap between the broad intention of the written law and the demands of fairness in particular cases.

There may be injuries to individuals, further, with respect to which the existing law is defective, in the law's failure to embrace basic principles of fairness such as the principle of the equality of all litigants as beneficiaries of the protection of the commonwealth. In the *Lex Salica* of the Franks, for example, the payment of a fine (*Wergeld*) in compensation for injury was determined according to the social status of the injured party. In cases of plunder, the offense of a Roman against a Frank was fixed at 63 shillings while the offense of a Frank against a Roman was fixed at 35 shillings.[13] In cases of murder, the slaying of a Frank who was in the king's service involved a fine of 600 shillings, this being three times the fine for slaying an ordinary free man.[14]

In the passing of the centuries, as a consequence of a variety of influences, the recognition of the person and his worth or dignity becomes separated from the facts of social status. The progress in this direction, particularly that development in social history which is a clear and distinct movement from the relations of family dependency to the relations of free individuals, has been noted by Sir Henry Maine in his *Ancient Law*.[15] Bernard Bosanquet, as philosopher rather than historian, has called attention to this development in his *Philosophical Theory of the State*. In commenting upon Hegel's *Philosophy of Right*, Bosanquet writes: "The system of law of a modern State is and still more ought to be, a fairly reasonable and intelligible definition of the rights and relations of persons. By this determination the economic system of particular wants and services enters upon a first approximation, as it were, to a unity of principle.[16] And one understands that in the affirmation of the rights of the person there is a direct and unequivocal appeal beyond any defective written law, however ancient, to a higher law, either constitutional or unwritten. In discussing the long and hard struggle through which the modern world has passed in the growth of the concept of just law, John Henry Merryman has written the following:

> With the growth of the nation-state . . . old restraints on government were removed, and in the new positivistic state the representative legislature was given an inflated role and encouraged to be the sole judge of the legality of its own action. In a sense the trend toward functionally rigid constitutions, with guarantees of individual rights against "unjust" legislative action, can be seen as a process of "codification of natural law" . . . to deflate the bloated image of the legislature that emerged from the revolutionary period.[17]

Challenges to legislative action have often been disparaged as being precipitous annd anarchical.[18] But if the written law is defective in its content, as judged by such a norm as the quality of persons, then it is in accordance with rather than contrary to the preservation of good order to appeal to what is morally and rationally superior to the existing law. There is the need to maintain that there is such a thing as abstract or absolute justice which is the very meaning of human freedom conceived, in Kant's terms, as *reciprocal freedom*. Abstract justice itself is distinguishable from constitutional justice, inasmuch as precise constitutions, for all of their pretension to declare the first principles of a just order, may be defective in articulating the rights of persons. Abstract justice is simply the norm of reciprocal freedom and, as such, cannot be irrelevant to any ordering of human affairs.

III

In the case of equity, the direct recognition of abstract justice as the norm of human affairs,[19] the focus in the administration of justice is upon the judge and upon judicial discretion. We have noted what Aristotle says about the function of the judge in dispensing justice which is real and expedient. In medieval England, from the time at least of Edward I, there emerges the notion of the "King's conscience." This is the right or prerogative of the King or Chancellor to introduce and apply rules of fairness to particular cases brought before the crown.[20] The declaration of Edward III, given in 1358, is as follows: "If any man feel that he have a grievance by breach of ordinances he should come before the mayor and the sheriffs to complain ... if they make default in justice, the person aggrieved should go to chancery, and the king after hearing his plaint will cause the complement of justice to be done."[21] In recent times one finds essentially the same appeal to the independent judgment and discretion of the judge in the writings of Francois Gény. In his *Science et technique en droit privé positif*, Gény speaks of the scrutiny to which the existing law must be subjected by judges and by others:

> Those who engage in the work of positive law as administrators, those who interpret or apply it, in the capacity of judges, are they bound by this form, by the text of the law? Ought they not to look beyond this, to penetrate to the sources, intimate and substantial, from whence they are derived, and those who obey the law ... are they obligated to submit without recourse to its injunctions? ... do they not have the

the right to interpret, to modify, to transform the existing law, indeed, in extreme cases to rebel against it; this implies that they appeal to aspirations defying by their nature the variations of particular legal formulas?[22]

And in another place, Gény says of the jurist that he is expected

to have the right to orient himself and to direct his interpretation toward a future postulate which is dictated to him by his conscience and his reason.

Appeals to higher law and to equity would be opposed by many legal theorists as introducing singularity or virtuosity into public matters and hindering the rule of law through extraneous and unworkable moral formulas. And it might be feared that the remedy which is promised through such judicial correction of the existing law will in most cases turn out to be worse than the disease. It would be said, accordingly, that the publicity of the existing law is a clear advantage over the obscurity, if not privacy, of the moral and juridical norms to which jurists and others are disposed to resort in the name of equity and conscience. And, further, one might argue that what is binding in reason or conscience cannot bind those who do not share the same philosophical insight or moral intuition. In order to take seriously the appeal to equity and to judicial discretion, it would appear that one must hold that there is a common moral sense or a common tradition of moral and legal reasoning.

There is, of course, a common reason or reasonableness which is active in all who engage in the discussion of human affairs. The "reason" which is involved in the criticism and correction of the existing law is the same "reason" which is involved initially in the establishment of the law. There is a presumption of *rationality* in the total legislative and judicial process, insofar as the rules under which individuals are to be governed are presented as the best that can be devised for a community or society. A law is just or unjust, valid or invalid, by virtue of its ordering of means to an end and not simply by virtue of the circumstances of its enactment and promulgation. Every just law would seem to owe its authority to the reasonableness of what is ordained as an action or program of action for free men. With respect to the binding force of just law upon the intelligence and conscience of the governed, the distinction between written and unwritten law is not really significant.[23] Every just law is a rule of equity.

IV

There are two kinds of injuries which have been suffered largely without compensation in the modern world, namely, injuries arising from economic exploitation and injuries arising from social station as fixed by ethnic origin or cultural identification. In distinguishing these injuries in kind, one recognizes that precise injuries have often come to particular individuals through a conjunction of economic and noneconomic circumstances. The individual who endures one kind of injury is likely to endure the other, in being generally powerless to hold his place as a free agent among equals and in lacking the protection of the laws of his society. We come around again to the matter of the worth or dignity of the individual and the recognition or denial of this worth in the administration of justice.

The setting for the correction of modern social injustice has been the breach between constitutional affirmations of principles of individual freedom and political democracy on the one side and the social and economic arrangements of commercial and industrial civilization on the other. The breach itself has been explored and described in the considerable literature of social criticism, particularly in the writings of socialists. In an early work, *On the Jewish Question*, Marx speaks of the problem of freedom and its solution in these words:

> *All* emancipation is *restoration* of the human world and the relationships of *men themselves*.
>
> Political emancipation is a reduction of man to a member of civil society, to an *egoistic independent* individual on the one hand and to a *citizen*, a moral person, on the other.
>
> Only when the actual individual has taken back into himself the abstract citizen and his everyday life, his individual work, and his individual relationships has become a *species-being*, only when he has recognized and organized his own

powers as *social* powers so that social force is no longer separated from his *political* power, only then is human emancipation complete.[24]

Socialist literature in general has called attention to the *social
character* of the wealth made available in a society.[25] Without seeking to support the socialist's case, one can accept the fact of cooperation in all human enterprise and the fact of increasing
collective effort in the expanding commercial and industrial operations of the modern world. One can think, then, of the resources of a society as the common yield of its total working people
and of the whole people as sharing in these resources under a
virtual common proprietorship. This suggests that there are common claims upon goods and services and that there is, at least for
a particular society, a minimum of "living well," to fall below
which must be considered injurious to any individual.

Injury incurred through social insensitivity is a particularly
embarrassing problem for a democratic order resting upon the
recognition of individuals as persons, as ends in themselves. What
becomes necessary is the application of sanctions to hold the members of a democracy to their own explicit pledges and tacit commitments concerning equality and fairness. How this is to be
done, given an imperfect system of justice which reflects imperfect
commitments to democratic principles, is the heavy task of social
and legal reform. Ultimately, this is a matter of correcting the
patterns of opportunity and reward of a free society. Immediately,
it is a matter of assessing the injuries which have come from historic practices of social and economic inequality and of seeking to
compensate the individuals who have suffered these injuries.

One recognizes at the outset that there is injury or deprivation
for which compensation is difficult if not impossible. A precise
deprivation of goods and services which an individual has a claim
to have and to enjoy at a given moment becomes more difficult to
remedy as more and more time intervenes between loss and gain.
To receive on Friday what one required on Monday or Tuesday is
not to recover fully what one has lost, if many of the opportunities
and options of Monday and Tuesday have vanished with the passing of the days. The difficulty intensifies, of course, as days become
years and years become decades. If remedy is not forthcoming in

the lifetime of the injured individual, there is the special difficulty of the *posthumous claim* and how such a claim can be "settled" in the succeeding generation or generations.

In spite of these difficulties, one seeks to know whether there is any manner of compensation for injury which can be recognized and accepted by an individual or his descendants as an expression of fairness. And it would seem that the answer lies in the awareness that injuries which arise from inequalities pervading the whole fabric of a society can be remedied only through a broad program of restitution which pervades the whole fabric of the same society. Such a program of restitution, resting upon principles of equity, would emerge from the courts and their justices and actualize itself through all suitable instrumentalities of remedy.

If there is a norm of "living well," conceived at least as minimum guarantees of freedom in a society of free and equal persons, then it is by this same norm that deprivations (e.g., in health, in education, in professional skill) can be measured at any point in the life of any individual. In putting the matter this way, the idea of compensation is extended to embrace the recent victims of injustice as well as those whose injuries are long standing. This may itself appear to be *unfair*. But what is important is the character of injury or deprivation, not its history, although historical information is significant in determining the precise character of any injury and the precise means pertaining to its correction. A man of fifty years who has endured the injuries of job discrimination and poor wages for a period of twenty-five years would not be justly compensated simply through new employment at a fair wage. Fairness or equity would seem to require that he be granted the economic security which in the ordinary course of events his employment at a fair wage would have gained for him in twenty-five years.

The issues raised by the recent *DeFunis* case pertain to compensatory justice and to guarantees of freedom in a free society. In the suit brought by Marco DeFunis against persons of the University of Washington, it was argued that the denial of admission to the plaintiff by the Law School was the denial of a constitutional right, inasmuch as the Law School had granted admission to "minority students" having a lower "Predicted First Year Average" than the plaintiff.[26]

The *DeFunis* case touches upon matters other than the correctness of the apparatus employed by the University of Washington to select the first-year class of the Law School. To grant the argument of Marco DeFunis concerning his constitutional right as a competent applicant to further his academic and professional aspirations is to defend the constitutional right of others to further similar aspirations even as less competent applicants. A fundamental right of human fulfillment thus transcends any claim to the opportunities of competence of one individual *vis-à-vis* other members of the same society. Concerning fairness or equity, there is the presumption that the resources of an organized society will be applied to support the freedom and fulfillment of all citizens. The distinction between advantaged and disadvantaged, as a *social* distinction, cannot be used to perpetuate social distinction, i.e., it cannot be used against the disadvantaged. The aspirations of the disadvantaged must be taken to be as genuine as those of the advantaged. Concerning fundamental right, the disadvantaged student must be extended educational opportunity without denying opportunity to the advantaged student, whatever expansion of present educational facilities this may require.

Compensatory justice, in summary, calls for a new allotment of the resources of a society which has tolerated an unequal extension of opportunity and an unequal distribution of the rewards of labor. For this allotment recent efforts at fairness in educational opportunity may well serve as a paradigm.

NOTES AND REFERENCES

1. *Corpus Iuris Civilis*, vol. 1: Institutions, ed. Paul Krueger (Berlin, 1877), book I, title I, 3: "Iustitia est constans et perpetua voluntas ius suum cuique tribuens."
2. Aristotle, *Nicomachean Ethics*, trans. H. Rackham (Cambridge, Mass.: Harvard University Press, 1934), V, ii, 10–11; X, ix, 12–13.
3. *Ibid.*, V, v, 17.
4. *Ibid.*, V, iii, 7.
5. *Ibid.*, V, ii, 13; V, iv, 2–14.
6. *Ibid.*, V, iv, 7.
7. Aristotle, *Rhetoric*, I, xv, 3–8.
8. Aristotle, *Nicomachean Ethics*, V, x, 6.
9. Aristotle, *Rhetoric*, I, xv, 9–12.
10. *Ibid.*, I, xv, 7.
11. *Ibid.*, I, xv, 9–12.

12. Cf. Aristotle, *Rhetoric*, I, xiii, 13: "For what is equitable seems to be just, and equity is justice which goes beyond the written law." Trans. John Henry Freese (Cambridge, Mass.: Harvard University Press, 1926).

13. E. F. Henderson, translator and editor, *Select Historical Documents of the Middle Ages* (London: George Bell and Sons, 1903), p. 179.

14. *Ibid.*, p. 182. Cf. Aristotle, *Nicomachean Ethics*, V, iv, 3: "The law looks only at the nature of the damage, treating the parties as equals."

15. Cf. Henry Sumner Maine, *Ancient Law* (Boston: Beacon Press, 1963), pp. 163–64: "In Western Europe the progress achieved in this direction has been considerable. Thus the status of the Slave has disappeared—it has been superseded by the contractual relation of the servant to his master. The status of the Female under Tutelage . . . has also ceased to exist."

16. Bernard Bosanquet, *The Philosophical Theory of the State* (London: Macmillan, 1965), p. 259.

17. John Henry Merryman, *The Civil Law Tradition* (Stanford: Stanford University Press, 1969), p. 143.

18. Cf. Jeremy Bentham, *Anarchical Fallacies*; in *Select Extracts from the Works of Bentham*, ed. J. H. Burton (Edinburgh: W. Tait, 1843), chapter 2.

19. This opposes the view of a writer such as Hans Kelsen, who has argued that the basic norm of justice is the ultimate competence to be obeyed which is presupposed in any legal order. According to Kelsen, the regulation of human affairs has its foundation in what is *voluntary* rather than *rational*. Cf. Hans Kelsen, *Reine Rechtslehre* (Vienna, 1960), pp. 196–200.

20. Cf. B. Wilkinson, *The Chancery Under Edward III* (Manchester: Manchester University Press, 1920), pp. 10, 25, 29, 40–53.

21. T.F.T. Plucknett, *Statutes and Their Interpretation in the First Half of the Fourteenth Century* (Cambridge: Cambridge University Press, 1922), pp. 121, 169.

22. Francois Gény, *Science et technique en droit privé positif* (Paris, 1921–30), 4: 213–14. Quoted in Charles Grove Haines, *The Revival of Natural Law Concepts* (New York: Russell and Russell, 1965), pp. 293–94.

23. Cf. Aristotle, *Nicomachean Ethics*, X, ix, 14: "Public regulations in any case must be clearly established by law, and only good laws will produce good regulations; but it would not seem to make any difference whether these laws are written or unwritten."

24. Karl Marx, *On the Jewish Question*; in *Writings of the Young Marx on Philosophy and Society*, ed. by Loyd D. Easton and Kurt H. Guddat (Garden City: Doubleday, 1967), p. 241.

25. Cf. R. H. Tawney, *The Acquisitive Society* (New York: Harcourt, Brace, 1920), pp. 70ff.

26. *DeFunis* v. *Odegaard*, 42 U.S. Law Week 4578 (U.S., April 23, 1974).

Selected Bibliography

BOOKS

Astin, Alexander W. *Predicting Academic Performance in College.* New York: Free Press, 1971.

Bardwick, Judith (ed.). *Readings on the Psychology of Women.* New York: Harper and Row, 1972.

Bittker, Boris J. *The Case for Black Reparations.* New York: Random House, 1973.

Blackstone, William T. (ed.). *The Concept of Equality.* Minneapolis, Minn.: Burgess, 1969.

Bowles, Frank H., and Frank A. DeCosta. *Between Two Worlds: A Profile of Negro Higher Education.* New York: McGraw-Hill, 1971.

Carnegie Commission on Higher Education. *Opportunities for Women in Higher Education: Their Current Participation, Prospects for the Future, and Recommendations for Action.* New York: McGraw-Hill, 1973.

Coleman, James S. et al. *Equality of Educational Opportunity Survey.* Washington, D.C.: U.S. Government Printing Office, 1966.

Davidson, Kenneth M., Ruth Bader Ginsburg, and Herma Hill Kay. *Text, Cases, and Materials on Sex-Based Discrimination.* St. Paul, Minn.: West, 1974.

Dorsen, N. (ed.). *The Rights of Americans.* New York: Random House, 1971.

Eysenck, H. J. *The I.Q. Argument.* New York: Library Press, 1971.

Feinberg, Joel. *Doing and Deserving.* Princeton, N.J.: Princeton University Press, 1970.

Feldman, Saul D. *Escape from the Doll's House: Women in Graduate and Professional School Education.* New York: McGraw-Hill, 1974.

Ginger, Ann Fagan (ed.). *DeFunis v. Odegaard and the Univer-*

sity of Washington: The University Admissions Case. Dobbs Ferry, N.Y.: Oceana Publications, 1974. 3 vols.

Jencks, Christopher et al. *Inequality: A Reassessment of the Effect of Family and Schooling in America.* New York: Basic Books, 1972.

Mattfeld, Jacquelyn A., and Carol G. Van Aken (eds.). *Women and the Scientific Professions: The M.I.T. Symposium on Women and the Scientific Professions.* Cambridge, Mass.: M.I.T. Press, 1965.

Moore, William, Jr., and Lonnie H. Wagstaff. *Black Educators in White Colleges.* San Francisco: Jossey-Bass, 1974.

Rawls, John. *A Theory of Justice.* Cambridge, Mass.: Harvard University Press, 1971.

Stacey, Judith, Susan Beraud, and Joan Daniels (eds.). *And Jill Came Tumbling After: Sexism in American Education.* New York: Dell, 1974.

Tesconi, Charles A., Jr., and Emanuel Hurwitz (eds.). *Education for Whom?* New York: Dodd, Mead, 1974.

U.S. Department of Health, Education, and Welfare. *Higher Education Guidelines, Executive Order 1246.* Washington, D.C.: Government Printing Office, 1972.

Wilson, Bryan R. (ed.). *Education, Equality, and Society.* London, Eng.: George Allen & Unwin, 1975.

ARTICLES

American Association of University Professors. "Affirmative Action in Higher Education: A Report by the Council Commission on Discrimination," *AAUP Bulletin,* 59 (1973), 178–83.

American Council on Higher Education. "Institutions; Faculty and Staff; Students: Characteristics and Finances," *A Fact Book on Higher Education,* No. 3 (1973).

American Council on Higher Education. "Population, Business Activity, and Employment," *A Fact Book on Higher Education,* No. 2 (1973).

Baker, Joan E. "The Impact of Title VII of the 1964 Civil Rights Act on Employment Discrimination against Women Lawyers," *American Bar Association Journal,* 54 (1973), 1029–32.

Bayles, Michael D. "Compensatory Reverse Discrimination in Hiring," *Social Theory and Practice*, 2 (1973), 301–12.

———. "Reparations to Wronged Groups," *Analysis*, 33 (1973), 182–84.

Bedau, H. A. "Compensatory Justice and the Black Manifesto," *The Monist*, 56 (1972), 20–42.

Black, Virginia. "The Erosion of Legal Principles in the Creation of Legal Policies," *Ethics*, 84 (1974), 93–115.

Block, N. R., and Gerald Dworkin. "IQ, Heritability and Inequality, Part 1," *Philosophy & Public Affairs*, 3 (1974), 331–409.

———. "IQ, Heritability and Inequality, Part 2," *Philosophy & Public Affairs*, 4 (1974), 40–99.

Brown, Barbara A., Thomas I. Emerson, Gail Falk, and Ann E. Freedman. "The Equal Rights Amendment: A Constitutional Basis for Equal Rights for Women," *Yale Law Journal*, 80 (1971), 871–985.

Cary, Eve. "Pregnancy without Penalty," *Civil Liberties Review*, 1 (1973), 31–48.

"Comment, Love's Labors Lost: New Conceptions on Maternity Leaves," *Harvard Civil Rights–Civil Liberties Law Review*, 7 (1972), 260.

Cooper, George. "Equal Employment Law Today," *Columbia Human Rights Law Review*, 5 (1973), 263–79.

Cowan, J. L. "Inverse Discrimination," *Analysis*, 33 (1972), 10–12.

Emerson, Thomas I. "In Support of the Equal Rights Amendment," *Harvard Civil Rights–Civil Liberties Law Review*, 6 (1971), 225–33.

Epps, Edgar. "Correlates of Academic Achievement among Northern and Southern Urban Negro Students," *Journal of Social Issues*, 25 (1969), 55–70.

Flew, Antony. "The Jensen Uproar," *Philosophy*, 48 (1973), 63–69.

Frankel, Charles. "Equality of Opportunity," *Ethics*, 81 (1971), 191–211.

Freund, Paul A. "The Equal Rights Amendment Is Not the Way," *Harvard Civil Rights–Civil Liberties Law Review*, 6 (1971), 234–42.

Goldstein, Jinny M. "Affirmative Action: Equal Employment Rights for Women in Academia," *Teachers College Record*, 74 (1973), pp. 395–422.

Golightly, Cornelius L. "Justice and 'Discrimination for' in Higher Education," *Philosophic Exchange*, 1 (1974), 5–14.

Govier, Trudy. "Woman's Place," *Philosophy*, 49 (1974), 303–9.

Green, Thomas F. "Equal Educational Opportunity: The Durable Injustice." In Robert D. Heslep (ed.), *Philosophy of Education, 1971: Proceedings of the Twenty-Seventh Annual Meeting of the Philosophy of Education Society* (Edwardsville, Ill.: Philosophy of Education Society, 1971), pp. 121–44.

Griffiths, Martha W. "Sex Discrimination in Income Security Programs," *Notre Dame Lawyer*, 49 (1974), 534–43.

Kleinig, John. "The Concept of Desert," *American Philosophical Quarterly*, 8 (1971), 71–78.

Ireland, Thomas R. "The Relevance of Race Research," *Ethics*, 84 (1974), 140–45.

Jaggar, Alison. "On Sexual Equality," *Ethics*, 84 (1974), 275–91.

Jensen, Arthur R. "How Much Can We Boost IQ and Scholastic Achievement?," *Harvard Educational Review*, 39 (1969), 1–123.

Johnston, John D., Jr. "Sex Discrimination and the Supreme Court, 1971–74," *New York University Law Review*, 49 (1974), 617–88.

Kagan, Jerome. "The Emergence of Sex Differences," *The School Review*, 80 (1972), 217–27.

Kapel, David E., and Norman Wexler. "Conceptual Structures of High Risk and Regular Freshmen toward College Related Stimuli," *The Journal of Negro Education*, 41 (1972), 16–25.

Lynn, David B. "Determinants of Intellectual Growth in Women," *The School Review*, 80 (1972), 241–60.

Matthews, Burnita Shelton. "Women Should Have Equal Rights with Men, A Reply," *American Bar Association Journal*, 12 (1926), 117–20.

Minuchin, Patricia. "The Schooling of Tomorrow's Women," *The School Review*, 80 (1972), 199–208.

Murray, Pauli. "The Negro Woman's Stake in the Equal Rights

Amendment," *Harvard Civil Rights–Civil Liberties Review*, 6 (1971), 253–59.

Nagel, Thomas. "Equal Treatment and Compensatory Discrimination," *Philosophy & Public Affairs*, 2 (1973), 348–63.

Newton, Lisa. "Reverse Discrimination as Unjustified," *Ethics*, 83 (1973), 308–12.

Nickel, James W. "Classification by Race in Compensatory Programs," *Ethics*, 84 (1974), 146–50.

Nozick, Robert. "Distributive Justice," *Philosophy & Public Affairs*, 3 (1973), 45–126.

Nunn, William A., III. "Reverse Discrimination," *Analysis*, 34 (1974), 151–54.

O'Neil, Robert M. "Preferential Admissions: Equalizing Access to Legal Education," *University of Toledo Law Review*, (1970), 281–320.

————. "Preferential Admissions: Equalizing the Access of Minority Groups to Higher Education," *The Yale Law Journal*, 80 (1971), 699–767.

Panos, Robert J. "Picking Winners or Developing Potential," *The School Review*, 81 (1973), 437–50.

Reid, Inez Smith. "Cast Aside by the Burger Court: Blacks in Quest of Justice and Education," *Notre Dame Lawyer*, 69 (1973–74), 105–21.

Rosen, Sanford J. "Equalizing Access to Legal Education: Special Programs for Law Students Who Are Not Admissable by Traditional Criteria," *Toledo Law Review* (1970), 321–77.

Ruud, Millard H. "That Burgeoning Law School Enrollment Is Portia," *American Bar Association Journal*, 60 (1974), 182–84.

Seabury, P. "HEW and the Universities," *Commentary* (February 1972), 38–44.

Sher, George. "Justifying Reverse Discrimination in Employment," *Philosophy & Public Affairs*, 4 (1975), 159–70.

Shiner, Roger A. "Individuals, Groups, and Inverse Discrimination," *Analysis*, 33 (1973), 185–87.

Silvestri, Philip. "The Justification of Inverse Discrimination," *Analysis*, 34 (1973), 31.

Simon, Robert. "Preferential Hiring: A Reply to Judith Jarvis Thomson," *Philosophy & Public Affairs*, 3 (1974), 312–20.

Slaughter, Diana T. "Becoming an Afro-American Woman," *The School Review*, 80 (1972), 299–318.

Stanley, Julian, and John R. Hills. "Easier Test Improves Prediction of Black Student's College Grades," *The Journal of Negro Education*, 39 (1970), 320–24.

Szaniawski, Klemens. "The Concept of Distribution of Goods," *Studia Filozoficzne*, 4 (1970), 255–66.

Taylor, Paul W. "Reverse Discrimination and Compensatory Justice," *Analysis*, 33 (1973), 177–82.

Thalberg, Irving. "Justifications of Institutional Racism," *Philosophical Forum*, 3 (1972), 243–63.

Thomson, Judith Jarvis. "Preferential Hiring," *Philosophy & Public Affairs*, 2 (1973), 364–84.

Vieira, Norman. "Racial Imbalance, Black Separatism, and Permissible Classification by Race," *Michigan Law Review*, 67 (1967), 1553–1626.

COURT CASES

Alevy v. Downstate Medical Center of the State of New York. *New York Supplements*, 359 (1974), 426–30.

Bakke v. Regents of the University of California. *California Reports*, 132 (1976), 680. *Pacific Reporter*, second series, 553 (1976), 1152.

Berkelman et al. v. San Francisco Unified School District et al. *Federal Reporter*, second series, 501 (1974), 1264–70.

Carter et al. v. Gallagher et al. *Federal Reporter*, second series, 452 (1972), 315–32.

Cleveland Board of Education et al. v. LeFleur et al. *United States Reports*, 414 (1973), 632–60.

DeFunis, et al. v. Odegaard et al. *United States Reports*, 416 (1973), 312–50.

Geduldig, Director, Department of Human Resources Development v. Aiello et al. *United States Reports*, 417 (1973), 484–505.

Griggs et al. v. Duke Power Co. *United States Reports*, 401 (1970), 424–36.

Keyes et al. v. School District No. 1, Denver, Colorado, et al. *United States Reports,* 413 (1972), 189–265.

Lau et al. v. Nichols et al. *United States Reports,* 414 (1973), 563–72.

McDonnell Douglas Corp. v. Green. *United States Reports,* 411 (1972), 792–807.

Morrow et al. v. Crisler et al. *Federal Reporter,* second series, 491 (1974), 1053–64.

Morton, Secretary of the Interior, et al. v. Maucari et al. *United States Reports,* 417 (1973), 535–55.

Roe et al. v. Wade, District Attorney of Dallas County. *United States Reports,* 410 (1972), 113–78.

The Contributors

RICHARD WASSERSTROM, professor of philosophy and law at the University of California at Los Angeles and former attorney in the U. S. Department of Justice, is the author of *The Judicial Decision: Toward a Theory of Legal Justification* and the editor of *Law and Morality*.

ROBERT D. HESLEP, professor of philosophy of education at the University of Georgia, is the author of *Thomas Jefferson and Education* and the editor of *Philosophy of Education, 1971*.

WILLIAM T. BLACKSTONE, professor of philosophy at the University of Georgia, is the author or editor of a number of books, including *The Concept of Equality*, *Political Philosophy*, and *Philosophy and Environmental Crisis*.

TOM L. BEAUCHAMP, associate professor of philosophy at Georgetown University, has edited *Ethics and Public Policy*.

ABRAHAM EDEL, Research Professor of Philosophy at the University of Pennsylvania, is the author of *Theory and Practice of Philosophy*, *Ethical Judgment*, *Method in Ethical Theory*, and others.

RUTH BADER GINSBURG, professor of law at Columbia University, is co-author of *Civil Procedure in Sweden* and *Swedish Code of Judicial Procedure* and co-editor of *Cases and Materials on Sex-Based Discrimination and the Law*.

DEAN RUSK, whose books include *The Winds of Freedom*, was formerly U. S. Secretary of State and is now Samuel H. Sibley Professor of International Law at the University of Georgia.

PRINCE E. WILSON is Vice-President for Academic Affairs at Atlanta University.

MAXINE GREENE, professor of English and educational philosophy at Teachers College, Columbia University, is the author of *The Public School and the Private Vision*, *Teacher as Stranger*, and others.

WILLIAM A. BANNER is professor of philosophy and Dean of the College of Liberal Arts at Howard University and the author of *Ethics: An Introduction to Moral Philosophy* and others.